GAME DEVELOPMENT
USING PYTHON

GAME DEVELOPMENT USING PYTHON

JAMES R. PARKER

MERCURY LEARNING AND INFORMATION
Dulles, Virginia
Boston, Massachusetts
New Delhi

Publisher: David Pallai
MERCURY LEARNING AND INFORMATION
22841 Quicksilver Drive
Dulles, VA 20166
info@merclearning.com
www.merclearning.com
800-232-0223

James R. Parker. *Game Development Using Python.*
ISBN: 978-1-683921-80-6

Library of Congress Control Number: 2018964986

The publisher recognizes and respects all marks used by companies, manufacturers, and developers as a means to distinguish their products. All brand names and product names mentioned in this book are trademarks or service marks of their respective companies. Any omission or misuse (of any kind) of service marks or trademarks, etc. is not an attempt to infringe on the property of others.

181920321   This book is printed on acid-free paper in the United States of America.

Our titles are available for adoption, license, or bulk purchase by institutions, corporations, etc. For additional information, please contact the Customer Service Dept. at 800-232-0223(toll free).

All of our titles are available in digital format at authorcloudware.com and other digital vendors. Companion files (figures and code listings) for this title are also available by contacting info@merclearning.com. The sole obligation of MERCURY LEARNING AND INFORMATION to the purchaser is to replace the disc, based on defective materials or faulty workmanship, but not based on the operation or functionality of the product.

Contents

Preface ....*xvii*

Chapter 0   Games 1

   Virtual Reality...4
   Game Genres..6
      Strategy...6
      Sports..6
      Simulation 7
      Role Playing 7
      Action 8
      Adventure..8
      Other Games..8
   Common Aspects of Computer Games.............................9
   Platforms...10
      Desktop Computers..10
      Tablets 11
      Game Consoles 11
      Portable Consoles 12
      Cellular Phones...13
   Aspects of Interesting Games 13
      Venue..13
      Conflict...14
      Graphics and Sound...15
      Props...15
      Interface 16
      Pace/Scale..17
      Fidelity 18
      Accuracy 18
   Exercises 19

Resources 19
References 20

Chapter 1   Introduction to How Games Work 21

Video Game Architecture 21
   The Graphics System 24
      Object Level 25
      Geometric Level 26
      Rasterization 27
      Comments on Optimization 27
   The Audio System 27
Game Design 28
   Mechanics 29
Playing the Game by the Rules 30
   Most of a Computer Game Is Hidden 30
   The Artificial Intelligence 31
   Game State 32
   Global State 32
   Push/Pull (client server) 32
   Managers 33
   Broadcast-listener 33
   Shared and Global Entities 34
Pong 35
The Game Design Document 39
   C2H6O Jet Boat Race 40
   C2H6O Jet Boat Race Design Document 41
Exercises 45
References 46

Chapter 2   Graphics and Images 47

Pygame Essentials 48
Simple Static Drawing 49
   Pixel Level Graphics 50
      Example: Create a Page of Note Paper 50
      Example: Creating a Color Gradient 51
   Lines and Curves 52
      Example: Note Paper Again 53
   Polygons 56
   Blitting 57
   Drawing Text 58

Transparent Colors..59
Images 61
Pixels..62
    Example: Negative Image 63
Image Transformations 64
    Rotation...65
Pixels and Color..67
The C2H6O Jet Boat Race Game 70
Exercises 72
Resources 73
References 73

Chapter 3   The Game Loop **74**

Time and Intervals 74
    The pygame.time Module 76
        A Game Loop: Bouncing a Simulated Ball.............78
Events 79
    The Mouse 81
    The Keyboard..82
    An On-Screen Button 84
    A Simple Game 85
    A Better Game 86
Randomness in Games...87
    Randomness Generally..88
Randomness in Games: Dice, Cards 90
    Probability for Beginners..92
    Probability Calculations...93
Generating Random Values 96
    Pseudorandom Numbers...97
Simulating Reality and Intelligence 98
Exercises 100
Resources..101
References..101

Chapter 4   Game AI: Collisions....................................**104**

Collision Detection 105
    Polygonal Objects 107
        An Example 108
Broad Phase Collision Detection..109
    "Operational" Methods...109

Geometric Tests 110
Using Enclosing Circles... 112
Sphere VS. Plane Collision (Circle – Line) 113
Circle-Circle Collisions 114
Finding the Closest Point on a Line to a Specified Point 115
Using Bounding Boxes... 116
Object Oriented Bounding Boxes... 117
Space Subdivision 118
Narrow Phase Collision Detection 120
Ray/Triangle Intersection 121
Collision Detection in the Boat Race... 123
Ray Casting 126
Exercises 127
References... 128

Chapter 5   Navigation and Control...129

Basic Autonomous Control 130
How to Control a Car 131
Cruising Behavior.. 132
Avoidance Behavior... 133
Waypoint Representation and Implementation 135
Finite State Machines 136
FSA in Practice 137
State and the "What Do We Do Now" Problem 140
Other Useful States... 141
Pathfinding 144
A* Search.. 146
Stochastic Navigation 151
Exercises 152
Resources.. 155
References... 155

Chapter 6   Sound 156

Basic Audio Concepts 157
Introduction to Sound in Pygame... 161
Sound Options 162
Sound Volume.. 163
Channels 164
Creating Your Own Sounds 165
Recording Using Cell Phones and MP3 Devices....................... 166

A Small Studio 167
Audio Software 168
Positional Audio 170
Example: Distance Attenuation 171
Example: 2D Positional Sound.. 172
Exercises 176
Resources.. 177
References 178

Chapter 7   C2H6O Jet Boat Race **179**
Implementing the Game: Prototypes.................................... 179
Prototype 0 180
Prototype 1 181
Screens 181
Buttons 182
Start Screen 184
Options Screen 185
Play Screen 186
End Screen 186
Prototype 2... 186
The Play Screen 187
User Control.. 190
The Boat Class 192
Artificial Intelligence 193
Collisions.. 193
Navigation 196
Waypoints... 197
Avoiding a Boat.. 199
Colliding with the Shore 200
Sound.. 201
Engine Sounds... 202
Collisions and Explosions... 203
Starting Gun 203
Finish 203
Testing... 203
Summary.. 206
Exercises 206
Resources.. 206
Sound Effects.. 206
Sound Editing 207

Graphics Editing 207
References 207

Chapter 8 Animation **208**

Creating Elementary Animations 209
Animation Math 214
   Motion Equations 216
Reactive Animations 219
   Using Real Images 224
Ambient Animations 225
Character Animation 228
Cut Scenes 229
Animations in the Boat Race Game 231
   Wakes 231
Summary 231
Exercises 233
Resources 234
References 234

Chapter 9 C2H6O – Final Steps **236**

Animations 237
   Wakes 237
   Explosions 238
      Determining a Boat Collision 240
Sounds 242
   Engine Sounds 242
   Starting Gun 243
   Finish 244
   Bing 244
   Audience 244
Gameplay 244
   Completing the Race 244
   Start 244
      Timer 245
   Intermediate Goals 246
   Finish 247
Mini-Map 247
   Game Data 248
Tuning 249
Exercises 249

Resources..250
References..250

Chapter 10   Networking **251**
The Game: Python Pong...252
The Paddle Class...253
The Ball Class 254
Communication between Processes.........................257
Example: Moving a Ball on the Screen 257
Network Pong..262
The Client 262
The Server 264
Blocking and Non-Blocking 265
Messages 267
The Pong Client...268
The Pong Server 270
Playing the Game...271
Resources..272
References..272

Appendix A: A* in Python **275**

Appendix B: *C2H6O Jet Boat Race* Game Design Document..........**281**

Appendix C: The NPC (Boat) Class for the Example Game...........**291**

Index **295**

ACKNOWLEDGMENTS

Thanks to the makers of *Audacity* for allowing me to include their sound editing software with the book.

Thanks also to the makers of *VideoMach* for allowing me to include their video editing software and providing a key especially for us.

Special thanks to Nigel Gebert for composing and playing a short jazz piano piece for me to use as an audio example. He even named it "Keys for Jim." How nice.

PREFACE

This book is about computer games. It's about how to develop them using the Python language, but the book also includes some design instruction, ideas about handling assets, and a host of things that should be useful for a game developer.

Python is a programmer's language, in that it provides features that programmers usually want and often recode again and again in their various programs. Lists, dictionaries, sets, arbitrary precision integers, dynamic typing – it's an encyclopedia of the tools a programmer uses all the time, or would if it were convenient. Well now it is. *PyGame*, the module used to help a programmer create games, adds to that a surface on which to draw, many graphics primitives, sound, animation, and interaction. It's a wonderful palette on which game developers can dip their brushes.

If you look up my name on the Internet you will see that I am a professor of Art. That's true, but I feel like a bit of a fraud, and the reason is that I have no training as an artist. I studied mathematics and computer science at university. So how did I end up in art?

I was known for work in image processing and vision in the 1990s as an academic. For some reason the Game Developer's Conference interested me. In 1998, I registered and attended, and my life was changed. The energy there was incredible. People everywhere were completely enthralled by their work. They were having *fun*. They were doing things and speaking about things that I had not heard about in my academic venues, and those things were *fascinating*. Moreover, their work had an immediate impact on people.

True, the companies were in competition for a share of the commercial games market, but the people at the conference were excited about what they knew and about sharing it. Sharing means, in this context, bringing back something as well as giving something to the others. Moreover, the group contained computer programmers, musicians and audio specialists, artists, designers, and business folks. A true meeting of multidisciplinary minds.

This book arose from my experience at GDC and my love of computer programming. I have written other books on game development, but for a casual programmer or home developer, I think that Python is a great way to proceed. Python is easy to learn, and *PyGame* has everything a 2D developer needs.

I do presume some proficiency in Python. That's necessary to keep the book under 1000 pages; to program games, one first needs to be a programmer. What the book will teach is still significant. Computer science degrees are useful, but few degree programs offer any treatment of *assets*: art, sound, graphics objects. Handling those is essential to any game, and assets are a key component of many practical computer programs.

The project in this book is by necessity incomplete. It is a boat race, 2D, and seen from above; but is has sound, animation, interaction, AI, and everything that a simple game should have. It could be more fun. It could have more features. I leave these things to you. As an instructional device I think it has everything that you need. As a *game* it still needs your touch.

There is a lot of code in the book. The code is also included in the companion files, along with the color figures and some very useful tools for asset creation. The programs are included so that you can play with them, modify them, and experiment. If you do not, then you are missing an element of the instruction that this book offers.

Playing games is fun. Making games is fun too, but can also be profitable, educational, and useful in a great many ways. The information you glean from studying game development applies also to other digital media. That's a bonus. As a marketer, web developer, artist, or app developer, what you can learn by studying game development is enormous.

And, of course, it's fun. If you are not having fun then you are doing it wrong.

Jim Parker
December 2018

GAMES

For all of recorded history, humans have played games. The earliest board game is possibly the Royal Game of Ur, named after one of the oldest human cities, having been established at about 3800 BC. This is what is called a two-player chase game, similar in basic concept to Parcheesi and likely a predecessor to Backgammon.

Why are people so interested in games? There are likely many reasons: a need to keep our minds occupied during periods of inactivity, an interest in social contact, and a desire for achievement are three. For whatever reasons, games have always been a part of human society.

But what is a *game*?

 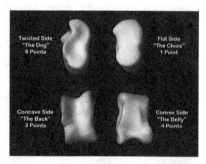

FIGURE 0.1(LEFT) The Royal Game of Ur. (Right) Knuckle bone dice.

Creating a perfect definition of the word *game* is not a profitable activity unless it leads to something practical. Here a game should be defined in a way that leads to a practical design and implementation process, and not more philosophical concerns. Some things that some people may consider to be a game may not be included in the definition, but the idea is not to exclude any particular thing. The idea is to include as many things as possible that we think of as games, and to provide clues for how one might begin to make one.

A game involves *play*, another term that is hard to define. Let's say that a game is an activity that people engage in voluntarily. A game is a structured activity, in that a game has rules and at least one goal. A game should involve variation or chance. Many simple games, like snakes and ladders, are purely games of chance; such games are often played by children, possibly as an introduction to how to play games. Most games have some chance and some skill, meaning players develop, over a period of time, a strategy for playing the game. Games like chess have very little chance. Chess uses chance to select the player who will move first, but that is all.

A game is *entertaining*. It can be other things also, but it must at least provide some degree of engagement for the player. As in other forms of entertainment, the feelings that a game imparts need not always be happy ones, but the game must encourage the player to continue playing in some interesting way.

By this definition *catch* is not a game, as there are no rules. A ball is simply thrown around. Yet it is an activity, and it is entertaining.

FIGURE 0.2 A play bow.

HTTP://WWW.PATRICIAMCCONNELL.COM/THEOTHERENDOFTHELEASH/A-NEW-LOOK-AT-PLAY-BOWS.

Games all use a mutual acceptance of the fact that what is occurring is play. The implication of this is that there should be *no real-world ramifications.*

While the game is being played, the players are operating under the game rules and not the rules of the world or society. Some people refer to this as being in the *magic circle*. This explains how a king and a peasant or an employer and employee can play chess together.

Games are also used to teach. This happens in the animal kingdom, where games played by cats, for example, teach hunting skills. This appears to contradict the "no consequence" rule, but it is always true that playing a game frequently makes one better at playing the game. Dogs also play, and that brings up the magic circle again. When a dog wishes to play with another, they begin with a play bow where the chest drops to the ground, the forelegs are extended, and the eyes are looking at the potential partner.

If the invitation is accepted, two dogs of differing status can play, and that means they can do things not normally allowed: staring, growling, even biting. The game can end quickly, though, if one of the dogs goes too far, perhaps biting too hard or taking the wrong toy. Then the magic circle disappears, and real life has resumed.

There are a few general game classes. *Kinetic games* are usually played outdoors with little in the way of equipment and, again, are often played by children. Tag and hide and seek are examples. However, charades could be in this category too. Such games involve the motion of the players.

Board games use a set of objects or *pieces* that are placed on a relatively small playing surface, a *board*. Players usually take turns moving the pieces to locations on the board following a set of rules.

Card games use a collection of paper or wooden chips that are marked in some way. The chips (cards) are usually handed out randomly at the outset of

The standard Nim game is for two players. It uses 16 matches in 4 rows . Two players alternately pick a certain number of matches, as many as they like from any one row.
The player who takes the last match loses.

Can also be played on paper, of course.

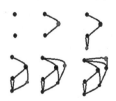

Sprouts is a two player game that begins with a few spots drawn on a sheet of paper. Players take turns, where each turn consists of drawing line between two spots (or from a spot to itself) and adding a new spot somewhere along the line. The players are constrained by the followir rules.

1. The line may be straight or curved but cannot touch any other line including itself.
2. The new spot must split the line into two shorter lines.
3. No spot may have more than three lines attached to it. A line from the spot to itself counts as two attached lines and new spots are counted as having two lines already attached to them.

FIGURE 0.3 **Examples of mathematical games.**

the game, and through following the rules they are collected into sets where some sets are more valuable than others. Dice games and games like dominos can be placed in this class.

Word games include guessing games, such as Yes and No (also called 20 questions); I Spy; How, When, and Where (from *A Christmas Carol*); and a host of others. These games use no props and can be played anywhere.

Mathematical games can use properties of shapes, numbers, or relationships to create puzzle-like games that can be very complex indeed. They are often played using a pencil and paper. Nim and Sprouts are two such games.

There are some other classes of games, but one that has developed in the past few decades is the computer game. These are not merely computer implementations of the other kinds of games, but they are games that use the specific characteristics of a computer to engage in play. Those properties include the ability to do many calculations each second, multimedia capabilities (images and sound), and many different ways of accepting use input. This means that a computer can display images and sounds under the control of a user (player). Objects that do not really exist except as images on a screen can be moved about and can interact with each other and a player. This opens a whole new range of possibilities for play.

It has been estimated that 69% of the human beings on this planet have played a video game. This seems a reasonable number given the popularity and ubiquity of games as observed in shopping malls, in movies, and in media generally. It amounts to about five billion people. What these players know about games varies quite a lot, but common knowledge concerns rules of specific games, interface issues such as what keys to press or buttons to push, and some tactical information about game play, like where to hide, when to jump, and so on. Very few of these people know how the games work at an implementation level though. The internal actions of the game, from key press to avatar motion, are a mystery to most people.

VIRTUAL REALITY

The term virtual means "almost" or "nearly." Virtual reality presents a form of reality that is not quite real but seems like it. Modern computer games often present a three-dimensional view of the game area and permit the player to navigate through this space, encountering friends and obstacles as they go. This presentation is similar to the virtual reality of books and films such as *The Lawnmower Man* and reached the peak of its form in the Holosuite of *Star Trek*. In *Star Trek* the suite is used for entertainment. Complex games are played and complex characters are created with which to interact in a natural way. Computer games are not yet at that stage, but they seem to be approaching it.

Both computer games and virtual reality are in some sense *simulations*. They are computer programs that present a realistic view of a nonexistent world, but a world that has the same or similar laws as the real one. This may include gravity, time, speed, physical contact, sounds, and even human reactions. All of these aspects of the virtual world must be simulated by the computer program that implements the game. When a character lets go of its grip on an object, the object falls to the ground because the software describes that process. When the object strikes the ground, the computer program plays a sound effect, because a sound would be produced by the impact. Nothing that happens in a computer game happens unless a computer program implemented it.

When we play cards or chess, there is really no discussion about how the game is implemented. Two people set up the board or deal the cards, and away you go. A computer game, on the other hand, has a very complex underlying implementation which is really the subject of the entire discussion here. How are computer games made? The nature of virtual reality gives some idea of what is needed. A video game needs what virtual reality needs:

- A video (graphical) display
- An audio display (speakers, sound card)
- A way for a player to communicate their moves to the computer
- A way for the computer to remember positions and make moves

If you examine what people *do* know about games, some internal structure can be inferred. That players know rules of games implies that games have a consistent set of rules that will be implemented by a computer program somehow. The players' knowledge of the user interface implies a level of consistency there too. We observe, for example, that the arrow keys, or sometimes the keys "W," "A," "S," and "D," are used to move the player's avatar, but not the keys "R," "G," "N," and "M"; there are conventions for user interfaces. The video game screens display images that move, and game actions result in sounds that the player can hear and use as cues. Thus, a video game must be able to display images and sounds and do so in response to user commands or internal events in the game.

On the other hand, what we need to know to design and build an original game is significantly more than that. There's only so much that you can learn from examining a game from the outside. Games are complex systems involving computer devices and software, art (textures, 3D models, sprites), music, sound effects, video and animation, story, and a designed structure for play. There are a great many existing games, and techniques and tools that will help a game developer in their task have evolved over the last few decades. If we're going to build a game, we should become familiar with at least some of those things.

Not all computer games are high-resolution, immersive (i.e., virtual reality), real-time games. In fact, each type or genre of game has a preferred style of representation.

GAME GENRES

Video games can be classified according to how the game is played rather than what the game is about, just as we did for games in general. A genre is defined by the kind of challenge the game offers to the player rather than the story it presents, if any. The games in a genre need not occur in the same locations, in the same time periods, or even have the same graphical style, although presentation style is more similar between games within a genre than in general. There are quite a few genres in the literature, but these are the most common ones.

Strategy

These games give the player a singular position in the game where they know nearly everything about the current state. By using plans involving placing and moving their objects (*forces*), the player opposes other player-controlled or game-controlled objects. Objects have specific powers within the game, and by clever opposition to the objects seen the player achieves a goal, which is usually domination of the other players. There is often an economy within which the player can acquire more objects.

Sub-genres include *tower defense* games, in which the player sets out static defenses along a path traveled by their opponent and *real-time strategy* games in which players act in real time against a dynamic game state (*Warcraft, Age of Empires*).

These games often use a medium-level resolution and have a point of view from above the playing area.

Sports

Sports games are the easiest to understand, because they reflect an activity that most people already know about, that being sports. Any sport can be made into a game. Golfing games use the rather clumsy mouse-keyboard interface to permit a player to control a golfer on a course, which is something of a solo activity. Team sports like football and hockey present more variation to the player, and often permit the switching of point of view between the individual team members. The games try to simulate the style of play of actual athletes so that a player can compete against their favorite individuals.

Racing games fall into this category. Actual racetracks are used in many of these, as are actual drivers and cars. A number of special interfaces have been devised to permit players to use a steering wheel and pedals, modeling the way cars are really driven.

Sports games are the most difficult to create. They tend to use high-resolution graphics to mimic what would be seen on television, which is the way many people view sports. Sport fans know quite a lot about their sport, so the game must be quite accurate. The fans in particular know how the real players actually play, and they will be critical of mistakes in this area. Each year players move between teams and new ones enter the sport, so the game must be regularly updated. And if that is not enough, the physics involved in sports games is very sophisticated. Consider the complexity of a collision between two hockey players skating at high speed (*rag doll physics*) or how a race car behaves when it crests a hill, leaves the ground, and then lands in a wet spot on the track.

Simulation

Simulation games have become more popular in the first part of the twenty-first century. While all games contain a simulation at their heart, a simulation game exposes that simulation and permits a player to manipulate it directly. The most obvious type of game in this genre is a *flight simulator*, in which the player flies an aircraft. As in sports games, flight simulators use real-world features: real airports, aircraft, and terrain. Air combat can sometimes be an aspect, as well as the distinct nature of each aircraft. There are also ship simulators and train simulators.

However, there are more complex simulation games where one simulates an ecosystem or an entire human or other lifetime. Games like *SimCity* allow the player to build and manage an entire city. Tycoon games (*Zoo Tycoon, Roller Coaster Tycoon*) are simulations of businesses and economies.

Role Playing

These games are referred to with an abbreviation, *RPG*. They are in some sense derived from the original non-computer game Dungeons and Dragons and cast the player in a role where they can pretend to be one of a number of characters, each having specialized abilities. There is a storyline and a set of goals, but the manner with which the player achieves the goals is up to them.

Action RPGs focus on combat and can be solo games (*Dragon Slayer*), multiplayer, or massively multiplayer (MMORPG), using the Internet to gather hundreds or more players into the same game at the same time (*Final Fantasy XI, Elder Scrolls Online*).

Action

This genre actually began the video game phenomenon. Action games are sometimes called *twitch* games because they require the player to respond quickly to the visual and auditory stimuli provided by the game. The player's viewpoint is central to these games, which often involve fighting of some kind.

Platformers have a two-dimensional presentation as seen from one side. The player controls a character who runs and jumps while collecting objects, fighting, and avoiding traps and enemies. *Donkey Kong* is the best known of these games. They require little in the way of complex graphics and can be played on very small, low-powered computers. *Shooters* are very popular because the game play is so obvious: enemies approach and you shoot them. They, of course, shoot back. Game developers like these because they are so simple in concept and easy to build, although more modern ones do have much better graphics and even complex narratives. *First-person shooters* (*Doom*) follow the player precisely, whereas third-person shooters render the scene from a distance.

Fighting games focus on individual combat. Various key press combinations correspond to actions that the avatar makes in a combat situation: punches, kicks, jumps, and so on. Memorizing the key sequences and speedy presses under real time actions make this style difficult for some.

Adventure

Adventure games use gameplay style that is relatively sedate. The player has some rather general goals and achieves them by solving puzzles and by interacting with game elements like other characters, terrain, or objects. These games use non-confrontation more than violence. Some of the earliest computer games were text-based adventures (*Advent, Zork*) that could be played on the early dumb terminals and telex interfaces. *Myst* is probably the best known of these games in the modern era.

Other Genres

There are many other genres in common use: *kinetic* or *rhythm* games (*Dance Dance Revolution*), *horror* and *survival horror* (*Silent Hill*), *casual*, *puzzle* games, *trivia* games, and others. Each has a typical implementation style in terms of the interface, and a preferred graphical presentation that is an advantage for that genre.

COMMON ASPECTS OF COMPUTER GAMES

Computer games have common requirements which have implications for the design of games. The need for participation and rules implies the existence of *objects*. A player manipulates some kind of object according to the rules, which defines *play*. The object could simply be the player's hand, or a ball, or a stone. There can be multiple objects and multiple object types. An object is manipulated by the player and can, in turn, affect the player, which provides *interaction*.

The way a player manipulates the objects is called *mechanics*, or *game mechanics*. The basic mechanics for basketball is *make the ball go through a hoop from above*, for example.

A game designer really designs mechanics.

The existence of objects implies the existence of some kind of playing area, volume, or space within which the game activity takes place. A game object needs space within which to act. A game space could be a board, as in checkers, or a table for card games, or a simulated 3D world for computer games like *Portal*, *Silent Hill*, or *Planetside*.

The game has a purpose, goal, or end point. The player must manipulate the objects according to the rules so as to accomplish the goal or reach the end point. The goal could be temporary, to be replaced by another goal when the old one is achieved. There could be multiple goals to be achieved, either collectively or optionally. Or, in some rare but popular instances, the goals could be selected by the player. That is the case in *The Sims*, where there is no designer-specified goal, but the players can manipulate the virtual worlds to achieve goals they have devised themselves. This the one of the most popular games ever made, but the concept of the *sandbox*, a place where players can manipulate the world freely, has relatively few examples. Most games have designer-specified goals and a way of keeping score.

A game should have these characteristics. What does this say about how a game, especially a computer game, should be built? What are the things that a computer game needs to implement, at a generic level? First, there must be a way of interacting with the game. How does a player interact? Usually by manipulating an object, or multiple objects, within the gameplay space. Interaction when using a personal computer usually means using a keyboard or mouse, although special-purpose game devices do exist. So, a computer game needs a straightforward way to accept input from those devices and use it to update the game.

Next, we require an *object* in an abstract sense. An object is manipulated by the user, so its location and state must be modifiable. The object might be able to interact with other objects. For example, it may collide with a wall. It should be able to create new objects (bullets, missiles, money, food) and destroy or drop objects (money again, traps, tools).

In the virtual space defined by the game, an object has a location and an orientation. It will normally have at least one graphical representation within that space so that the player can see its location and orientation and modify it as wanted.

While most games have these characteristics, computer games certainly do. They define the structure of a video game as a piece of software, and that structure is referred to as the *architecture*. In order to visualize how a computer game works, we'll look at a specific game and then generalize what is learned there to all video games in the next chapter.

PLATFORMS

Computer games are played using a computer—everyone knows that. But there are many kinds of computers, and each one presents special advantages and disadvantages for hosting a game. The features of importance include the speed of the processor; the nature of the graphics area, including its size, color, space, and speed of access; the nature of the user interface; speed and cost of Internet access; and the amount of memory available. Games are usually developed for a particular platform, but they may expand their range of platforms with time.

Desktop Computers

PCs and Macs are good devices on which to play games. PCs in particular have a large variety of devices that can be used to supplement the gaming interfaces. Desktops typically have a large amount of memory, run at 3 GHz and more, and multiple processors and most importantly possess a high-powered graphics card. Modern graphics cards are much faster than the processors on the computer and are programmed to respond to a game's specific needs. Programming a PC can be done in any of dozens of languages.

PCs have a range of video and audio output devices. Color quality of monitors is now excellent, although each monitor is just a little different from the others. Multiple high-quality speakers can be fed by 5.1 and 7.1 channel sound cards to create a compelling 3D sound display. By the way, the ".1" in "5.1" refers to the subwoofer, which is not really a distinct channel. The quality of the displays places a responsibility on the developers to provide good sound and images. Defects will be obvious.

Of course, computers are all sold with high-speed Ethernet cards, so Internet access is not a problem. Also, games are now often downloaded to a PC from the Internet using services such as Steam. This means that software updates to games, something that was once impossible, are now done while the player sleeps.

There are some pitfalls when using desktop computers as gaming devices. After someone has owned a computer for a few weeks, it is unlike any other computer in the world, because users always customize them. New programs are installed, special devices are connected to the bus, security measures are taken, and a host of small modifications are made. The fact that no two PCs are the same does make it difficult for developers to guarantee that their games will work. Then there are software upgrades from the system vendors and the simple variation in operating system levels and versions. What can the developer depend on? Not much. So, they must provide it for themselves.

Tablets

Tablets are not quite computers. They have a smaller, slower processor, less memory, and no extendability. The screens are small and have small, slow graphics cards. Their Internet is restricted to wireless. There is no keyboard or mouse, usually just a touch screen.

This means that the touch screen has to be used for most user input. A touch screen maps onto a mouse pretty easily in terms of the operations it can perform, but avatars are usually controlled using the "w," "a," "s," and "d" keys, which are not available.

Tablets have sound capability but are limited to stereo. Headphones would be the rule. Some tablet games have been downsized from a desktop, but the advanced ones simply will not work.

Game Consoles

A game console is a specialized computer designed to run games. The system is optimized for game performance in every regard. Because a console has no other job, it has limited customizability and a much smaller range of things it can do, but it does those things very fast. It generally has multiple processors, an advanced graphics card, and some disk space so as to store a few games and high scores. Games can be distributed on disks and on the Internet.

A computer game that executes on a console is sometimes called a video game, possibly because they used to use the television as a monitor.

Programming a game for a console is actually a quite complex task involving a lot of specific knowledge of the architecture of the machine and some parallel programming. The results can be spectacular.

Popular consoles are the PlayStation (now at version 4), Xbox (multiple versions), and Nintendo Switch.

Portable Consoles

Portable consoles are handheld computers that only play video games. The king of the portables is the Game Boy by Nintendo. That version has sold over 118 million units, although it is no longer made. It has an 8-bit computer, meaning the graphics and sound were very primitive indeed. However, you could play it on a school bus or in a subway.

The Game Boy has been replaced by the DS and 3DS with 32-bit processors, which have sold 152 million units. The bestselling game was Super Mario Bros. at 31 million copies. Financially this would be the device to create games for, but Nintendo keeps a very tight reign on who can create for these devices. They keep control partly because they own the patent on the game distribution device, a small chip that fits into the body of the console. Nobody else can make those.

Other portables include the PlayStation Vita and the Sony PSP Slim.

FIGURE 0.4 **The original Game Boy.**

Cellular Phones

Cell phones are ubiquitous and have multiple purposes, so it makes sense that games would be created for them. The problem is that they are really just very small tablets. This means that the screen size (what developers call "real estate") is a limiting factor. Playing a game like *Civilization* or *World of Warcraft* could be tricky. It would certainly be constraining. Yet the advantages are clear. A phone has Internet access, it has many built-in devices like GPS, tilt sensors, and accelerometers, and it has sound.

Cellular phones are frequently based on the Android operating system, although iPhones are not. This means that a developer has some clear choices to make when building a game, and the Android operating system is upward compatible for at least a few versions.

Building a game for a phone must take into account the specific constraints, although there are a few games that can be played on nearly any device; *Angry Birds* comes to mind.

ASPECTS OF INTERESTING GAMES

Games that have had an enduring quality tend to have things in common. Very few games have all of these, and some have only one, but these are things that should be thought of when designing and building a new game. Genre is an important consideration when incorporating features, as is the style and quality level of the graphics, the nature of the sound, and so on.

Venue

Some games take place in interesting locations, often real places that you may have visited: San Francisco, New York, Paris. People like to see new and interesting places, and people who have been to those places like to see spots they can recognize within the game. Of course, many people have seen these places in movies and on television, so that gives the sites an extra degree of familiarity. This is important, and not just because the locations are often distant and exotic to many of us. If we could create a game that would drive through your own hometown, for instance, that might interest you. The makers of the *Monopoly* game have done this by customizing their game for various cities, and it seems to work.

Naturally, simply placing the action in an exciting place is not good enough—you must portray that place using graphics and sound well enough so that the player can identify it. This is an implementation issue more than a design issue, but is important, and it will be discussed in more detail.

If the game is a driving game, then placing it on a racetrack is an obvious thing to do and can actually take away from the fun *unless* that track is familiar to the player. The track at Indianapolis is well known, for example, and a racing fan would identify it in a moment. In a basketball or hockey game, the designers and implementers go to some significant efforts to try to make the players look and act like the real players and to have the venues be accurate representations of the real thing. Fans know their sport and can be very critical when the game does not look right.

It is a little unusual to permit the player to get too far away from the path that the game designers have set out. In some games you can go anywhere in the simulated world and manipulate objects—this is an essential aspect of play in *The Sims*, for instance. Such games are sometimes called sandboxes, because the player, rather than the designer, defines the way the game is played. It is a feature of most games that the player *appears to have much more freedom than they really do*; they appear to have choices, but for simplicity's sake the choices all seem to lead to the same few consequences. This appearance of freedom is very important to computer games in general, not just racing games. It is necessary because we just can't simulate the entire universe.

Not *yet*, anyway.

Conflict

A game most often has winners and losers; games keep score. Clearly the goal is to win, and any game that does not allow the player to win will not be popular. This is the minimum conflict requirement of any game, even ones that involve collaboration. Perhaps the term *challenge* should be used in place of conflict. In any case, a game presents the player with obstacles to be overcome, and success is a matter of learning how to deal with these obstacles.

There are a variety of conflict sources in games, and variety can be essential to game play. Indeed, any narrative depends on a degree of conflict to be interesting. While narrative in some games is usually there only to provide background, or an excuse for the action, other times the conflict is fundamental to the story (World War II, for instance) as it defines both the goals and the means of achieving them.

So, what kind of conflict are we talking about? First-person shooters have one of the obvious forms of conflict, where the goals are achieved by shooting your opponents. Sports games have obvious conflicts, as do racing games: to defeat an opponent using the rules of the sport. In *Crazy Taxi* we have customers refusing to pay if we get there late, and they berate us for going too fast or slow. In the *Tycoon* series of games (e.g., *Zoo Tycoon*), conflict is created by forcing the player to balance costs and income through building attractions. Not all games use competition as conflict, but most do. *Little Big Planet* is a cooperative game in which the players can create new content, but there are still goals to be achieved that present challenges; it lacks the incentive to defeat an opponent, and so in that way it is not competitive.

Graphics and Sound

All really good games excel in some aspects of graphics or sound or both. Graphics do not have to be high resolution and three dimensional, but they do have to be appropriate for the specific game. Games like *Halo* offer high-quality graphics and good animation, but we should not mistake "high resolution" for "interesting." *The Simpsons Hit & Run* offers the players the ability to explore a town that they know fairly well—Springfield, home of the Simpsons. Do not underestimate the value of *sandbox mode*; if the world is interesting, then just looking around can be entertaining.

Sound may be more important than graphics, especially for imparting mood. This includes excitement, and a fast-moving rock and roll audio background adds energy to a game in the same way the ethereal themes from *Half Life* make its world seem dangerous and spooky. It is not usually a trade-off, and we can have good graphics and audio if we just have the wherewithal to create them.

Naturally some games require better graphics, because they need to be more faithful simulations, whereas others can be very cartoony, like *Double Dash*, and still offer a huge degree of entertainment value. As a result of these considerations, the best games have in common an appropriate level of detail in graphics, with good audio and appropriate and entertaining objects and backdrops rendered predictably.

Props

Props are items that can be manipulated in the game. All games have props of some kind. Sports games in general have fewer props than most games, and simulation games often have many. A ball is a prop; so is a bullet or a missile, and they can move on their own. Power-ups and penalty objects are props too. Props have an immense potential for making a game more interesting. Without the possibility of picking up weapons and speedups, the *Double Dash* game is just a cartoon race game. Being able to slow down an opponent from a distance, and have him be a threat from behind, adds an element of excitement.

Props also allow a more interesting narrative, since entire missions and levels can depend on moving props from one place to another. They can impart important properties that remain from level to level, like magic icons, fuel, and skill points. This leads to the conclusion that complexity makes a game more interesting. There is some truth to this, so long as the game remains playable, but it is more likely that a degree of unpredictability makes the game more interesting. The game must be consistent, but it is best if it does not repeat itself exactly each time it is played. Props can be used both to make a game more complex and to make it less predictable. The location of the props can change along with a repeatable character that otherwise could become dull. A pattern of play can be useful sometimes, but it's rarely entertaining.

Interface

Games are fundamentally an interactive medium, and interfaces are at the heart of interaction. There has been a significant effort to standardize some game interfaces. For example, on consoles we find very similar controls doing similar jobs, especially on games that run on multiple consoles. Also, games of a specific genre tend to use consistent control sequences, like arrow keys for motion. Games vary a little on use of keys/buttons and mouse gestures, and there is still too much variation generally for identical mechanics.

Some racing games use the mouse to control speed and direction. The mouse has more degrees of freedom in directional control, and the faster the car goes, the harder it is to control it with a mouse. One tends to oversteer, and mouse position is relative, not absolute. Still, given the popularity of games for tablets and smartphones, the use of the mouse is increasing. The touch gestures on tablets translate into mouse clicks and motions directly. Anyway, most tablets and phones don't have keyboards, so using keys is a bad idea.

There are now many special game interfaces available at low cost, most of which use the USB interface. This is much better than the old parallel port or, even older, the "game port" that used to be available on PCs. These were almost always used to plug in a "joystick," a curious term for a game control.

One such special-purpose interface is the steering wheel-pedal set that converts wheel and pedal motions into character sequences. The fact that they can be configured to send any sequence you like means that game interfaces don't have to be standard anymore, at least in the long run. More and more people will acquire the special interfaces until the keyboard becomes old-fashioned. Figure 0.5 shows one particular brand, the Logitech.

Another USB interface device is the flight stick; the idea is to make the interface look more like that of an airplane by giving it a similar control device.

FIGURE 0.5 Special-purpose game controllers for specific genres. (Left) A driving controller that emulates a steering wheel. (Right) A flight stick for aircraft and other vehicle simulations.

The Logitech Wingman shown in Figure 0.5 is one example, which again can be configured to provide specific control sequences for any possible action.

A problem is that there is no "feel," in that the action is from the player to the game only. In a real airplane or car, the control—wheel or stick—provides a force that counters the player's actions, and that can be relative to the speed, direction, driving surface, or even wind. Few game controllers do this. Some can vibrate, which gives a limited feedback. The Reactive Grip controller (Provancher, 2012) simulates responses of various weapons, like swords and guns, and is probably the best example of a reactive device right now.

There are many other possibilities, and progress is proceeding rapidly. At a recent Game Developer's Conference, for example, there was an interface for sale that input brain waves from a couple of small electrodes attached to the skull and used the signals to play some simple games. The price? One hundred dollars. There is university research that includes some work on hand gesture recognition as applied to controlling games on the PC—hand motions are interpreted as requests to move, pick something up, and so on. Ultimately games will become an invisible technology, like telephones and TV. They will be anywhere we like and will require no special knowledge or hardware to play.

Pace/Scale

The driving games that are the most fun typically allow you to go *fast*. Submarines move slowly but inevitably and cannot turn or stop in any reasonable time. The pace of the game must be appropriate (that word again) for the kind of situation being simulated by the game. In addition, as the player gains experience, the game should present more and more difficulties. In some games this means that the game speeds up; other times there are more or stronger opponents.

An impression of speed can be given by placing objects near the player that move past at a high speed. Buildings are good for this because they have a lot of detail that flashes past in a similar way to what we'd see on movies or in real life. In fact, a variety of objects in a range of distances is effective in conveying the illusion.

Sound is crucial as well. Play a fast tempo game with the sound off to see the difference. A fast-moving music track helps a lot, as does a good set of speed implying sound effects: positional sound, Doppler effects, and so on.

One nice idea that is simple to implement and is now a standard in games is a backdrop with scenery painted on it. This effect is used in movies too; the shots of the inside of Borg ships on *Star Trek* are actors in front of paintings, and quite a lot of science fiction depends on paintings to convey distance and strange environments. The use of drops in a game can add depth that is noticed if absent, but usually draws no comment otherwise.

A 3D game consists of a terrain model on top of which we have both moving and stationary objects. There is usually a distance beyond which objects will not be rendered (*far clipping plane*), and as objects get closer they seem to "pop" into existence when they pass that distance. In the far distance we have an image painted on a surface that passes for the horizon. This often has hills and sky painted on it, or an urban backdrop. In any case, the drop has no real depth. A game will have the drop rotate as the player turns so as to give the illusion that the car changes direction.

Fidelity/Accuracy

When we create a game, we create an entire universe. We get to decide where things are, how big they are, what they eat, and so on. In particular, the rules of physics as we understand them in the *real* universe are flexible, and we decide how they work in *our* universe. In many kinds of games, the accuracy of the physics takes a back seat to playability and entertainment value. So, if you have ever played *Doom*, you will probably know that the player can seem to run pretty quickly through a level. You may not know that if you measured it, you would see the character has a top speed of 60 mph! This does not detract from the fun; on the contrary, restricting game objects to normal speeds will slow the game down a lot.

Physics includes a variety of topics, including how collisions are handled, how fuel is consumed, how fast the vehicles can accelerate and what the top speeds are, how fast cars can enter a turn before they skid, and how a vehicle can become airborne if it reaches the peak of a hill. Most games do take liberties with physics to enhance game play, especially the more cartoon-style games. We will discuss this further after there has been a chance to look at how physics is implemented in a game. Just remember that any rule can be violated if it makes the game more fun.

EXERCISES

The following problems will exercise your knowledge of the material in this chapter, and they will sometimes require that you do some more research before you are able to complete them.

1. Describe the venue, conflict, pace, scale, and fidelity of two games that you currently play. Think about other games you enjoy—do they have common elements?

2. The game Nim has a known strategy for winning. Any game for which a win or draw can be forced is said to be strongly solved. What other games are strongly solved? Name two.

3. A *serious game* is one that has some function in addition to entertainment, such as education. Name at least one serious game.

4. Describe the interface to *Angry Birds*. How does the interface contribute to the fact that the game can be found on so many different platforms?

5. Art style can be an important aspect of a game. Sketch two possible visual interfaces for a computer-based Nim game.

6. The game Snakes and Ladders is purely random. There is no strategy that can be used; it all depends on the throw of the dice. Suggest rules that would allow some degree of strategy in this game.

7. Consider the kind of materials that can be found in a dollar store or craft store. Make up a game that uses such easily found materials, write a set of rules, and play the game with at least two other people. Did the game play the way that you thought it would?

RESOURCES

Yale Game Theory class, *http://oyc.yale.edu/economics/econ-159.*

MIT course on Computer Games and Simulations for Investigation and Education, *https://ocw.mit.edu/courses/urban-studies-and-planning/11-127j-computer-games-and-simulations-for-education-and-exploration-spring-2015/*

MIT Game Design course, *http://ocw.mit.edu/courses/comparative-media-studies/cms-608-game-design-fall-2010/.*

Raph Koster, Theory of Fun for Game Design, *http://www.theoryoffun.com/theoryoffun.pdf.*

https://www.archimedes-lab.org/game_nim/play_nim_game.html.

REFERENCES

1. Elwyn R. Berlekamp, John H. Conway, and Richard K. Guy. (2001). *Winning Ways for Your Mathematical Plays*, Vol. 1–4. A K Peters/CRC Press. Boca Raton, FLA.

2. Johann Huizinga. (2016). *Homo Ludens: A Study of the Play-Element in Culture.* Kettering, OH: Angelico Press.

3. Aki Järvinen. (2008). *Games without Frontiers: Theories and Methods for Game Studies and Design.* Tampere, Finland: Tampere University Press.

4. William Provancher. (2011). Multidirectional controller with shear feedback. US Patent 13/269,948, filed October 10, 2011, and issued August 14, 2013, Publication number US 2012/0038468 A1.

5. Miguel Sicart. (2008). "Defining Game Mechanics." *The International Journal of Computer Game Research* 8, no. 2 (December). *http://www.gamestudies.org/0802/articles/sicart*

6. John von Neumann and Oskar Morgenstern. (1947). *Theory of Games and Economic Behavior*, 2nd edition. Princeton, NJ: Princeton University Press.

7. Dan Whitehead. (2018). *Game Over: The Games We Loved to Play and the Consoles Time Forgot.* Studio Press.

1

INTRODUCTION TO HOW GAMES WORK

Computer games are first of all games, and second computer based. A good way to begin as a student of game development is to examine a real game to see how it functions in some detail. We can take it apart and take a look at how a computer game is structured at the design and implementation level. A simple game that everyone knows is ideal for this purpose. *Pong* is one of the first computer games, and it has all of the elements of other games, except that it is simple enough to understand completely. First, let's take a look at how a game operates at the computer level.

VIDEO GAME ARCHITECTURE

The word "architecture" can be defined as construction or structure generally; any ordered arrangement of the parts of a system: the *architecture* of the universe.[1]

According to this definition, game architecture should be about the internal structure of a game, its general organization as a functional system in terms of the way that the parts are arranged to create a working game. In order to truly understand the structure of a game, you pretty much have to know something about computer programming, because the computer is the enabling technology and any computer game is a piece of software at the core. Without being a programmer, it is only possible to have a general appreciation of how a game functions. You need to know what the parts are—not the visible parts like cars and roads, but the structural and functional parts, like the audio system and the renderer. You need to understand how the parts communicate with one another and what one part needs to know to accomplish its task.

A game player cannot be required to know this. The player needs only to know the rules of the game, the task, the interface; those things needed to *play*. In fact, my students have told me that after studying games and writing one, they never look at a game in the same way. They still play games, but they find themselves asking, "why did they put that building there?" and "how do they implement those torches?" So, knowing how games function "under the hood" can sometimes interfere with, or other times enhance, the experience of playing them.

In a technical sense, a computer game is an interactive real-time simulation with a graphical and audio display. If you accept this definition, then there are already a number of identifiable components that comprise the game system: the graphics system, the audio system, the user, and the scheduler. The only essential part that is missing is the artificial intelligence (or *AI*), whose job is to keep track of the simulated objects in the game.

Figure 1.1 shows a diagram of the basic components and how they are connected. It is not the only organization, and it certainly does not show too many details, but it should be good enough for now, and it will form the basis of this discussion. So, the remainder of this chapter will describe each of these components of a game and how and what they communicate with each other. This will give you a much clearer idea of how the overall game functions as a software system.

A computer game offers the player a world that does not really exist. Without getting too philosophical about it, what you see through the computer screen is a rendition of data that represents a simulated situation. What you see is a real screen with real images, but the situation and what is being drawn do not exist in the real world—it is an analogy, a virtual environment in which you control the laws that dictate how objects interact (for instance, gravity or the results of a collision). A significant part of a game, in terms of code and time required to create it, is the part that displays images and sounds from the imaginary world for the player to evaluate.

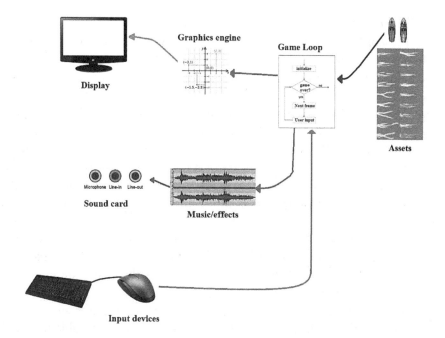

Display

Graphics engine

Game Loop

Assets

Microphone   Line-in   Line-out

Sound card

Music/effects

Input devices

FIGURE 1.1 General architecture of a computer game.

Before proceeding, it should be noted that there are many types of games and that each has its own specific needs. This means that the viewpoint, or the place from which the simulated universe is seen, will vary from game to game and genre to genre, and so the discussion must be sufficiently general to allow many perspectives. Many games that are played online, through browsers, are effectively two-dimensional (2D), and so the discussion will eventually focus on ways to render 2D games effectively.

In a three-dimensional (3D) environment, we perceive the game universe from our particular point in space and project the view from that point onto a 2D plane for display on the screen. What is going on a great distance away is unlikely to be relevant to us, and so the graphics system might not bother displaying it. The region ahead for the next few feet or meters or yards is crucial, and how we respond to that will influence the meters following that. The important thing as a game programmer is to display the things that the player needs to make gameplay decisions and to feel that the simulated world is real. The display of key data involves two main aspects: visual data, requiring a computer graphics system, and sound data, which requires an audio display system. Most games have both of these things.

The Graphics System

Many people still think that games are all about graphics. They are not, really, but many games use more CPU time in drawing the scene than for anything else. An efficient graphics system can leave a reasonable number of CPU cycles for use by other aspects of the game system, and that is very important. A good game uses an appropriate level of detail for the application, and that's important too. The basic problem addressed by game graphics systems is placing enough frames (images) on the screen every second to give the illusion of motion and realism. Movies use 24 frames per second to achieve their degree of realism, while television uses almost 30 per second. However, a television displays an image that is about 525 x 525 pixels, while a motion picture has a much higher resolution.

Another aspect of picture display that must be considered is the number of distinct colors that can be shown. This is sometimes called *quantization*, and television, for example, can display far fewer colors than can a motion picture, and a computer screen falls in between.

Some simple math: at 24 frames per second, with a computer screen having a resolution of 1024 x 768 and using 24-bit colors, we need to be able to calculate and write out 56 megabytes of data per second. This seems like quite a lot, even on a modern PC, so we have to use a few little tricks. First, and most importantly, the video card has been taking a larger role in the calculation of screen updates for games. Video cards can draw millions of polygons per second and can do more advanced and esoteric operations like texture mapping, support for stencil buffers, and *mip-mapping*. This means that the CPU does not have to do these things but simply organizes the data for the video card.

The fundamental differences between 2D and 3D games can be summarized by saying that in a 3D game all objects are 3D and need to be viewed from a particular point in space. The graphics system will flatten the scene by projecting it onto a flat surface, and this means that some objects will be hidden by others, some will be too far away to see, some will be behind us and so not visible, and all objects will be transformed so that the usual visual cues will apply for the viewer (player). This last item usually means something called a perspective transformation, in which objects farther away from us appear to be smaller and parallel lines appear to meet at a distance point. For example, in a driving game if we are driving a car and looking through the front windshield, then our field of view is restricted to the region in front of us, say 60 degrees to each side of dead ahead. Objects that are not in that region can be ignored and should not require any significant amount of computation. Also, objects that are too far away are also to be ignored, as they will be too small to see. Of course, figuring out what can and cannot be seen requires computational effort.

In a 2D game we usually view all objects from the side or from above. Sometimes the gameplay area is bigger than the screen, and the background scrolls as the player's character moves about. Objects in a 2D game are simpler and easier to draw, and perspective is not an issue.

Some of the work in drawing the views must be done by you as the game programmer, but much of it can be handled by your graphics card. There are quite a few such cards out there, and each has its own capabilities and interfaces. If you want your game to run on more than one computer, you cannot code your graphics system for a specific device. Fortunately, there are software packages that form a layer between us and the graphics card, hiding the differences between the cards while presenting us with a consistent interface. This is really essential for a commercial game, and it is pretty important for us too.

The programming language Python has no built-in support for graphics or game development. It's a very popular language for teaching introductory courses and is popular in the programming community, especially the *Linux* community. However, associated with Python is a very useful package called Pygame that provides all of the facilities needed to build almost any computer game, and that begins with a very usable graphics library. It allows 2D graphics and a 3D library that looks like *OpenGL*; this book will rely heavily on what Pygame supplies for graphics support generally. Since Python runs on all major operating systems, this means that a game developed using that language is playable effectively everywhere. The thing to remember about most game graphics systems is that the 3D systems are based on polygons, since polygons can be drawn quickly using a graphics card. We can represent any object as a collection of polygons, as well as shade them, place textures on them, rotate and scale them, and so on using very fast algorithms.

If you read a lot of game programming books, you will frequently encounter the phrase *graphics pipeline*. The idea is that if you can keep a number of software modules busy at the same time, you can achieve an increase in the number of polygons you can process per second. There are a few ways that the pipeline can be organized, but here the view will be taken that there are three basic parts: the object level, the geometric level, and the rasterization level.

Object Level

At this stage the objects are still understood as such, rather than as collections of primitive graphic entities like polygons and lines. We do animation at this level, as well as morphing and collision detection—basically, any operation that needs to know about the objects themselves. At the end of this phase, a set of polygons or lines is sent to the geometric level.

This part of the pipeline is the most sensitive to the game itself. It is implemented in software, most often by the game designers and creators, because it is they who understand the game objects best.

Geometric Level

The geometry part of the pipeline has a variety of functions that can be broken off into distinct modules, as seen in Figure 1.2. 3D geometry is much more complex than 2D, and the figure illustrates the more complicated situation. The first step converts model-based coordinates, which are often based on an object-centered coordinate system, into a more global system of coordinates so that objects can interact.

Next, based on the position of the viewer (camera), we compute a coordinate transformation that aligns the polygons of the objects to a common system based on the viewer. One result of this is that some polygons become impossible to see; they may be behind us or too far away.

Now we consider the position and color of the lights and create appropriate shading and color transformations of the object's polygons. The sun, for example, is positioned a great distance away and is colored yellow-white, while a nearby headlight might be a brighter blue. The color of a pixel is a function of its own intrinsic color and of the brightness, color, and position of the illumination sources.

Now we compute the viewing transformation, most often a perspective transform. This gives us the view we would expect of a three-dimensional object, including the fact that distant objects look smaller than near ones. The view of the scene will be realistic if it represents what we expect, and we expect a perspective view. The objects that used to be 3D polygons are now two-dimensional ones.

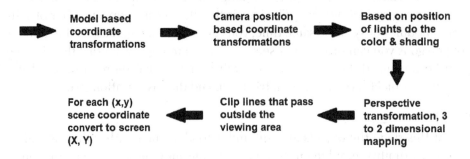

FIGURE 1.2 The Geometry Pipeline

The polygons that fall outside of the computer screen area, or viewing area, must be eliminated, or *clipped*. This is the next stage. Polygons that are too close or far away would have been clipped in the previous stage. Clipping is a non-trivial operation. For example, a triangle that is partly outside of the screen area is cut by a vertical or horizontal line, and this often means that it is not a triangle anymore. Finally, all coordinates of all lines and polygons are converted in screen (or window) X,Y coordinates so they can be drawn quickly.

Rasterization

In this stage, we convert lines and polygons into pixels. The only thing that a screen can display is pixels, so it is essential that this step be performed accurately as well as quickly. After this is done, we can do any other operations that need to be done on a per-pixel basis. Much of this is done by the graphics card.

Comments on Optimization

It should be obvious that the code must be efficiently written, because the graphics system must render a sufficient number of frames per second so that the game appears to be smooth. The algorithms we choose must able to deal with the number of polygons likely to appear in the objects, in both space and time considerations.

The game we are going to create will, first and foremost, have to display scenes on the screen with the correct positions and colors, follow the game rules as designed, and play sounds at correct moments. While we will not be intentionally wasteful, efficiency will not be the most important thing. Why? Because code optimization can become boring very quickly, and it is not our main interest. There are many reference works on the subject for those interested, including *Game Coding Complete* and *Core Techniques and Algorithms in Game Programming*.

The Audio System

In general, the purpose of the game's audio system is to play music and sound effects. This is supposed to be a simplistic view, and yet even after decades of technological changes in game technology and design, the game audio system still does pretty much what it always did, and still works in a similar way. Huge steps forward have been made in the area of graphics, but standards are still weak and there are a lot of ad hoc schemes out there.

Most sounds that we will need, like an engine sound, a door opening and closing, crashes and scrapes, and even the music, will be read in from files, usually one file per sound. A very common format for sound files is the WAV file, basically a Microsoft standard that is supported on most platforms. These can contain compressed or uncompressed audio, can have mono or stereo, and can store audio at a variety of sample rates, including the CD standards. It is a simple file format and very convenient for our purposes.

However, there may be a need for more sophistication on the part of the audio system. It may be asked to play positional audio, in which each sound appears to originate from a particular point in space. This can be done with stereo, but it is much better suited to modern 5.1 channel audio systems, which can be truly impressive. Sound cards have recently been designed with some capacity for sound synthesis, and some degree of synthetic sound and music, especially using MIDI, can now be found on games. However, the basic function of the audio system is simple, and its job is obvious: we need to play and stop a sound on cue. How this is done will be the subject of Chapter 3.

GAME DESIGN

Being a game designer is not as cool as many people believe. Yes, the very best get some attention, but few people know the name or face of the person who designed their favorite game. Moreover, a game designer's job mostly involves creating written design documents. Yes, they must have ideas about how the game will operate, but the key job of a designer is to communicate those concepts in detail to the people who will implement them. Not just programmers, but especially artists, musicians, and other designers such as level designers and character designers.

Earlier it was said that a game designer really created game mechanics. That's true. A designer either creates novel mechanics, as was done in the game *Portal*, or fits existing mechanics together into a new game. Really new mechanics are rare, but they do occur from time to time. The important thing is to incorporate simple mechanics into a novel and interesting situation. *Angry Birds* did that very well. The use of one's finger to specify the direction and force of a throw combined with the interesting concept of knocking down a structure made of blocks made for a compelling game. There's really no way to specify a formula for accomplishing that.

Fortunately, that's not needed. A game programmer has relatively little creative input to a game. The programmer is given the game design document and is assigned a part of the game to implement (i.e., write the code for). A game is a special kind of program, though, and there is a specific set of knowledge that one needs in order to be good at the task.

Mechanics

The subject of *game mechanics* is going to arise again and again, so a good definition would be useful. Unfortunately, this term is more generally understood by designers, but it is hard to define for people who don't build games, and it is impossible to explain to people who don't play them. A commonly quoted definition, and the one appearing in Wikipedia, is:

> *A game mechanic is a construct of rules intended to produce a game or gameplay.*

This is a bit circular—games use mechanics and mechanics make a game, as it were. Also, not everyone would agree than rules must be directly involved in the definition. Järvinen (2008) defines mechanics as

> *means to guide the player into particular behavior by constraining the space of possible plans to attain goals.*

This is possibly better because it puts rules into a subservient position to player actions. There is an instinctive view that a mechanic is something that a player *does*, and something that is *designed* into the game. Another possible definition (Sicart, 2008) is:

> *Game mechanics are methods invoked by agents for interacting with the game world.*

By looking at a collection of definitions, we might get an instinctive idea of mechanics. It is a key concept. The idea appears to be that *a game mechanic is a design feature of a game that allows the player to progress toward the goal.* There can be mechanics that interfere with forward progress too. So, one example mechanic could be called *dodge*, in which players must avoid objects moving toward their avatars. *Space Invaders* is one example of this. The *shoot* mechanic is a common one, where you must hit your opponent or a target with a thrown missile of some type. The *race* mechanic involves a player getting to a particular spot in the game before any opponents, and so on.

A game mechanic should be interesting to the player and simple to use. A button press or mouse gesture is usually all that is possible in a game, so these must be converted into game elements that implement the mechanic—press space to shoot, up arrow to move ahead. The mechanic is not specifically about the interface though. One of the better game mechanics in recent memory is the one used in the game *Portal*, where the player creates (using a mouse click) two circular doorways through any floor, ceiling, or wall. Walk the player's avatar into one doorway and it exits through the other! This can be used for quite complex maze puzzles. The mouse click, however, is not the issue—it is about the possibilities created by the click.

PLAYING THE GAME BY THE RULES

What we have seen of game architecture up to this point is what can be called the *game board*, the part that the user sees and manipulates. There are many programs that have very sophisticated graphical and audio interfaces that are not games. What's the difference? A game, the kind of game we are discussing, works in real time, processing user choices and updating the display accordingly. A game is a simulation and, most importantly, is one that has a goal. To be a game, there must be a way to at least keep score, and usually there is a way to win. The part of the game program that does this is variously called the *game logic* section, the *artificial intelligence*, and some other things too.

The graphics and audio parts of a game can largely be shared between games that are quite different from each other. The game logic is what makes each game what it is. It is the code that reflects the game designer's intent. Even here, the structure of this program has a certain consistency from game to game; it is in the details that the code differs.

Most of a Computer Game Is Hidden

The player actually sees a world drawn by the graphics system, but this world is particular to the game at hand and changes according to rules that are largely invisible to the player, at least at first. Part of the game play is figuring out what the rules are. For example, how fast can someone drive into that corner before skidding? That is actually a kind of rule. What's the ratio of brake to gas pedal for a proper 180-degree turn? Again, this is a rule that is discovered. The number of damage points you can take before your car blows up is an *explicit* rule that is stated up front, a slightly different thing. Most game players don't read a lot of rules before starting to play, and instead discover a lot of the explicit rules as they go along.

So when we say that a lot of the game is hidden, we mean that the rules, interrelationships between game objects, goals, and even your particular progress through the game are saved in code and internal data structures and are not necessarily displayed. Indeed, their internal representation does not lend itself to display.

The Artificial Intelligence

The artificial intelligence (AI) subsystem of a game is responsible for many things that the game does that are not seen directly but are reflected in game play and realism aspects. The AI does object management, including physics, and the direction of independent simulated objects like opponents, in our case opposing drivers. Specifically, the AI keeps track of the current position and velocity of all objects. Thus, it is the logical place to do collision detection. It keeps track of attributes of objects, including earned attributes like hit points, damage, and found objects (ammunition, money, etc.).

Artificial intelligence has a connotation among the general population, supported by movies and TV, of computers that can think. In the movies they are also frequently evil, but we'll leave that for later. Computer scientists and programmers know more about the details, and they realize that AI is about making a computer *appear* to be intelligent. The techniques that computer professionals use are many and varied, but the truth is that game AI is very simplistic compared with the techniques found in research labs, and the goals are quite different too.

The basic problem is that the game AI has to function in real time, and it must steal CPU cycles from what is perceived to be really important—the graphics system. Thus, the really complex and sexy functions of an advanced real AI system are simply too time consuming for a game. Good thing they are mostly not required. For example, a voice recognition system would be cool on some games, but really isn't needed. Games AI is rarely required to prove theorems, recognize faces, or invent novel answers to complex questions. It *is* required to decide what to do next and to plan a route through a building or a forest to a goal. Maybe it will have to decide how best to pass you on a hairpin curve. Although it is sometimes useful to use an advanced technique like a neural network to accomplish a game goal, it is unusual.

However, one thing that all AI systems must do is keep track of everything on the screen and most things that are not. Not only does the game have to decide when you hit the wall, but it must also keep track of all of the other cars, even the ones you cannot see, and slow them down when they hit an obstacle. Most of the AI system is about simple rules implying simple choices. The most common implementation of such a choice is:

```
if (condition is true) then { do this thing }
```

This is not especially sophisticated, but it does the job quickly. The same thing can be implemented as a table or a tree, as you will see in Chapter 5.

Game State

The state of a game is a collection of information that represents the game at any given time. Given the state, a game can be started from that point. The information needed in the state includes:

- position, orientation, velocity of all dynamic entities
- behavior and intentions of AI-controlled characters
- dynamic and static attributes of all gameplay entities
- scores, health, power-ups, damage levels, etc.

All subsystems in the game are interested in some aspect of the game state, because the state variables are exactly those things that are essential to the look of the game and the play options possible from any point. For instance, the renderer needs to know the position of objects to draw, their damage levels, and so on.

How is the game state made available to subsystems? As always there are many options, each with their own advantages and disadvantages, but for a straightforward driving game, there are only a few that make sense. In most cases an object is coded as an integer.

Global State

This is just what it sounds like. State variables are global, shared by all of the modules. A lot of programming language design and software engineering has gone into trying to show why this is a poor idea. After all, imagine every module having access—complete access, mind you—to every other module's variables. Chaos!

On the other hand, there is a certain convenience to this scheme. If the graphics system wants to know where a tree is, it simply gets it from where it is stored. The problem is that it can change it, of course. Really, if you are writing a quite small system with pretty clear modules, and you are relatively disciplined, then this will work out OK. The more complex the game is, the more likely this scheme is (exponentially!) to result in problems.

Push/Pull (client server)

Here, subsystems have incomplete knowledge of one another, and can request information from each other in a structured fashion (a *pull*) or send a new value to a module (a *push*). This is what we will use in our sample game, and it is what we often see in Java and C++ as accessors and modifiers. For example, if we want to find the location of a ball, we ask for it using a function:

```
getPosition (BALL, x, y);
```
which is a pull. If we wish to notify the AI system that an object has been destroyed, we do a push:

```
setExist (object[i], FALSE);
```

which sets the *exist* attribute of the object to false.

This scheme is elegant, but it has another big advantage: it can be used across great distances with equal simplicity. For online multiple player games, the push-pull scheme operates on a server at a remote site, and one of various remote invocation schemes can be used, transparently.

Managers

In some sense this is like the push-pull model with an intermediate system for handling the requests. The AI system does not own position and orientation attributes in this scheme, for example. They are owned by a management subsystem that has the simple task of hiding the variables and structures and permitting access to them using standard accessor and modifier functions.

So, using this scheme the AI system would have to ask for the position of an object just like the graphics system, and would also have to request a modification to a position from the manager:

```
manager.getPos (OBJECT1, x, y);
manager.setPos (OBJECT1, x+1, y+1);
```

This is not much more complex than the client server approach, and it has a similar feel. There are few tools that support this model, and so discipline is needed to maintain it. There are few situations this scheme would avoid that the client-server scheme would not also avoid, and so that's not a distinction between the two.

Broadcast-listener

For a certain amount of overhead, we can change the client-server model into one in which modifications to state attributes can be sent to other subsystems by issuing an event. So, when the position of an opponent changes, for example, an "opponent-change" event can be sent to the graphics system so that it may be drawn correctly. Given a system similar to the Java **interface** scheme that uses *listeners*, all subsystems interested in this change can be alerted at the same time! Objects or subsystems interested in a particular event, like position change of police cars for instance, would register with the listener so that they would receive the events.

So, using a Java-like syntax, we could have:

```
public class Z extends q implements BallListener
{
...
    t1.addBallListener(this);
...
}
public void ballMotion (GameEvent e)
{
    if (e.getSource() == t1) ...
}
```

This shows the three essential parts of the setup: declaring the use of the **BallListener** interface in the class header, adding this class instance to the list of those interested in receiving police motion events, and writing a handler (a callback, really) named **ballMotion** that will be called when a police motion event takes place. There is no direct communication between subsystems in this scheme. Information is sent to those interested, and only those, and is queued in the case where there are multiple events occurring simultaneously.

Now, this is pretty clever, and if you can make it work properly in a language not offering specific support, it is sure to give you a programmer rush. On almost all PC systems, a process generally uses *only one CPU*. We can pretend that processes are independent if we like, but switching between software processes takes time on our single CPU, and treating software events like variable modifications as if they were asynchronous processes is a little wasteful and obscures the flow of the code. This system works efficiently on a multiple-processor console like the PlayStation. Still, some systems profit from using threads and such, and this is the way to deal with state on such systems.

Shared and Global Entities

This uses the inheritance characteristic of the language, object-oriented, of course, in which the game is implemented. Think of it as global state, but with references to classes and inheritance. So, both the AI and the graphics system would have a reference (pointer) to a police car object, and could, by manipulating the accessor and modifier methods, get and change the object's position, orientation, and other attributes. This is the classic object-oriented way—cleaner than using globals.

Within this scheme there are many options: a single rooted hierarchy, ownership, multiple inheritance, and so on. This kind of thing has, in fact, become the standard practice in many colleges and universities that teach programming (mine too!), and as a result this method, or family of methods, has become the most common scheme for manipulating game objects and system state.

An important complaint with this set of schemes is that they tend to become dependent on a particular language, usually C++, and then decisions become "religious." This is because of many an argument with "software engineers" over things like the proper use of multiple inheritance, for example. Since C++ is one of the few languages that permits multiple inheritance, a scheme that depends upon it has limited options for implementation. The problem is that a single rooted class hierarchy does not scale well, and the inheritance structure starts looking like nonsense after a while. Therefore, the most complex system (graphics, in general) tends to be able to specify the structure of the rest. Multiple inheritance scales better, but it is hard to change later and becomes hard to manage when the system gets complex enough. There are also performance issues in all of these schemes.

There is no best scheme, but one based on a client-server scheme or on managers can work well using object-oriented languages like C++ and Java, and even in C where object orientation is hand coded. Each module contains a set of variables and data structures that cannot be accessed from the other modules except through the accessor functions provided by the module. However, when needed for testing or while merging modules, there can be globals and shared entities; a log file, for example, for dumping test information while debugging. There is nothing to prevent the user of this scheme from using Java or a scripting language like Lua as a tool for creating small, specific-purpose sub-modules—as the controller for an opponent, for instance.

However we do it, the management and control of the system state in a complex system like a computer game must be done carefully and with discipline. While the best way has yet to be determined with certainty, it is absolutely clear that modularity, planning, and discipline must be used if success is to be achieved. Sitting down in front of the computer and starting to enter code is sure to fail, later if not sooner. A game design document is essential so that more than one programmer/developer can work on the game at the same time.

PONG

Pong is sufficiently old that it's possible now that some people don't know what it is. The idea is to create a basic simulation of table tennis or ping pong. It is a game by the definition given previously:

- It is an *activity*, certainly.
- It is *entertaining* by some standard. It has no other purpose.
- It has *rules*. There is a ball that moves about the screen according to basic rules of interaction. It bounces off of walls, basically.
- It has *objects*. There is a ball and two paddles.
- There is a *playing area*, a window on the screen meant to represent a table-tennis table.
- The rules are:

A ball will be created and will be moving in a specific direction.

Each player (there are two) controls a paddle, which is just a vertical line on the screen near the left or right end of the playing area.

By using keys on the keyboard, the player can make the paddle go up and down.

The key mechanic is to block the passage of the ball so that it does not reach the left or right end of the playing area, that is, hitting the ball with your paddle.

If the ball passes your paddle and gets to the side of the playing area you are protecting, then your opponent gets a *point*. A new ball is created when this happens.

The objects each have a graphical rendition that is displayed on the screen at the location where they are supposed to be in the play area. The paddles are simply lines, and the ball is just a circle. The program that implements the game has to keep updating the screen to make it seem as if the ball and paddles are moving.

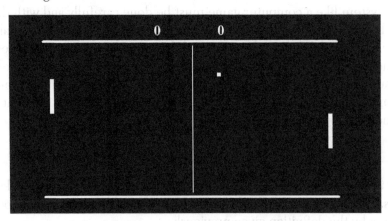

FIGURE 1.3 The Pong display.

This is an optical illusion much like the one used by motion pictures and television. If the human visual system is presented with repeated still images where objects appear in slightly different positions, it has the appearance of movement.

What the game does is to move the objects to new positions based on the movements specified by the game and the user and then draw the objects again. It does this many times each second.

The game software does other things too, of course. It keeps track of *events* that happen in the game. When the ball hits a wall, that's an event. When a ball hits a paddle, it's an event. When the ball reaches one end of the table, that's an event. These are the basic events in *Pong*, but the end of the game should probably be an event, although it can only happen once, and the resetting if the ball after a point could be thought of as an event.

It should be clear that this computer game is implemented by proper handling of all of the events that can occur. Let's make it into a principle:

The software involved in a computer game keeps track of all objects and implements the interactions between them according to the rules.

A game is really a simulation. In *Pong* there's no real ball or paddles, only a simulation of a ball and paddles. There can be no actual impact between a ball and a paddle, only an event that indicates their geometry has overlapped and a response by the game program to do something, in this case change the velocity of the ball. *Pong* is a real-time simulation of table tennis with sound and a graphical display.

It is a willing suspension of disbelief on our part that objects in a game behave as real objects in the world do. When that fails to happen, we notice immediately, the game is now flawed, and the fourth wall is broken. The player is now using a piece of software and is no longer immersed in a game.

Going back to the game *Pong*, Figure 1.4 shows a potential starting point for the game. The ball starts at a location (x_b, y_b) with a velocity (d_x, d_y). The paddle locations are also known. This situation (state) can be drawn immediately as the first image (frame) in the game. The next situation has the ball moved into a new position. This is done quite simply:

$$x_b = x_b + d_x$$
$$y_b = y_b + d_y$$

If the paddles are not being moved, then this will be the only change in the game, and the next image (frame) will be drawn with the ball in the new position.

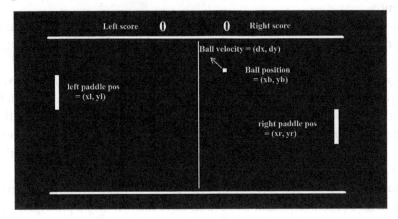

FIGURE 1.4 **The objects in the** *Pong* **game space.**

If the left paddle is being moved, it will be because the left player made it happen by pressing a key. Let the key that moves the left paddle upward be "w" and the one that moves it downward be "s," although this is a design decision. If the left player presses "w," the left paddle will move up. How much? That's another design choice, so let's call that distance dp_y. The program would do this:

$$y_1 = y_1 - dp_y$$

If the "s" key had been pressed, then the left paddle would move down by the same amount:

$$y_1 = y_1 + dp_y$$

This works the same way for the right paddle. The up-arrow key will move it up, and the down-arrow key will move it down. If the up-arrow is pressed:

$$y_r = y_r - dp_y$$

and if the down-arrow is pressed then:

$$y_r = y_r - dp_y$$

When the new frame is drawn, the paddles will be drawn in their new positions. This process continues for step after step, frame after frame, until the ball's x position become smaller than 0 (went past the left paddle) or greater than the screen width (went past the right paddle) or the ball collides with something. Colliding with a wall changes the ball's y velocity, so it changes direction. Colliding with a paddle changes its x velocity. That's basically the game.

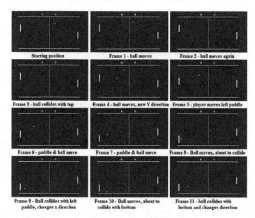

FIGURE 1.5 Sequence of consecutive frames from the game Pong.

Figure 1.5 shows a set of consecutive frames from the game illustrating what the game software must do between each pair of frames. Things that should be moved must be moved, collisions must be resolved—velocity changes, for example. Other things could occur, like a change in score or a new ball, but the point is clear: the software must look for any possible event that happens between any two frames and work that into the game display.

THE GAME DESIGN DOCUMENT

A game design document (GDD) should specify everything that can happen in a game and how it will be resolved. Each interaction between each pair of objects needs to be defined in a careful manner, and in enough detail so that a programmer can implement it in the way that the designer anticipated. Each event must be carefully and fully characterized. It is a software specification and much more, because it defines sounds and artistic assets as well. Programmers, artists, musicians, and level designers all have access to this same document. It's like a Bible.

A programmer does not create this document; the game designer does. The programmer needs to know how to read it though. A book about game programming should teach how to read a design document. So let's do that.

C2H6O Jet Boat Race

A game starts with an idea. Ideas are relatively common in creative industries, but *good* ideas are less common. In the games arena, ideas have to be winnowed down to a very few that may be worth implementing. It's not clear that the idea for a game being presented here is in fact a *good* idea, but for the purposes of explaining a design document and how to use one, it serves the purpose.

The idea concerns a boat racing game. Some number of boats begin at a wharf and have to round a circuit three times and pass a finish line. There will be natural hazards—fishing boats, ducks and geese, whales, wind, waves, and so on. They will have to perform one pit stop, so fuel will be a consideration. There will be opponents which will be controlled by the game AI system, and which will be designed to be entertaining.

That's just an idea though. To turn this into a design, one must define what the objects are, what the mechanics are, what the events are, what the goals are, how the events move the player toward the end (goal), and what the art assets and sound assets are, as well as complete a detailed assessment of everything that can happen in the game. A game cannot crash. An accounting program shouldn't, but sometimes does, and while there are consequences, the crashing of an accounting program is not seen as so much of an issue as is the crashing of a game. Games, except online ones, do not usually have updates or bug fixes, so the interactions and event handling must be carefully defined.

The game design document (GDD) for the Jet Boat game will be developed further in each chapter. It is typical for the GDD to evolve as the game development progresses, but it is essential that there is only one version of the game that is current and shared by all of the developers at any given moment, and that everyone knows where it is. A version control system could be used, but there are document management and share systems such as Google Docs that work very well for this purpose.

The following document is incomplete and will be filled in as more is understood about aspects of the game such as pathfinding, collision detection, audio, and so on. It is clear from the document that artistic assets are a key part of the game and specialist talent is needed to develop a compelling game. In the final document some images will be included, as well as file names and locations for all assets.

C2H6O Jet Boat Race **Design Document**

1. Game Overview

1.1. Concept – This game will involve the player guiding a jet boat through a course down a river and around a lake and over a finish line, while escaping traps, avoiding obstacles, and picking up boosts and fuel.

1.2. Genre – This is a basic race style game, 2D with overhead view.

1.3. Audience – Any age, but with a younger demographic.

1.4. Game Flow – After moving through the initial screens, the player is signaled to begin the race. The game begins at a small dock with three other boats, and initially all move down the river and jockey for position. A lake is entered that has floating pylons to guide the player, each having a number and a color. The number indicates the next pylon to pass in sequence, and the color indicates what side of the pylon the boat must pass; green means pass on the right, red means pass on the left. The first boat to pass the final pylon wins the race.

1.5. Visual Style – The view of the playing area is from above, and it scrolls to follow the player. It is a typical 2D race game in that aspect. Boats are 21st century jet boats.

2. Gameplay and Mechanics

2.1. Gameplay

    2.1.1. Game Progression – There is one level, and one goal.

    2.1.2. Mission/Challenge Structure – no specific missions.

    2.1.3. Objectives – The overall objective is to cross the finish line before any of the other (NPC) boats. Other goals include:
- To pick up flags along the route
- To fuel up to avoid running out of fuel
- To interfere, if possible, with the other boats

    2.1.4. Play Flow – The game is focused on the human player. Other boats will attempt to interfere by bumping into the boat, dropping obstacles, and otherwise getting in the way. The player must move through the obstacles, pass the markers correctly, and pass over the finish line.

2.2. Mechanics –

The player can control their boat, making it accelerate or turn left or right.

Hitting land slows the boat, which will bounce back into the water.

Each boat begins the race with two (2) obstacle floats that can be deployed in the path of an opponent. When struck by a boat, the boat slows 50%.

Each boat begins with insufficient fuel to finish the race, so each boat must stop to refuel (pit stop) at least once. There are two locations on the lake where that can be accomplished, simply by stopping there.

The race begins on a river, enters a lake where three laps must be made, and ends on another river where the finish line is.

Small flags are floating near the boat's path and can be picked up by driving over them. They are worth random numbers of points, each point representing an amount of time that will be removed from the player's finishing time.

A clock keeps track of the time that the boat has spent on the race so far. The boat with the smallest time at the finish wins, irrespective of their physical place in the race.

2.2.1. Physics – The game takes place on the surface of the water, which is a high friction surface. Acceleration can be quick, but slacking off on the accelerator will slow the boat quickly. Turning too quickly can flip the boat over, slowing the player's progress.

2.2.2. Movement in the game – The "q" key accelerates the boat forward, and releasing it will slow the boat. Turns are performed using the "a" key (left) and the "d" key (right).

2.2.3. Objects – Running over objects enables their action on the boat (Collision).

2.2.4. Conflict – Other boats can release their obstacles to interfere with the player's boat and may collide with it either on purpose or through alcohol-fueled accidents. This slows both boats.

2.2.5. Economy – There is no in-game economy.

2.2.6. Screen Flow – A graphical description of how each screen is related to every other and a description of the purpose of each screen.

There will be an opening screen (load game assets)
Start screen (play, exit, options, sound)
Options screen – select boats, sound on/off
Play screen
End – win/lose, save score, replay/exit

2.3. Game Options – The player can select a boat that has specific properties of top speed, acceleration, and maneuverability from a small list.

2.4. Replaying and Saving – The game can't be saved, but it can be replayed, and a list of players and scores can be maintained.

3. Story, Setting, and Character

3.1. Story and Narrative – There is no narrative here, just a race. Cut scenes before and after the race are real boat racing scenes from actual jet boat races.

3.2. Game World

   3.2.1. General look and feel of world – A 2D plane showing water and land areas, flags, boats, refueling area, and obstacles.

   3.2.2. The start area is a dock along a river. When the game begins, the player and NPCs accelerate to the left along the river.

   3.2.3. The river opens into a lake that has refueling areas and colored pylons. The first pylon is red, meaning it is to be passed on the left side OF THE BOAT. The second pylon is to the left, meaning that boats will circle the lake in a clockwise direction.

   3.2.4. There are islands in the lake, spectators, other boats, and two refueling areas, one on each side of the lake.

   3.2.5. There is another river entering the lake which contains the finish line, and it is to be used after three circuits of the lake have been performed.

3.3. Characters. NPC boats have various colors and shapes.

4. Levels –

4.1. Levels. Only the one
4.2. Tutorial Level – Later

5. Interface

5.1. Windows and Transitions
5.2. Visual Assist. HUD (Head's Up Display)
5.3. Camera is above the player's boat.

HUD is in the lower right corner, and shows a wider area with other boats, pylons, and scene features.

5.4. Control System – Keyboard
5.5. Audio

Music
At the beginning of the game and the end.
sound effects –
sounds of impacts
other boats
terrain
pylons
flags
water sounds
Starting gun
End indicator
ambiance
engine noises
voice of an announcer (script)
crowd
5.6. Help System – a single help screen can be opened at any time by typing the "h" key. Contents later.

6. Artificial Intelligence

6.1. Player and Collision Detection – Later
6.2. Pathfinding – later
6.3. Opponent AI – later
6.4. Friendly AI – none

7. Technical

7.1. Target Hardware – Any desktop
7.2. Development hardware and software, including Game Engine –
    Python and Pygame
7.3. Network requirements – Later

8. Game Art – Key assets, how they are being developed. Intended
    style.
    Terrain
    4 player boats
    NPC boats
    Pylons
    Flags
    Obstacles
    Water trail animations

EXERCISES

The following problems will exercise your knowledge of the material in this chapter, and they sometimes require that you do some research before you are able to complete them.

1. Give your own definition of *fun*. Don't think too long about it—try to be instinctive. Can fun be measured, using your definition? Is it possible to predict how much fun something will be, or is it only observable after the fact? How is *engagement* different from *fun*?

2. Explain the conflict/challenge in *Tetris*, *Mortal Kombat*, *Frogger*, and *Defender*. How is it maintained?

3. What is the (a) goal of the game *Mario Kart*? *Pac Man*? *The Sims*?

4. Describe, as concisely as possible, the major mechanic of *Angry Birds*, *Portal*, and *Space Invaders*.

5. Examine ten or more web-based games and list the controls (buttons, sliders) found on the *open* (splash) screen and on any *options* screen. List this in order of frequency, most common first.

6. Many games are *zero-sum* games, in which there is a win and a loss for each choice and situation. Each gain for one player is offset by a corresponding

loss for another. Give three examples of a zero-sum game, and explain why they fall into this category.

7. Sketch a game loop for *Tetris*, stating in simple English at each step what needs to be done for this game in particular.

8. Write a short GDD for any computer game you have played, but do not name the game. Give this to another person; can they figure out what the game is?

REFERENCES

1. Pippin Barr. Games Blog. (n.d.). http://www.pippinbarr.com/games/pongs/Pongs.html

2. Aki Järvinen. (2008). *Games without Frontiers: Theories and Methods for Game Studies and Design*. Tampere, Finland: Tampere University Press.

3. Mike McShaffry and David Graham. (2013). *Game Coding Complete*. Boston, MA: Course Technology.

4. Katie Salen and Eric Zimmerman. (2004). *Rules of Play: Game Design Fundamentals*. Cambridge, MA: MIT Press.

5. Daniel Sanchez-Crespo. (2004). *Core Techniques and Algorithms in Game Programming*. Indianapolis, IN: New Riders Publishing.

6. Thomas Schelling. (1980). *The Strategy of Conflict*, revised edition. Cambridge, MA: Harvard University Press.

7. Brian Yap. (1999). *Analytical Perspectives in Game Design: Architecture*. http:// numbat.sourceforge.net/numbbatV2/architecture.html.

## CHAPTER 2

GRAPHICS AND IMAGES

As a game programmer one of the first skills required is to be able to display renderings of the playing volume. This means that the volume itself and all objects must be drawn in their correct locations, orientations, and sizes. Each game object has a distinct set of colors and textures, and consists of a collection of simpler geometric shapes. Some are drawn as those basic shapes, while others may be pre-drawn images that are pasted into place. In any case, the game must be updated many times per second, meaning that every object has to be drawn that often. A game programmer needs the software tools to accomplish that effectively.

Graphics software is organized as a set of levels, with higher levels allowing the most complex tasks to be performed and lower levels offering the most detailed modification. At the bottom layer of software are functions that manipulate *pixels*. At the next level are *lines* and *curves*; these are the basic components of drawings and sketches. An artist with a pencil uses lines and curves to represent scenes. At the level above lines are functions that use lines to create other objects, such as *rectangles*, *circles*, and *ellipses*. These can be line drawings or can be filled with colors. The next higher levels can be argued about, but *text* is probably in the next software layer and then shading and images followed by 3D objects, which includes perspective transformation and textures.

Python itself does not have graphics tools, but various modules that are associated with Python do. The standard graphical user interface library for use with Python is *tkinter*. There are many features of this module, including the creation of windows, drawing, user interface widgets such as buttons, and a host of other features. It is free and is normally included in the Python distribution.

Another library that allows graphics programming is called *Pygame*, and this is designed for building computer games using Python. Let's look in detail at

Pygame, as it will allow us to draw pictures, manage interfaces, and do animations.

PYGAME ESSENTIALS

To start creating computer graphics, it is necessary to understand how Pygame manages the screen and other resources. There is a distinct set of steps that must be followed in order for even the simplest Pygame program to work. After the basic steps are accomplished, we can draw into a graphics window and have it appear on the screen.

It will be assumed that the Pygame module has been installed correctly on the computer. For some instruction on doing, this see Appendix A.

The first step in using Pygame in a program is to import the Pygame module. Assuming that it has been installed correctly, this is a matter of beginning with the following statement:

```
import pygame
```

Next, there are variables that need to be initialized and storage that has to be allocated for Pygame to work. One example is that fonts must be loaded and placed into a data structure. This is done with the following statement:

```
pygame.init()
```

Nothing seems to happen, but Pygame is now ready to work. Next, we create a drawing structure called a *surface*:

```
surf = pygame.display.set_mode((400, 450))
```

The variable **surf** will now contain a reference to a *surface* object, and in this case it will be the *display surface*, because we accessed it through the display part of the Pygame object. The display surface is the place where things are drawn if we want them to be visible on the screen; think of it as the playing area. There are other surfaces that can be drawn on that will not display by default, so in general a surface in Pygame is a thing that we can draw into. The method *set_mode* takes a tuple as a parameter that gives the size of the surface. This surface will be 400 pixels wide by 450 pixels high, and it will appear briefly on the screen and will then vanish. Why does it vanish? Because the program ends after the last statement, taking the window with it.

How can we keep the drawing area on the screen? Don't end the program until told! We could, as one example, read something from the keyboard and then terminate the program. Here's the first full Pygame program, which is non-standard but functional:

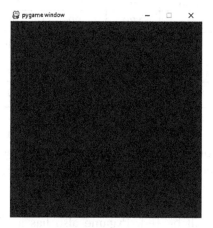

FIGURE 2.1 An empty Pygame drawing window.

```
import pygame
pygame.init()
surf = pygame.display.set_mode((400, 400))
pygame.display.update()
input()
```

The window will stay on the screen until a character is typed in the input region (not the drawing window!), at which point the program continues to execute and terminates, taking the window with it. This is not suitable for playing a game, but it illustrates a problem: we'll need to execute the game loop and accept user input somehow while keeping the drawing window open. This is something Pygame was designed to do.

SIMPLE STATIC DRAWING

Everything drawn on the display surface has a color, and it is a tuple consisting of the red, green, and blue component of the color. Thus, the tuple (255,255,255) would be the color white. (0,0,0 would be black.) To humans, colors have names. Here's a list of some named colors and their RGB equivalents:

Color	Red	Green	Blue	Color	Red	Green	Blue
Black	0	0	0	Olive	128	128	0
White	255	255	255	Khaki	240	230	140

Color	Red	Green	Blue	Color	Red	Green	Blue
Red	255	0	0	Teal	0	128	128
Green	0	255	0	Sienna	160	83	45
Blue	0	0	255	Tan	210	180	140
Yellow	255	255	0	Indigo	75	0	130
Magenta	255	0	255	Orange	255	165	0

The background is black by default. Assuming that the display surface is named **surf**, then the background color can be changed by a call to the fill method, passing a tuple specifying the color:

```
surf.fill ((255, 0, 0))
```

In this case the background color will be red. Pygame also has a *Color* class that has red, green, and blue components and methods for converting to non-RGB color specifications like HSV. After:

```
c = pygame.Color(255,0,0)
surf.fill (c)
```

the color stored in **c** will be red as well as the background color.

Pixel Level Graphics

The only pixel level operation draws a pixel at a specified location; so, for example, the call:

```
surf.set_at ((x, y), c)
```

will set the pixel at coordinates (**x**,**y**) to the color **c**. Setting a collection of pixels that are adjacent to each other will create a line.

Example: Create a Page of Note Paper

Note paper has blue lines separated by enough space to write or print text between them. It often has a red vertical line indicating an indentation level, a place to begin writing. Drawing this is a matter of drawing a set of connected blue pixels in vertically separated rows and then making a vertical column of red pixels. Here is one way to code this:

```
import pygame
pygame.init()
surf = pygame.display.set_mode((400, 400))
c = pygame.Color(0,0,200)
```

```
surf.fill ((255,255,255))
y = 60                          # Height at which to start
for n in range (0, 27):         # Draw 30 horizontal blue lines
    for x in range (0,400): # Draw all pixels in one line
        surf.set_at ((x, y),c)  # Draw a blue pixel
    y = y + 20                  # The next line is 20 pixels down
c = (200, 0, 0)                 # Pixel color red
for y in range (0, 400):    # Draw connected vertical pixels
    surf.set_at ((25, y), c)    #  to form the margin line
pygame.display.update()
input()
```

FIGURE 2.2 A graphic of a sheet of lined paper.

FIGURE 2.3 A color gradient drawn as pixels.

The output of this program is shown in Figure 2.2. When pixels are drawn immediately next to each other they appear to be connected, and so in this case they form horizontal and vertical lines. This is not easy to do for arbitrary lines; it is not obvious exactly which pixels to fill for a line between, say, (10, 20) and (99, 17). That's why the line drawing functions exist. Note that we're still using a call to input() to postpone the end of the program. This will continue for a few examples, and then the standard method will be explained.

Example: Creating a Color Gradient

When creating a visual on a computer, the first step is to have a clear picture of what it will look like. For this example, imagine the sky on a clear day. The horizon shows a lighter blue than the sky directly above, and the color changes continuously all the way from horizon to zenith. If a realistic sky background were needed, then it would be necessary to draw this using the tools available. What would the method be?

First, decide on what the color is at the horizon (y=ymax) and at the highest point in the scene (y=ymin). Now ask: "how many pixels between those points?" The change in pixel color will be the color difference from ymax to ymin divided by the number of pixels. Now simply draw rows of pixels beginning with the horizon and move up the image (i.e., decreasing Y value), changing the color by this amount each time.

As an implementation, assume that the color at the horizon will be blue = (40, 40, 255) and the top of the image will be (40, 40, 128), a darker blue. The height of the image will be 400 pixels; the change in blue over that range is 127 units. Thus, the color change over each pixel is going to be 255.0/400. A color can't change a fractional amount, of course, but what this means is that the blue value will decrease by approximately 1 unit with every increase of a couple of pixels in height. Do not forget that the horizon is at the bottom of the image, which has the greatest Y coordinate value, so that an increase in Y means a decrease in height and vice versa.

The example program that implements this is:

```
import pygame
pygame.init()
surf = pygame.display.set_mode((400, 400))
surf.fill ((255,255,255))
blue = 0
delta = 255.0/400
for y in range (0, 400):
    yy = 400-y
    c = (40, 40, blue)
    for x in range(0, 400):
        surf.set_at   ((x, y), c)
    blue = blue + delta
pygame.display.update()
input()
```

Figure 2.3 shows what the gradient image looks like as a grey level image.

Lines and Curves

Straight lines and curves are more complex objects than pixels, consisting of many pixels in an organized arrangement. A line is actually drawn by setting pixels though. The fact that a **line()** function exists means that the programmer does not have to figure out what pixels to draw and can focus on the higher level construct, the line or curve.

A line is drawn by specifying the endpoints of the line. Using *Pygame* the call is:

```
pygame.draw.line ( surf, col, (x0, y0), (x1, y1))
```

where one end of the line is at (x0,y0) and the other is at (x1,y1). The color of the line is specified by the second parameter **col**. If any part of the line extends past the boundary of the window that's OK; the line will be clipped to fit.

Example: Note Paper Again

The example of drawing a piece of note paper can be done using lines instead of pixels, and it will be a lot faster. Draw a collection of horizontal lines (i.e., that have the same Y coordinate at the endpoints) separated by 20 pixels, as before having a blue color. Then draw a vertical red line for the margin. The program is a variation on the previous version:

```
import pygame
pygame.init()
y = 60                    # Height at which to start
width = 400
height = 400
surf = pygame.display.set_mode((width, height),
                        pygame.SRCALPHA)
surf.fill ((255,255,255))
y = 60                            # Height at which to start
for n in range (0, 27):    # Draw 30 horizontal blue lines
    pygame.draw.line (surf, (0,0,200), (0, y), (width, y))
    y = y + 20                    # The next line is 20 pixels down
c = (200, 0, 0)                   # Pixel color red
pygame.draw.line (surf, c, (25,0), (25,height))
pygame.display.update()
input()
```

The output from this program is the same as that for the version that drew pixels, which is shown in Figure 2.2.

A *curve* is trickier than a line, in that it is harder to specify. The method used in Pygame is common: a curve (arc) is defined as a portion of an ellipse from a starting angle for a specified number of degrees, as referenced from the center of the ellipse. Here's a call to **arc**:

```
pygame.draw.arc (surf, c, box, start_angle, end_angle)
```

The parameter **surf** is the surface to draw on, **c** is the color, **box** is an enclosing bounding box as a tuple (upper left x, upper left Y, width, height), **start _angle** is an angle between 0 and 2π radians, and **stop_angle** is an angle in the same range. The angle 0 is to the right, 90 degrees is up, 180 degrees (π radians) is left, and 270 degrees is down. The angle specifies the part of the ellipse to draw. Figure 2.4 shows some example calls to curve and their results. The curves are drawn counterclockwise. The value **conv** is $\pi/180$ and converts an angle in degrees into radians when multiplied.

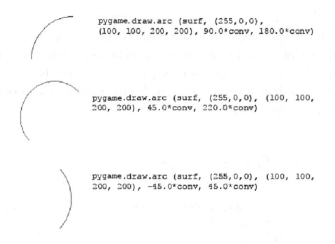

```
pygame.draw.arc (surf, (255,0,0),
(100, 100, 200, 200), 90.0*conv, 180.0*conv)
```

```
pygame.draw.arc (surf, (255,0,0), (100, 100,
200, 200), 45.0*conv, 220.0*conv)
```

```
pygame.draw.arc (surf, (255,0,0), (100, 100,
200, 200), -45.0*conv, 45.0*conv)
```

FIGURE 2.4 Examples of the curve method

Before proceeding, we have a few examples of drawing in Pygame now, and some generalizations can be made about the structure of the module. The variable *pygame* here is an instance of a class that contains most of the code that implements Pygame. Within that class can be seen some methods and other class instances, as follows:

init()	Initialize Pygame
SRCALPHA	A constant, indicating a pixel format with an alpha channel (opacity)

init( )	Initialize Pygame
color	A class representing color
display	a variable, a class reference
set_mode( )	Modify display size; Returns THE display reference
update( )	Draw this display to the screen
surface	A class representing a place one can draw
fill ( )	Set the color for filling polygons on this surface
set_at( )	Set a pixel specified by (x,y) to the fill color
draw	A module for drawing simple objects
line( )	Draw a line
arc( )	Draw a curve

Online documentation for Pygame is extensive, and a quick search should locate anything that the system can provide. The key web site right now is *https://www.pygame.org*. Looking up the *draw* module on that site we find:

pygame.draw.rect	—	draw a rectangle shape
pygame.draw.polygon	—	draw a shape with any number of sides
pygame.draw.circle	—	draw a circle around a point
pygame.draw.ellipse	—	draw a round shape inside a rectangle
pygame.draw.arc	—	draw a partial section of an ellipse
pygame.draw.line	—	draw a straight line segment
pygame.draw.lines	—	draw multiple contiguous line segments
pygame.draw.aaline	—	draw fine antialiased lines
pygame.draw.aalines	—	draw a connected sequence of antialiased lines

That's everything that *draw* can do.

Polygons

For the purposes of discussion, a polygon will include all closed regions, including ellipses and circles. A rectangle is drawn using the **rect** method, as shown in Figure 2.5a.

```
pygame.draw.rect (surf, ((0,200, 50), (100, 100, 200, 300))
```

The **surf** and **color** parameters are as before, and the **box** is specified as the upper left coordinates, the width, and the height. By default, the rectangle is filled with the specified color. An additional final argument specifies the line thickness with which to draw the rectangle, and if this is specified then the rectangle is not filled with color (Figure 2.5b):

```
pygame.draw.rect (surf, (0,200, 50), (100, 100, 200, 100), 1)
```

The **ellipse** method takes the same parameters as does **rect**, and it draws an ellipse within the rectangle defined by the third parameter (Figure 2.5c).

```
pygame.draw.rect (surf, (230,230, 0), (100, 100, 200, 100), 1)
pygame.draw.ellipse (surf, (0,200, 50), (100, 100, 200, 100), 1)
```

A circle is an ellipse drawn in a square. This makes the center and radius rather implicit. There is a **circle** method also (Figure 2.5d):

```
pygame.draw.rect (surf, (230,230, 0), (50, 50, 100, 100), 1)
pygame.draw.circle (surf, (0,200, 50), (100, 100), 50)
```

The third parameter to circle is a tuple defining the center, and the fourth is the radius. A fifth would be the line thickness, and filling would turn off. In the case here of a circle at (100,100) and radius of 50, the enclosing

FIGURE 2.5 (a) A Filled Rectangle; (B) Unfilled Rectangle; (C) An Ellipse; (D) A Circle, Filled

square would be from (100-50, 100-50), which is (50, 50), for (100,100) pixels.

Blitting

To *blit* is to combine several graphics or bitmaps into a single one. It is often accomplished using a Boolean function, and often is very fast due to hardware assistance. Pygame has one special Surface that is the display Surface, but it allows us to draw on other surfaces too. To display what is drawn on these surfaces, we would *blit* them to the display Surface.

Blitting has consequences and requires specifications that are not usually appreciated by the definition. Consider the creation of two Surfaces named **s1** and **s2** in addition to the display surface, and draw into each of those:

```
s1 = pygame.Surface((400,400)) # New Surface
pygame.draw.rect (s1, (230,230, 0), (50, 50, 100, 100), 1)
s2 = pygame.Surface((400,400)) # New Surface
pygame.draw.circle (s2, (0,200, 50), (100, 100), 50)
```

The Surface **s1** contains a rectangle, and the Surface **s2** contains a circle. Neither appears on the display Surface, which already exists due to a previous call and is named **surf**. A *blit* is a copy from one Surface to another. Some questions are:

- Which part of the Surface being blitted is copied?
- Where (coordinates) is the surface being blitted to?
- What happens to the pixels that already exist in the region being blitted to?

The method that copies (*blits*) one surface to another is *blit*, the simplest form of which is:

```
surf.blit (s1, (0,0))
```

This copies all of Surface **s1** to **surf** so that the upper left of **s1** is at (0,0) of **surf**. We can copy **s1** to any pixel coordinate in **surf**. To draw a circle and a rectangle in different Surfaces and then blit them to the display Surface would involve creating the surfaces, drawing in them, and blitting them:

```
s1 = pygame.Surface((200,200))   # S1 is 200x200
s1.fill ((255,255,255))          # White background
pygame.draw.rect (s1, (230,230, 0), (50, 50, 100, 100), 1)

s2 = pygame.Surface((200,200))   #s2 is also 200x200 pixels
s2.fill ((255,255,255))          # White background too
```

```
pygame.draw.circle (s2, (0,200, 50), (60, 60), 50)

# Blit rectangle to (0,0) and circle to (100,100)
surf.blit (s1, (0,0))     # s1 has a rectangle: blit
surf.blit (s2, (100,100)) # s2 has a circle: blit  pygame.display.
update()
```

Here **s1** is blitted before **s2** (i.e., is drawn first), and there is overlap between the drawn regions. Thus, the one drawn last (**s2**) appears to be drawn *over* **s1**. If we think in terms of layers, the last surface drawn is the top layer and is visible. Layers beneath may be partly or completely covered by layers above. A Surface is rectangular, so notice that the background surrounding the circle is also drawn over the square below. Figure 2.6 shows the result.

The blit function has other parameters that we'll get into shortly.

Drawing Text

Drawing text is accomplished by loading a font and then drawing (rendering) a text string to a surface using that font as a guide. An instance of the Font class, and there is a default for that, can render text onto a surface. That surface is

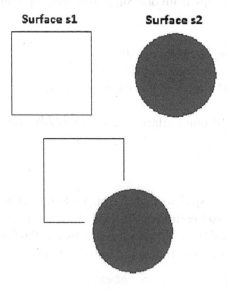

Surface s1　　**Surface s2**

FIGURE 2.6 (a) A filled rectangle; (b) Unfilled rectangle; (c) An ellipse; (d) A circle, filled.

then blitted to the target surface, possibly the display. A simple example involves placing the text "Hello there" at location (100,100):

```
font = pygame.font.Font(None, 36)
text = font.render("Hello There", 1, (10, 10, 10))
surf.blit (text, (100,100))
```

The method **pygame.font.Font** selects a font to be used and returns an instance. A font has a name, in this case **None**, indicating that we should use the default, and a size, in this case 36. Each computer system has a different set of fonts available, so we'll use the default. Next, the font class can draw (render) the text onto a surface. The call:

```
text = font.render("Hello There", 1, (0,0,255))
```

renders the text "Hello there" in the color (0,0,255), which is blue. The second parameter 1 means to anti-alias, which will yield nice smooth characters. Finally:

```
surf.blit (text, (100,100))
```

will blit the text to the display Surface **surf** at location (100,100). The coordinates (100,100) are those of the upper left of the text Surface, which will be a rectangle large enough to enclose the string.

A problem is that this text Surface will write over anything underneath as a rectangular area. This can be fixed by using a transparent background. The key things to know about drawing text are that **font.render** draws a text string into a Surface and returns that Surface, which then must be blitted to the place it belongs.

Transparent Colors

When one pixel is drawn over top of (i.e., at the same location as) another, the one drawn most recently will be visible. This may not always be what is needed. Background pixels of text images being blitted should be invisible so that the background can be seen with the text on top.

Transparency is a value that can be numerical. Let's say that a value of 0 means that the drawn pixel is invisible and a value of 255 means that it is opaque. Values in between have degrees of transparency. Then we want the background of a text box to have the value 0 for this parameter, and the text to have a value of 255. Looking at this value it has the same properties as does a color component, and so it is generally implemented as a fourth component called *alpha*. A color can be specified as RGBA, which means four components: red, green, blue, and alpha.

Not all Surface objects can implement transparency. They must have a property called 32-bit color and have the **SCRALPHA** property. Creating a Surface like this is done as follows:

```
surf = pygame.display.set_mode((w, h), pygame.SRCALPHA, 32)
```

where the third parameter means that the Surface can support transparency and the final one means that it has thirty-two bit colors: four values of eight bits each.

The previous example having a rectangle and a circle drawn and then blitted to the display Surface can now be implemented using transparency:

```
import pygame

pygame.init()
surf = pygame.display.set_mode((400, 400))
s1 = pygame.Surface((200,200), pygame.SRCALPHA, 32)
s1.fill ((255,255,255, 0))
pygame.draw.rect (s1, (230,230, 0), (50, 50, 100, 100), 1)
s2 = pygame.Surface((200,200), pygame.SRCALPHA, 32)
s2.fill ((255,255,255, 0))
pygame.draw.circle (s2, (0,200, 50), (60, 60), 50)
surf.blit (s1, (0,0))
surf.blit (s2, (100,100))
pygame.display.update()
input()
```

The fill color value of (255,255,255,0) yields a fully transparent color that will comprise the background of the circle and the rectangle Surface, allowing the background to show through. Notice that the background color is black; this

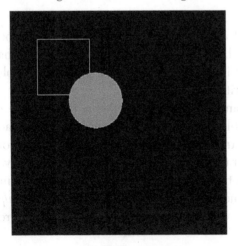

FIGURE 2.7 **Example of transparent colors.**

is the default on the display surface. To change it to white, as an example, call **surf.fill**:

```
surf.fill ((255,255,255))
```

Images

Unlike the graphical components displayed so far, an *image* is fundamentally a collection of pixels. A camera captures an image and stores it digitally as pixels, and so it was never anything else. Displaying an image means drawing each pixel in the appropriate color, as captured. *Pygame* can load and display images in files of various formats: JPEG, GIF, BMP, and PNG.

Unlike languages such as Java, Python has no image class. An image is read from a file using the function **pygame.image.load** and is returned as a Surface. This means that it can be displayed immediately using a blit and that individual pixels can be accessed using the Surface method **get_at()**.

The file "charlie.gif" is a photo of Checkpoint Charlie in Berlin (Figure 2.8). It could be read in to a Python program with the call:

```
im = pygame.image.load ("charlie.gif")
```

The variable **im** now holds the image, and can be displayed using:

```
surf.blit (im, (0,0))
```

While the details are not completely relevant, it is good to know that **im.get_width()** and **im.get_height()** give the width and height of the image in pixels.

The complete Python program (using *Pygame*) that can load and display the image is thus:

```
import pygame
pygame.init()

im = pygame.image.load ("charlie.gif")
width = im.get_width()
height = im.get_height()
surf = pygame.display.set_mode((width, height),
                        pygame.SRCALPHA)
surf.fill ((255,255,255))
surf.blit (im, (0,0))
pygame.display.update()
input()
```

This displays the image in a window that is exactly the correct size.

The module *Pygame.image* has functions for loading and saving images, but none for manipulating them. The other important function is one that saves data into an image file:

```
Pygame.image.save( Surface, filename)
```

FIGURE 2.8 Checkpoint Charlie image displayed in a Pygame window.

Pixels

An image is just a Surface after it has been read from a file. Individual pixels can be accessed using the method **get_at** passing the **x** and **y** coordinates. The code

```
pix = im.get_at ((i,j))  # Parameter is a tuple
```

returns the color of the pixels at (i,j), which is a tuple containing red, green, blue, and alpha components.

Changing the value of the pixel at location (x,y) is accomplished by calling im.set_at()

```
im.set_at ((x,y), color)
```

where again, *color* is a tuple.

Pygame does not have facilities for modifying images directly, but requires they be placed into a Surface first. Now the pixels can be accessed individually through that Surface.

Example: Negative Image

A photographic negative is not something that is encountered much in the age of digital photography. A negative is the intensity inverse of the image: black pixels are white in the negative, and white pixels are black. In between pixels are reversed in value, usually on a scale of 0 to 255. So, if a specific pixel has a value x, then its value in the negative image will be 255-x.

Using the Checkpoint Charlie image again, let's create a negative image using this pixel value range. First, we have to convert the color pixels into grey values. An easy way to do this is to average the R, G, and B values. For a pixel value **pix**:

```
grey = (pix[0]+pix[1]+pix[2])/3
```

Now this value is subtracted from 255 and is replaced into the image:

```
grey = 255 - grey
im.set_at (x, y, grey)
```

The whole program is:

```
import pygame
pygame.init()
im = pygame.image.load ("charlie.gif")
width = im.get_width()
height = im.get_height()

for i in range (0,width):
    for j in range(0,height):
        pix = im.get_at ((i,j))
        grey = (pix[0]+pix[1]+pix[2])/3
        grey = 255-grey
        im.set_at ((i,j), (grey, grey, grey))
surf = pygame.display.set_mode((width, height), pygame.SRCALPHA)
```

```
surf.blit (im, (0,0))
pygame.display.update()
input()
```

The color (grey,grey,grey) is a grey pixel, the same color intensity for each of red, green, and blue. The **for** loop is used to examine every pixel in the image.

FIGURE 2.9 Checkpoint Charlie image: (a) grey; (b) negative (greys reversed).

Image Transformations

An image is read into a Surface prior to display, but it may not be the correct size for the display window. It's possible that the display window will be used to display many images of various sizes consecutively, of display thumbnails of a collection. It will be necessary to resize images from time to time. Pygame has a module named **transform** that can do this and more.

To resize an image named *im*, a call to scale will do the job:

```
im = pygame.transform.scale (im, (newx, newy))
```

where *newx* is the new width that we want the image to have and *newy* is the new height. To create a new image that is 1/4 the area of the old one, reduce the width and height by a factor of 2:

```
im = pygame.transform.scale (im, (im.get_width()//2, im.get_
height()//2))
```

Images have an *aspect ratio*, the ratio of the image's width to its height. If this is changed then the image will look different, perhaps stretched or squashed. When scaling an image, care should be taken to ensure that the aspect ratio *A* stays the same. An easy way to do this is to set one dimension to a needed value and then compute the other so *A* is not modified. If you want the width to be 100 pixels, then set the height to *100/A*. If you want the height to be 100 pixels, then set the width to *A *100*.

Using *scale*, one can make the image either larger or smaller.

Rotation

An image in a **Surface** can also be rotated using the **transform** module. pygame.transform.rotate (surf, angle) will perform a counterclockwise rotation of the image in the Surface surf by the specified angle. Angle is in degrees and is a real number. Rotating an image *im* by 30 degrees would be coded as:

```
s = pygame.transform.rotate(im, 30)
```

The returned image *s* will have the rotated image centered in a new **Surface** large enough to contain it. A rectangle that is rotated will require a larger bounding box to hold it, so *s* will inevitably be larger than *im* (Figure 2.10b).

Rotating an image requires that it be completely resampled. Few if any pixels will have the same values. An image is seen as a 2D rectangular grid, and when rotated it becomes a new grid with the new pixels interpolated from the neighbors of the old image. What this means is that *an image should never be rotated multiple times.* If so, each image will be a little more distorted than the previous one until the result holds no relation to the original.

Omitting some of the initial setup code, here's a program that rotates an image by 2 degrees ten times, and then back:

```
surf = pygame.display.set_mode((width, height), pygame.SRCALPHA)
im = pygame.transform.scale (im, (width//2, height//2))
for i in range (0,10):
  im = pygame.transform.rotate(im, 2)
for i in range (0,10):
  im = pygame.transform.rotate(im, -2)
surf.blit (im, (0, 0))
pygame.display.update()
```

The result in Figure 2.10a is quite distorted. The correct way to do multiple rotations is to rotate the original image by a larger angle each time:

```
for i in range (0,10):
  s = pygame.transform.rotate(im, 2*i)
```

FIGURE 2.10 Checkpoint Charlie image: (a) after multiple rotations; (b) after one 30-degree rotation.

Because a game often requires that sprites, represented as small raster images, be rotated, we need to understand the rotation method pretty well. Consider a small image of a boat, which will used as a sprite in the boat race-game. As visualized in Figure 2.11, the boat image initially points to the right, which is the 0 degree orientation. The boat always moves in the direction it is facing, so if it makes a change in direction, the sprite will have to be rotated to face in that direction.

The rotate method will rotate the image about its center. This often makes the bounding box larger at first, and so the point that is the center of the image changes. If the image is to be rotated many times, this becomes obvious. Figure 2.11 was created using the code:

```
boatr = pygame.transform.rotate(boat, angle)
display.blit(boatr, (250, 200))
```

where the image of the boat is in a *Surface* named **boat**. This image is rotated by the specified angle and is returned as a new *Surface* **boatr**, which is then blitted to the center of the screen. In order to have this rotation appear to be about the center of the boat, the image must be translated to the origin. By "the image" we mean the rotated boat image, which changes in size.

```
boatr = pygame.transform.rotate(boat, angle)
sx = boatr.get_width()
sy = boatr.get_height()
display.blit(boatr, (250-sx/2, 200-sy/2))
```

The values of sx and sy reflect the size of the rotated image, and so (sx/2, sy/2) would be the center of that image. This places the center of the rotated boat image at the center of the display. It could, of course, be placed anywhere.

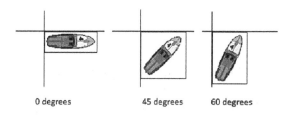

0 degrees   45 degrees   60 degrees

FIGURE 2.11 Rotation of a boat sprite. The bounding box and axis have been added.

PIXELS AND COLOR

Colors are important in graphics, of course, because lines, shapes, and regions will be drawn in different colors. On a computer screen and in memory, graphics are drawn as individual pixels, even if we don't specify individual pixels directly. We know that a pixel is a color or intensity value that is measured or drawn at a particular location in an image. The key to representing a pixel is to represent the color, and color on a computer is usually specified by its red, green, and blue components (RGB). The choice of how to implement a pixel would seem to be made for us: it will be a collection of three values, one holding the amount of red at that location, one holding the amount of green, and one holding the amount of blue.

The Pygame **color** class represents colors as described thus far, and so a pixel would be of that type. A variable of type **color** has a red, green, and blue component, each of which is an unsigned integer. Each component, red for instance, can have a value between 0 and 255. A value of 0 means that no red is present in the color, and a value of 255 represents the most red that is possible (saturated).

The **color** type in *Pygame* is really just a tuple with three (or four) values. Setting a color value is easy:

```
c = pygame.Color (128, 90, 20)
```

causes the color in c to be a medium brown. It can now be used to set color values, such as:

```
surf.fill (c)
```

The red component of *c* can be accessed using either *c[0]*, which is the first component of *c*, or *c.r*. The latter is preferred, and it can be used to modify the color component. The code:

```
c.r = 255
```

sets the red component of *c* to the largest possible value. Similarly, for green and blue, the components *c.g* and *c.b* would be used.

In addition to the red, green, and blue components of a pixel, there is a fourth property that is of interest. It's called *alpha*, and it refers to the degree to which the pixel is opaque or transparent. A pixel that is completely transparent would be effectively invisible, since anything drawn before (i.e., underneath) it would show through. Conversely, a pixel that is opaque would cover anything beneath it. The use of an alpha value to control the degree of transparency allows objects underneath any pixel to be visible to a greater or lesser degree. This usually appears as a color change in overlap areas.

It is important to remember that an alpha of 0 means that the pixel is completely transparent. An alpha value of 255 means that the pixel is opaque. This is the opposite of what one would expect if alpha is the degree of transparency, since 0 transparency would seem to mean it is not transparent. Figure 2.12 shows the effect of changing the alpha value. The green (rightmost) circle in each overlapping pair has a specified alpha value of (left to right) 255, 200, 128, and 96. Note that the color of the other circle shows through more and more as the alpha of the green circle gets smaller.

Alpha is a more difficult aspect of color to use in Pygame than in some other languages and graphics systems. The standard display **Surface** in Pygame does not display the alpha color channel, and so trying to draw transparent colors directly will fail. A **Surface** can be created that permits transparent colors, and this could be blitted to the display surface.

Consider the program that created Figure 2.12. The red circles are all opaque, having an alpha of 255, and can be drawn directly on to the display surface. So can the first circle. The second circle has an alpha of 200. What needs to be done is to create a new Surface having the property that it can display alpha. It needs to be large enough to hold the circle as well. The code is:

```
surf = pygame.Surface((60,60), flags=pygame.SRCALPHA)
```

The flag SRCALPHA indicates that this new surface must deal correctly with alpha values. Next, draw the circle in this Surface, specifying the alpha value as the fourth component in the color:

```
pygame.draw.circle (surf, (0, 255, 0, 128), (30,30), 30)
```

In this case the alpha is 128. Notice that the **Surface** is just large enough to hold the circle, and that the circle is drawn in the center of the **Surface.** The final step is to blit this Surface to the display:

```
display.blit (surf, (250, 40))
```

FIGURE 2.12 The effect of the alpha value on pixel color.

The location to which this surface is blitted dictates where in the display the circle will appear, so some planning is needed. Drawing the situation using some graph paper is always a useful measure.

A new Surface should be created each time; that is, for each circle. The code that creates Figure 2.12 is:

```
import pygame

pygame.init()

display = pygame.display.set_mode((500, 150), pygame.SRCALPHA,
32)
display.fill ((255,255,255))

pygame.draw.circle (display, (255, 0,0, 255), (50, 50), 30)
pygame.draw.circle (display, (0, 255,0, 255), (75, 75), 30)

surf = pygame.Surface((60,60), flags=pygame.SRCALPHA)
pygame.draw.circle (display, (255, 0,0), (150, 50), 30)
pygame.draw.circle (surf, (0, 255, 0, 200), (30,30), 30)
display.blit(surf,(150,40))

surf = pygame.Surface((60,60), flags=pygame.SRCALPHA)
pygame.draw.circle (display, (255, 0,0), (250, 50), 30)
```

```
pygame.draw.circle (surf, (0, 255, 0, 128), (30,30), 30)
display.blit (surf, (250, 40))

surf = pygame.Surface((60,60), flags=pygame.SRCALPHA)
pygame.draw.circle (display, (255, 0,0), (350, 50), 30)
pygame.draw.circle (surf, (0, 255, 0, 96), (30,30), 30)
display.blit (surf, (350, 40))

pygame.display.update()
input()
```

THE C2H6O JET BOAT RACE GAME

Much of the information communicated from a game back to the player is done visually. Our ability to display images and draw graphics is essential to this communication, and immediately demonstrates the dependence of a game on artistic assets and good design. The case of the Jet Boat Game we are developing is a good example.

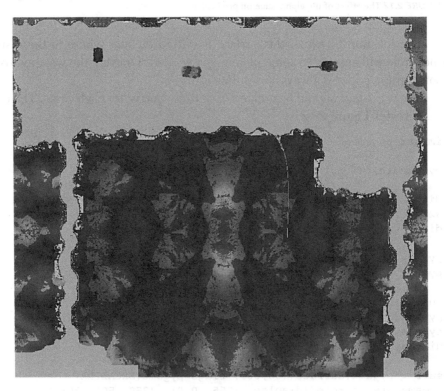

FIGURE 2.13 Terrain image for the boat race game.

The game requires art assets, and those must be described first by the designer and then placed into the design document for use by artists and developers. The most significant piece of art is the terrain. This is the stage on which the game is played, or the board on which checkers or Backgammon is played. It will show the lake and rivers on which the boats will be raced. Figure 2.13 shows the terrain image that our game will use, but there are many other possibilities. Having a competent artist is essential for this task, and good artists are worth just as much as good programmers.

The terrain art in Figure 2.13 was created by a programmer, using a terrain texture generation tool *(http://cpetry.github.io/TextureGenerator-Online/)*.

When the game is executing, a portion of the terrain image is displayed, usually one within which the player's avatar (in this case a boat) is found. The game display is a window within the much larger terrain image, which in this instance is 8000 x 7000 pixels. The mobile elements of the game, boats for example, are objects having a position and speed, the speed being specified ultimately in pixels per frame. These are drawn over the terrain image. The first image drawn is the one further in the background, and the more recent object drawn will be on top of this (Figure 2.14). The objects that can move could be drawn in new positions in each frame.

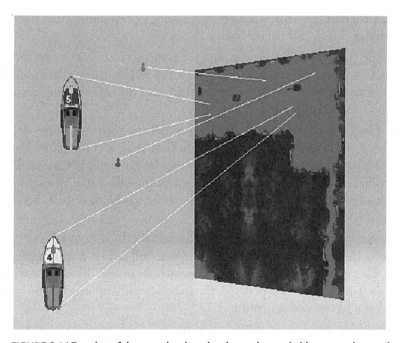

FIGURE 2.14 Drawing of the game involves drawing sprites and objects over the terrain.

The game thus has a background, static objects (i.e., trees, walls, piers, rocks), and dynamic objects (i.e., boats, buoys, markers, power-ups). An artist creates them and places them into an image file, and the programmer must read those images and draw them where they belong.

EXERCISES

The following problems will exercise your knowledge of the material in this chapter and sometimes require that you do more research before you are able to complete them. Solutions to some of these are available.

1. Write a function that will draw a regular hexagon. Assume that the hexagon has sides of length **h**, and will be drawn in such a way that the upper left corner of the bounding box is specific as a parameter **pos**. The call would be:

```
hex (display, col, h, pos)
```

   where **col** is the color and **display** is the surface on which to draw.

2. Create a program that will display an image that is specified when a user types the file name of that image on their keyboard.

3. Write a program that draws a target consisting of ten alternating white and black circles.

4. Write a program that displays an image on the screen. When the mouse is clicked a rectangle is drawn within which the image appears magnified 2x. This magnifying window can be dragged around the screen, magnifying the image beneath it as it moves.

5. Image file formats GIF, JPG, and BMP differ in how they store data and compress it. Find an image and save it as a GIF, JPG, and BMP file. Using an image display utility of your choice, examine those images at various degrees of magnification. What can you observe about the effect of different formats on the image data? (Not all images will illustrate the likely distortions of each format.)

6. Create a program that displays an image and allows the user to select a portion of it using the mouse: click, drag, and release will define a rectangular sub-image. This sub-image now becomes the whole image, filling the window. When the RETURN key is pressed, the image being displayed in the window is saved as a file named "output.jpg."

7. Make bubbles. Bubbles in a liquid are basically spherical, but get larger as they rise to the surface, where they eventually burst. Create a sketch that

makes bubbles that look more or less real. They should rise to the surface and increase in size as they do. (Look up the function `random`.)

8. Find an image of a television set and make a copy in a file. Find any other image you want and display the two images so that it looks like the second image is being displayed on the television. What did you have to do to make this appear natural?

RESOURCES

2D Game graphics tutorial: *http://gamebanana.com/tuts/11225*
Intro to 2D Graphics: *http://rbwhitaker.wikidot.com/introduction-to-2d-graphics*
Processing documentation: http://processing.org/reference/
Techniques for fancy and lightweight 2d graphics (game producer blog): *http://www.gameproducer.net/2008/03/03/techniques-for-fancy-and-lightweight-2d-graphics/*
Sprite Database: *http://spritedatabase.net/*. Useful information and downloads.
Open Game Art: *http://opengameart.org/*. Downloadable sprites and 2D art.

REFERENCES

1. Charles Kelly. (2012). *Programming 2D Games*. Boca Raton, FL: A K Peters (Taylor & Francis).

2. J. R. Parker. (2011). *Algorithms for Image Processing and Computer Vision*, 2nd edition. Indianapolis, IN: Wiley.

3. John Pile Jr.. (2013). *2D Graphics Programming for Games*. CRC Press (Taylor & Francis).

4. Allen Sherrod. (2008). *Game Graphics Programming*. Boston, MA: Course Technology (Cengage Learning).

5. Daniel Shiffman. (2008). *Learning Processing*. Burlington, MA: Morgan-Kaufman. *http://www.learningprocessing.com/*.

CHAPTER 3

THE GAME LOOP

In Chapter 2, all of the Pygame programs ended with an input request. This was so the window would stay open long enough so that the graphical output could be seen. This is not the correct way to do this. Pygame has devised a scheme that not only keeps the graphics on the display window, but repeats the drawing process as often as needed so that the game can progress frame by frame and permit the user to interact using the mouse and keyboard.

Because Pygame was specifically designed to be used in making games, it allows the programmer to easily do what was suggested in Chapter 1: *to keep track of all objects and implement the interactions between them according to the rules*. This means that Pygame allows for fixed-time intervals to pass between frames and has an implementation of an *event*.

TIME AND INTERVALS

The game loop is the heart of any game. A high-level abstraction of what it does is:

Loop forever
   Move objects
      Check for collisions
   Handle Events
   Handle Sounds
   Draw all objects at current positions

A potential problem with this loop is that it will not always take the same amount of time to execute. This can result in gameplay issues that interfere with parts of the design. A classic example is the old arcade game *Space Invaders*. Figure 3.1 shows how this game could look, although this is not a screen shot for copyright reasons. The player controls the football shaped icon at the bottom of the screen, which can fire little square missiles upward when a button is pressed. If the missile hits one of the shapes (representing spaceships) above, the missile and ship will disappear. The entire array of ships is moving left, then down, then right, then down, and so on to create moving targets. The problem was that as the targets were shot and vanished there were fewer objects remaining in the game, and the game loop would execute a little faster. When there were only a couple of ships left, they were moving very quickly indeed and were hard to hit. Although this was in fact a bug, it was kept in the game as a feature.

The game loop should take about the same amount of time no matter how much work must be done. It's not possible to speed the execution up, so we'll have to slow it down to a steady pace. In the previous game loop sketch, this can be done by adding one more statement at the beginning, making it look like this:

Loop forever
    Wait until the current fixed time interval is complete
    Move objects
        Check for collisions
    Handle Events
    Handle Sounds
    Draw all objects at current positions

The *wait* will ensure that a fixed frame rate is assured. If, for example, the frame rate is set to 30 per second, then each frame will take 0.333 seconds, and when that period has expired, the *move objects* step can be done.

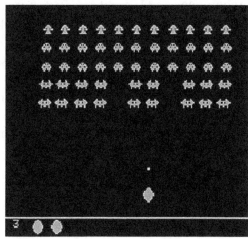

FIGURE 3.1 *Space Invaders* had a bug that made the game run faster as objects were removed from play.

The pygame.time Module

Pygame has a module named **time** that monitors the passage of real time. This is something that most programming classes do not get involved with. Yet operating systems, networking, and games require close attention to the passage of time. The time module offers four functions and a class that offer the programmer a way to keep close track of time, mainly elapsed time or *intervals*.

The function *pygame.time.get_2ticks()* returns the number of milliseconds that have passed since *pygame.init* was called. This function could be used for timing the main loop, but it would not be the best choice. If we wanted to print a message every second, then here's code that would do it:

```
import pygame
pygame.init()
t = 1000                  # 1000 milliseconds = 1 second
while True:               # Loop forever

# Other code here          Game code

    if pygame.time.get_ticks() < t:    # Time since init < t millisecs?
        continue          # No. loop again.
    print (t//999)        # Print seconds
    t = t + 1000          # Add one second to t
    if t > 10000:         # Stop after 10 seconds
        break;
```

This will print a message each second for ten seconds. The comment that says "Other code here" could have some Python code that would execute each second. Changing the constant 1000 to 33 would give the period of time that would accommodate one frame at 30 frames per second. This would work, but the problem is that the loop will execute constantly, burning up CPU time doing nothing at all. This is usually considered to be a bad thing. Other processes on the computer would suffer.

The function *pygame.time.delay()* does some of that work for the programmer. It pauses for the specified number of milliseconds using the same method—running a loop, executing CPU cycles, until the specified duration has passed. The previous loop would be executed in the following way:

```
import pygame
pygame.init()
t = 1000

while True:
```

```
# Other code here
    delta = t - pygame.time.get_ticks() # Calculate time remaining
    if delta > 0:                        # Wait for that time period
        pygame.time.delay(delta)
    print (t//999)
    t = t + 1000
    if t > 10000:
        break;
```

The value of the expression t - pygame.time.get_ticks() will be the time remaining in the current frame. Each time through the loop this will get smaller as real time advances. The problem with both of these code snippets is that the CPU is active during the time delay. It's eating up CPU cycles for no reason; a CPU can be made to pause, to switch to another process for a while and then return. The function *pygame.time.wait()* makes the process "go to sleep" to share the processor with other programs. A program that waits for even a few milliseconds will consume very little processor time, but it is slightly less accurate than the function *pygame.time.delay()*. The new code would be:

```
import pygame
pygame.init()
t = 1000

while True:
# Other code here
    delta = t - pygame.time.get_ticks() # Calculate time remaining
    if delta > 0:                        # Wait for that time period
        pygame.time.wait(delta)
    print (t//999)
    t = t + 1000
    if t > 10000:
        break;
```

This is the best version so far. *Wait* allows other processes like your browser and email reader to execute while the game is waiting. It does require that the programmer keep track of the remaining time pretty carefully. There is another choice, one that is frequently used in Pygame.

The **time** module has within it a class named **Clock**. This class has methods that can return real time values and time intervals, but it has one method that is exactly what we need for the game loop: it's called *tick(x)*. It will compute how many milliseconds have passed since the previous call, but the important thing is that it will wait for as long as you want and do so in a way that a game program would find convenient. If a value for the parameter x is passed, the parameter will be considered to be the desired frame rate. The function will delay to keep the game running slower than the given ticks per second. So, by calling the method *Clock.tick(40)* once per frame, the program will never run at more than 40 frames per second. The previous code written to use *clock.tick* would be:

```
import pygame
pygame.init()

clock = pygame.time.Clock()
while True:
  clock.tick(1)

# Other game code here
    print (t)
    t = t + 1
    if t > 10:
        break;
```

This snippet is the typical Pygame main loop, but the frame rate is usually faster, meaning that the parameter to tick would be perhaps 30 or 40 (frames per second) rather than 1.

Game Loop: Bouncing a Simulated Ball

Using *clock.tick()* a practical game loop can be created. In this case, a ball, indicated by a circle, will move around the screen. It will change direction when it reaches the edge of the window.

The position of the ball on the display surface, indicated by a variable named *display*, will be indicated by variables x and y. The number of pixels the ball moves during one frame is indicated by the variables dx and dy. The main action that takes place each pass through the game loop would be to update the ball's position and display it:

```
x = x + dx
y = y + dy
pygame.draw.circle (display, (200,200,200), (x,y), 20)
```

Of course, within a very few iterations, the position of the ball will be outside of the screen and thus will not be visible. Consider the horizontal dimension, for example. If the value of x becomes larger than the width of the screen, then the ball should not move any further right. The simple way to do that is to change the sign on the variable dx so that the x value now decreases with each frame. If the value of x becomes smaller than 0, meaning it has moved past the left side of the screen, then the same action, changing the sign of dx, with have the effect of moving the ball to the right in each frame, again keeping the ball on the screen. The same can be done for the vertical motion using *y* and *dy*.

The game loop would look like this:

```
import pygame
dx = 3      # Speed in X direction
dy = 4      # Speed in Y direction
x = 100     # X position
y = 100     # Y position
radius = 20
pygame.init()
clock = pygame.time.Clock()
display = pygame.display.set_mode((500, 300), pygame.SRCALPHA, 32)
while True:
    clock.tick(30)                      # Make sure 1/30 second has passed
    display.fill((100, 100, 100))       # Clear the screen
    x = x + dx                          # Move objects
    y = y + dy
    pygame.draw.circle (display, (200,200,200), (x,y), radius) # Draw the ball
    if (x< radius or x>500- radius): # Outside of the screen in x?
        dx = -dx                        # Change the motion direction in x
    if (y< radius) or (y>300- radius):  # Outside of the screen in y?
        dy = -dy                        # Change the motion direction in x
    pygame.display.update()             # Update the screen
```

In the code, checking the *x* and *y* values is done, accounting for the radius of the circle so that it looks like the ball is bouncing off of the sides. A screen shot from this program appears in Figure 3.2.

This program executes forever, and it requires the user to stop it from the keyboard. There's a better way to end a program in Pygame.

EVENTS

As pointed out before in this book, an *event* can be defined as *something that happens*. In Python and Pygame, an event is also a **class** and a **module**, each one representing something specific that can happen while a program executes.

What is meant by *something that happens?* It's usually something unpredictable, such as a key press or mouse gesture. Accordingly, one of the most important uses for events in Pygame is user input.

The **pygame.event** module contains thirteen functions, but the most important one is *get()*. When an event occurs, like a key press, a record of that is placed into a queue. The *get()* function returns the list of **event** objects in that queue and removes those from the queue. What is returned is a list (actually, an *eventlist* object reference) of things that have happened since the past time it was called. Each of these events may need to be handled differently, in a loop that looks at them all.

The typical event handling loop is (in pseudocode):

FIGURE 3.2 **Screenshot of the bouncing ball program.**

```
for event in pygame.event.get():
    if event.type == some event type:
        # do something
    if event.type == some other event type:
        #do something else
    ...
```

This gets each event from the list and checks to see what to do with it until there are no more events. The variable *event.type* indicates which specific event has been encountered. There are fifteen of those, but most are not common. They are:

Event Name	What Happened?
QUIT	Game is over
ACTIVEEVENT	Pygame has been activated or hidden, perhaps by mouse
KEYDOWN	A key has been pressed
KEYUP	A key has been released
MOUSEMOTION	The mouse has been moved

Event Name	What Happened?
MOUSEBUTTONDOWN	A mouse button has been pressed
MOUSEBUTTONUP	A mouse button has been released
JOYAXISMOTION	Joystick was moved
JOYBALLMOTION	Joy ball was moved
JOYHATMOTION	Joystick hat was moved
JOYBUTTONDOWN	A joystick or pad button was pressed
JOYBUTTONUP	A joystick or pad button was released
VIDEORESIZE	Pygame window was resized
VIDEOEXPOSE	Part of the Pygame window was exposed
USEREVENT	A user defined event

The names in boldface are the most important ones for most situations. These are constants inside the **event** module, so the full name of the *QUIT* event would be *pygame.QUIT*.

The bouncing ball loop complete with a *QUIT* event handler would be written:

```
while True:
    clock.tick(30)                      # Make sure 1/30 second has passed

  for event in pygame.event.get():
     if event.type == pygame.QUIT:
        exit()

  display.fill((100, 100, 100))       # Clear the screen
  x = x + dx                          # Move objects
  y = y + dy
     .   .   .
  pygame.display.update()             # Update the screen
```

This exits the program when the QUIT event is encountered.

The Mouse

The three basic mouse events, *MOUSEMOTION, MOUSEBUTTON-DOWN,* and *MOUSEBUTTONUP,* give all that is needed to deal with mouse input, and because finger gestures on a touch screen are essentially the same as mouse gestures, the same events are used for those as well.

The *QUIT* event has no other data connected with it, but other events do. These are called parameters even though they are variables local to the *event* module. In the case of mouse events, the parameters are the position of the mouse in the display surface, the distance the mouse has moved since the last event, and which button was pressed or released.

The parameters are named and can be accessed via the object reference returned by **get()**.

Event.buttons	A tuple having an entry for each mouse button. So, *buttons[0]* is 1 if the left button is pressed and 0 otherwise. **Buttons[1]** is the middle button and **buttons[2]** is the right
Event.pos	A tuple holding the position of the mouse when the event occurred as (x,y).
Event.rel	A tuple holding the distance the mouse has moved since the previous mouse event (dx, dy).

The event can be printed, so a program that allows the viewing of the parameters while a program executes would be:

```
import pygame
pygame.init()
clock = pygame.time.Clock()
display = pygame.display.set_mode((500, 250), pygame.SRCALPHA, 32)
while True:
    clock.tick(30)
    for event in pygame.event.get():
        print (event)
        if event.type == pygame.QUIT:
            exit()
```

A typical output line would be:

<Event(4-MouseMotion {'pos': (465, 82), 'rel': (-31, -1), 'buttons': (0, 0, 0)})> which shows the current mouse position, the motion since the previous event (to the left), and that none of the buttons are pressed.

The Keyboard

Another important kind of event is a key press. The event KEYDOWN occurs when any key is pressed, and KEYUP occurs when a key is released. This means that a key could be depressed for multiple frames (iterations). The key that was pressed is identified in the event object itself as the variable **event.key**. This variable holds a pygame constant that represents the key, and it is ***not*** a character constant. Every character has a corresponding constant within pygame that identifies it. The character "a" is represented as **pygame.K_a**, for example (a complete list can be found at *https://www.pygame.org/docs/ref/key.html*).

Consider that a game will allow the player to accelerate an object forward when the **"w"** key is pressed and slow it down as long as the **"s"** key is pressed, which is a standard scheme. A loop that detects these key presses is:

```
for event in pygame.event.get():
    if event.type == pygame.KEYDOWN:
        if event.key == pygame.K_w:
            forward = True
        elif event.key == pygame.K_d:
            backward = True
    if event.type == pygame.KEYUP:
        if event.key == pygame.K_w:
            forward = False
        elif event.key == pygame.K_d:
            backward = False
```

Another way to detect key presses is to use the **key_pressed** method. This is a part of the key class of pygame, and it returns a tuple of flags that indicate the state of every key: False (or 0) means the key is not pressed, and True (1) indicates that it is pressed. Testing to see if the "w" key is pressed would be accomplished as follows:

```
pygame.key.get_pressed() [pygame.K_w]
```

This method does not require the use of the **event** class and can be used anywhere in the code. It is also interesting to note that the pygame constants for characters are actually indices into the tuple. Code that is equivalent to that in the previous event loop could be written, using **key_pressed**, as:

```
z = pygame.key.get_pressed()
forward = False
backward = False
if z[pygame.K_w]:
    forward = True
elif z[pygame.K_s]:
    backward = True
```

An On-Screen Button

A *button*, in the user interface sense, is usually a rectangle that is drawn within a window. When a mouse button is clicked while the cursor is within this rectangular area, some task is performed. Almost everyone who has used a computer has "clicked on a button." Here's how it works.

The mouse position is tested after each time it is moved to see if the cursor, which is the icon that represents the mouse position, lies within the rectangular area defined by the button. The button itself can be defined by its upper left coordinates ULX and ULY, its width, and its height. If *mouseX* is the x coordinate of the mouse and *mouseY* is the y coordinate, then the cursor is within the button if

```
(mouseX >= ULX) and (mouseX <= ULX+width) and
    (mouseY >= ULY) and (mouseY <= ULY+height)
```

If this is true the button is said to be *armed*, meaning that the button on the mouse will now cause an action. Let's assume that the action desired is to change the background color of the drawing surface to red. The loop will be the same as the previous one until the event loop is encountered. Then:

```
for event in pygame.event.get():
    if event.type == pygame.MOUSEBUTTONDOWN:
```

When the mouse button is pressed, this event will occur and the code that follows will be executed. Was the mouse button clicked within the rectangular region defined by the screen button? Let the screen button have an upper left corner at (100,100), a width of 100, and a height 0f 50. Then:

```
mouseX = event.pos[0]
mouseY = event.pos[1]
if (mouseX >= ULX) and (mouseX <= ULX+width) and
            (mouseY >= ULY) and (mouseY <= ULY+height):
display.fill ((255,0,0))
```

because we want to change the color of the display surface to red. When the screen is updated, the color change will occur:

```
pygame.display.update()              # Update the screen</CODE>
```

This works, but it is customary to draw the rectangle on the screen so users can see it and know where to click. This has to be done every time the screen is refreshed. Somewhere before the call to update should be a line that draws the rectangle:

```
pygame.draw.rect(display, (0,255, 255),(100,100,100,50))
```

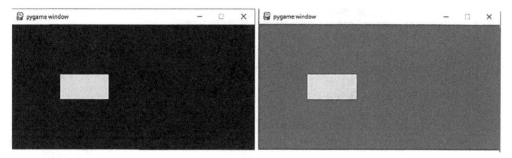

FIGURE 3.3 The "button." Left – The button can be seen but has not been pressed. Right – After pressing the button.

A Simple Game

Until now, we could not really build a computer game because input from the user was not possible. Interaction is essential in a game. Now we have mouse input, and that's almost all we need.

Here's a simple idea: we have a bouncing ball, as we made before. When the mouse is clicked while the cursor in inside the ball, it disappears and reappears somewhere else on the screen. This is not much of a game in terms of its being fun, but it has many of the needed components. Also, a lot of the code already exists.

Beginning with the existing program from earlier in the chapter gives the bouncing ball part. Adding the mouse interface means testing to see if a mouse click finds the cursor within the circle on the screen. The circle is drawn at location *x,y* and its radius is given by the variable *radius*, so what we need to do is to add a mouse click event and then check to see whether the location of that mouse click is within distance *radius* of the point (x,y).

```
for event in pygame.event.get():
        if event.type == pygame.MOUSEBUTTONDOWN:
            mouseX = event.pos[0]
            mouseY = event.pos[1]
    if distance ( (mouseX,mouseY), (x,y) ) <= radius :
    #    do something.
```

The function distance is simply the Euclidean distance function, and the two locations between which the distance is to be determined are tuples. The comment "do something" is where the ball is removed and placed in a new location. That can be done simply by changing the values of x and y. Let's place the ball at 100,100 again:

```
for event in pygame.event.get():
        if event.type == pygame.MOUSEBUTTONDOWN:
            mouseX = event.pos[0]
            mouseY = event.pos[1]
        if distance ( (mouseX,mouseY), (x,y) ) <= radius :
x = 100  # X position
y = 100  # Y position
```

This program is called **game01**. It lacks a few things to make it a complete game. There are no intro and extro screens and no score keeping. It's basically a toy.

A Better Game

Score keeping is an important part of a game, but it can sometimes be tricky. A simple way to do it is to have the player continue until they fail and count the number of times they succeeded. A better game than the previous one would allow the player to keep clicking and to make the task harder each time they are successful. A successful click is a point, and the game is over when they fail.

Making the game harder can be as simple as making the motion of the ball faster or making the ball smaller. The former is better because it has a more generous challenge. One can only make the ball so small, after all. Making the ball move faster means increasing the values of *dx* and *dy* by some amount, which is easy to do.

A problem is that *dx* and *dy* can be positive or negative, so just adding a fixed value to them may slow them down, rather than speed them up. A function named *sign(x)* can be used that returns 1 if the sign of x is positive and -1 if it is negative. Now speeding up the ball is accomplished by:

```
dx = dx+sign(dx)
dy = dy+sign(dy)
```

Now we need a score. This is simply an integer count of the number of successful clicks. It should be displayed on the screen and updated after each frame. The variable will be named *score*:

```
t = font.render ("Score: "+str(score), 1, (255,255,255))
```

```
display.blit (t, (20,20))
```

The final modification to game01 is to quit the game if the user misses the ball. The event loop is now:

```
for event in pygame.event.get():
    if event.type == pygame.MOUSEBUTTONDOWN:
        mouseX = event.pos[0]
        mouseY = event.pos[1]
        if distance((mouseX, mouseY), (x, y)) <= radius:
            dx = dx+sign(dx)   # X speed
            dy = dy+sign(dy)   # Y speed
            score = score + 1
        else:
            exit()
```

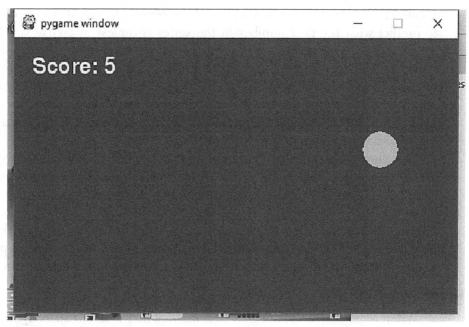

FIGURE 3.4 Game02, click in on the moving ball to get points.

This is **game02**, and a screen capture of the game being played is shown in Figure 3.4.

RANDOMNESS IN GAMES

Randomness has a huge role in games, not just computer games but all games. A deck of playing cards is always shuffled so that the cards are dealt in a random order. Dice are used in many games to create random integers. In computer games, random numbers are used to resolve battles, to place opponents on a playing area, to determine how to evaluate a player's choice, and to provide realistic patterns of traffic, movement, and other aspects of realism in a game. Why? Because a sufficiently complex situation has the appearance of being random.

How often will a bus arrive at a specific stop? Of course, there is a schedule, but do busses arrive at the stop exactly on time? Always? If they did, would that seem like a realistic situation? Probably not. So, a game that involved busses arriving would likely add a random number to the scheduled time to determine when the next bus would arrive. The variability makes it seem more real.

If we use a machine (the computer) to generate random numbers, it is actually not possible to produce *truly* random numbers. It is however possible to create a set of equations that when used repeatedly will produce a series of numbers where no matter how much of the series you see, it is not possible to predict what the next number in the series is (unless of course you have access to the set of equations). One very useful aspect of these *pseudorandom* number generators is that if you start with the same seed, you are guaranteed to produce the identical sequence of numbers. Now, this is not good for games and gambling, but it is extremely useful when testing a program and in some simulations. When testing a program it is important to be able to reproduce the identical statement execution sequence.

For other applications, it is just as important that we be unable to reproduce the sequence. If Video Lottery Terminals or other gambling machines went through an identical sequence each time they were turned on, it would probably be a lot less fun and the operators of these machines would no longer be able to count on the fact that many more people will lose than will win, as is the case in all gambling (i.e., it wouldn't be gambling anymore). In these applications the sequence of numbers used must be as close to random as we can get.

Randomness Generally

When we say that something is *random*, what do we mean? In everyday life, things that we call random are things that are unpredictable. Objects that are moving at random have no identifiable pattern; events that occur at random cannot be anticipated or predicted. That the event *will* occur may not be random, but precisely *when* it will occur might be. When will the next red pickup truck pass by? When will the next customer arrive at the bank teller's window? Who will win the next civic election? These are things that are commonly thought of as random events. The technical meaning of random relates to these things, but it is more specific and less intuitive.

Consider a guessing game in which a player is asked to provide a number between 1 and 10. If the player guesses correctly, they win some money, perhaps $8. Otherwise they lose $1. The player chooses the number 7. Is 7 a random number? How can this be established? One way to look at it is that the randomness of that particular number 7 is determined by the process used to get that 7. Perhaps dice were rolled, or maybe the answer is always 7. This is a part of the common meaning implied when we say something is random, and so it has some value, but it's not a technical or mathematical definition, because it cannot be accurately defined or tested. You may believe that 7 was random, but if you did not know how that number was arrived at you would have no way of determining if it was.

Let's repeat the experiment. **The number 7 is chosen** again. Is *this* one random? The same arguments apply here as applied to the first experiment. Does anything change if we look at the whole set of experiments (in other words, both of them together)? It produced a pair of numbers, "7 7"; are these random? Some might say that they start to detect a pattern (that I am picking only sevens) and that this is not random. Of course it is easily possible that I selected two sevens in a row, and that it happened by chance. What if this experiment is repeated a hundred times and produces a six each time? Now it's pretty clear that these numbers are not random and that the pattern can be defined with some confidence. The point of this exercise is to underscore the idea that numbers, and things in general, are random relative to one another only. Randomness exists only in *context*, as a relative property of sequences of numbers.

What if the 7 that I picked is the result of a die roll and you can watch me roll it? Does that violate the rule that random things are random in relation to others? Not at all. Randomness is a property of a collection of events or objects, preferably a large collection. This is true even if the collection we are using was produced at another time, as is the case with my die roll. We assume that the roll in question is like all the other rolls we know, and so we can say this one is random too. Looking at the properties of large collections of numbers is essentially what statistics is all about.

When we look at human behavior, it is in fact difficult for a human to behave in a random fashion. People have learned connections between events: things that are related to each other can't be random with respect to each other. We also have misunderstandings about randomness, make correlations between perceptions and actions, and possess a host of instinctive actions that preclude random behavior. Individuals can be trained to behave randomly, but we don't do it instinctively. The behavior of groups of people can *seem* random because it is so complex, but the appearance of randomness does not necessarily imply that something is indeed random. For example, if a large group of people is asked to pick "heads" or "tails" in a coin toss, it may be that the number of people selecting "heads" is almost the same as the number selecting "tails." The complex patterns of the individual lives that produced the specific decision of "heads" or "tails" that they made that day would be impossible to analyze and can seem random. However, if those selecting "heads" are moved to another room and asked to repeat the selection many times, it is likely that this group will end up selecting heads more often than chance would dictate. Therefore, their choice of "heads" was not random.

When implementing things on a computer, it is important to realize that underneath it all everything is represented using numbers. That's because the only things that computers can manipulate directly are numbers. This means that if we want to create a random color, for example, we first need to come up with a way to represent colors as numbers and then generate some random numbers. The first step is easy: you simply create a mapping of numbers and colors. Often, it doesn't even matter if you are organized about it so long as the same number always refers to the same color (5 = red, 8 = blue, 0 = white, etc.). Once we have our mapping, we can choose random numbers just like we would for anything else and then "translate" those numbers into their representative colors. If the numbers are random, then the colors are too. This applies to any element we want to be able to select at random.

Random can be a tricky word in that it means something to most people but also has a more specific, technical meaning in science generally, and in simulation in particular. The main purpose of this chapter is to explain what is meant by the word "random" in the more technical context.

RANDOMNESS IN GAMES: DICE, CARDS

When discussing randomness, many people think of gambling or of games that involve random selections and actions. Gambling has had an appeal to humans throughout recorded history and naturally involves chance. No sensible person would bet against an event that was certain to occur or even for one that was unlikely. So it is that when discussing randomness, the subject very quickly turns to gambling.

The simplest example of gambling is that of a coin toss. Two-choice decisions (also called *binary* decisions) are sometimes made by assigning a decision to each side and then determining the "winner" by flipping a coin. Football teams flip a coin to decide which side kicks off. The name for the city of Portland, Oregon was chosen based on the toss of a coin (it could have been named

Boston). In 1959, a member of Buddy Holly's band flipped a coin with Richie Valens to see who would get the last seat on a small plane flying out of Fargo, North Dakota after a concert when their bus broke down. Valens won, and he died when the plane crashed. Because a coin has two sides, and because it is presumed that the coin is fair and that flipping it creates a random selection between the two sides, this seems a natural way to make a random choice. Even the ancient Romans flipped coins as a gambling game *Capita vel Navia* (heads or ships). We've apparently been deciding things this way for quite a long time.

We all know that a die is a cube with different numbers on each of the six faces, and it should behave like a six-sided coin. Throwing a die properly, where the cube tumbles and then bounces off of another surface, should create a trajectory so complicated that predicting the number that will appear of the top face would be impossible. The random nature of dice has appealed to human gamblers since prehistoric times. The oldest die known is 5,000 years old and is from Iran, but references to gambling with dice are even older than that.

Playing cards are also common gambling tools, and they are thought to have originated in China in about the eight to tenth century, well after the invention of paper. Before that devices like dominoes were used to play similar games. The number of cards in the deck varies with time and geography, but the first decks appeared to have four suits just like modern decks. Contemporary card decks have fifty-two cards (plus jokers), and that means that there is a 1 in 52 chance of picking a specific card from the deck and a huge number of different five-card hands that can be dealt.

The progression from coin to die to cards constitutes an increase in complexity and an increasing difficulty in predicting the result of simple events. Events that are very complex in terms of the number of possible combinations provide a more interesting basis for gambling, at least partly because the results are hard to predict. In addition, the value of a card drawn from a deck of cards *seems* more random than does the result of a coin flip. So, not only are there different degrees of randomness, but there is a commonly held apprehension of this fact.

The modern discipline that concerns the likelihood of events is called probability, and it quantifies these degrees of randomness. A coin toss has two possible outcomes. One outcome is heads, and the probability of heads on any given toss is 0.5, or 1/2—one out of the two possible outcomes. Similarly, the probability of rolling a die and having six appear on top is 1/6 (one in six), and the probability of drawing a King of Clubs from a shuffled deck of cards is 1/52. The probability of drawing a King from the deck is 4/52, though, or 1/13, because there are four kings in the deck. Thus, the probability of drawing a heart is 13/52, or 1/4. Another way to express this is to say that a quarter of the time we expect to pick a heart. These simple definitions make sense to most people, but in order to make use of random numbers in simulations, we need to be able to manipulate probabilities, and the rules for manipulating probabilities are less intuitive.

Probability for Beginners

When dealing with complex situations such as are common in the real world and in simulations, there are many events that occur, and probabilities become more difficult to determine. Fortunately, there are straightforward rules for dealing with multiple events. For example, what is the probability of rolling a die twice and getting a six each time? The probability is 1/6 (one in 6) for each trial; for both it will be 1/6 * 1/6, or 1/36. The individual probabilities are multiplied together to produce the combined probability. Looking at the diagram of this situation in **Figure 3.5**, it should be fairly easy to see why this is. For the first roll, each possible outcome has a probability of 1/6, including the target roll of "6." For the second roll, each outcome also has a probability of 1/6, and for each individual outcome of roll 1 there are six possible outcomes for roll 2. This means there are thirty-six possibilities for the two rolls, and a six followed by a six is just one of those. Thus, the probability is 1/36. This is also the probability of rolling two sixes simultaneously on two dice.

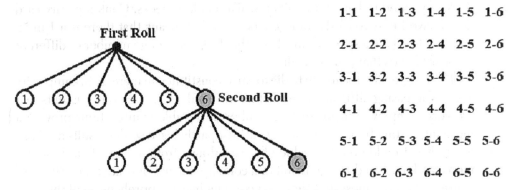

FIGURE 3.5 The set of outcomes for the tossing of a pair of six-sided dice.

Figure 3.5 shows the possibilities available when rolling a die twice, showing the specific path that has two consecutive "6" rolls. This is the same as rolling two dice simultaneously. All possible outcomes are listed on the left, and 6-6 is one of thirty-six possible outcomes (1/36).

Now let's look at a gambling game that involves dice to see how the calculation of probabilities gets more complex. The game of craps is played with two dice where the numbers on the dice are added together. A player's turn in craps is a sequence of one or more rolls determined by the rules. If the player (shooter) throws a 2, 3, or 12, then they lose immediately. If they roll a 7 or 11, then they win immediately. If a 4, 5, 6, 8, 9, or 10 shows, then that number becomes the "point," and the player rolls the dice again until that number is rolled again (win) or a 7 is rolled (lose). There's more to it, but that is the basic set of rules. Here's your question: what is the probability that the player will lose on the first roll?

This is a harder question to answer than the previous ones, because there is more than one way to roll a particular number. On two dice, a 3 can be made in two different ways: by having the first die show a 1 and the second a 2, or the first die could be a 2 and the second a 1. The probability of rolling a three is therefore 2/36, or 1/18. In general, the probability of a particular sum is found by looking at the possibilities in Figure 3.5. To find the probability of getting any particular number, count the number of times the sum of two numbers equals the number you wish to roll, and divide your count by 36 to give the probability. A "2" can only be rolled by having both dice be "1," so the probability is 1/36, and a "12" can be rolled only as "6" and a "6," so that's 1/36. The chances of rolling any one of a "2" or a "3" or a "12" is the sum of the individual probabilities, which is 1/36 + 2/36 + 1/36 = 4/36 (or 1/9). In craps, this is the probability of losing on the first roll.

On the other hand, there are lots of ways to roll a "7": 1+6, 2+5, 3+4, 4+3, 5+2, and 6+1 for a total of 6/36. There are two ways to roll an "11." The probability of rolling a "7" or an "11" on the first roll is thus 6/36 + 2/36 = 8/36, or 2/9. This means that the probability of winning on the first roll is twice the probability of losing on the first roll. This process of calculating probabilities can be repeated for every outcome, so it turns out that the likelihood of winning at craps is well known and can be found on the Internet and in books. These likelihoods, that is of gambling and day to day activities, are generally expressed not as probabilities but as *odds*.

Probability Calculations

Probabilities are used both in real life and in simulations to estimate how likely events are to occur. Simple events, like the flip of a coin, have a simple interpretation in probability terms. More complicated events, especially combinations of events, require a degree of calculation. In these cases it is sometimes useful to think of a probability as a special kind of number, a kind that requires a special arithmetic. Consider two coin tosses, one after another. The probability of the first coin showing "heads" is 1/2, and the second coin is the same. What is the probability that both coins show "heads"? The answer is 1/4, which is the product of the individual probabilities of each coin showing heads. This is in general the correct way to calculate the overall probability of a series of events—to multiply the individual probabilities together.

There is a simple algebra for this. The letter **P** means "probability of," and the expression **P(heads)** means the probability of a coin showing heads. The event involved is inside the parentheses. We get to invent some of our own notation here so long as it is consistent, so **P(H)** will be the probability of heads too, **P(H1)** will be the probability of heads showing on the first coin, and **P(H2)** is the same situation for coin 2. The situation where heads is showing on two tossed coins will be written as **P(H1 and H2)**, and if the coins are fair the rule can be written:

$$P(H_1 \text{ and } H_2) = P(H_1) \times P(H_2)$$

This rule applies to all independent events, and can be expanded to any number of them, not just two. The probability of three independently tossed coins all showing "heads," for example, is

$$P(H_1 \text{ and } H_2 \text{ and } H_3) = P(H_1) \times P(H_2) \times P(H_3)$$

The rule expands in a logical way for any number of events. It works for mixed events too, of course. The nature of the event is not at all important here, only that the events do not depend on one another and have known probabilities. So, if **P(D=6)** is the probability of rolling a 6 on a single die, then

$$P(H_1 \text{ and } D = 6) = P(H_1) \times P(D = 6) = (1/2) \times (1/6) = 1/12 = 0.08333$$

which is the probability of both tossing heads and rolling a six.

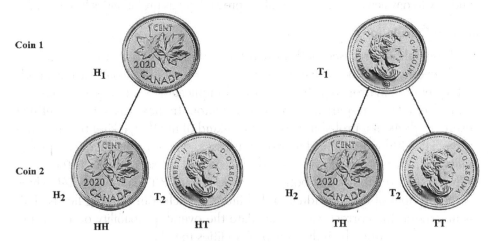

FIGURE 3.6 **The complete set of outcomes for the toss of two coins.**

The probability that one or the other of two events will occur is a little bit more difficult to calculate, but it is not past high school math. The simplest example is the probability that heads will be thrown on any one of two coins. Using the notation just devised, this could be written as **P(H1 or H2)**, and the obvious answer, that it is **P(H1)+P(H2)**, must be incorrect. If it were correct then **P(H1 or H2) = P(H1) + P(H2) = 0.5 + 0.5 = 1.0.** This can't be correct because it means that it is certain that one of the coins would be heads.

In order to sort out a way to calculate the probability of at least one of a specified set of events occurring, look at Figure 3.6 which shows a diagram of the possible outcomes of two coin tosses. The top part of the figure shows the two results possible for the first coin, and below that the results of the second coin are enumerated based on the first toss. There are four possible outcomes, and each can be described as one of the paths through the outcomes in the figure. These outcomes are:

H1 and H2 means that heads is visible on both coin1 and coin2. Recall that **H1** is the symbol that means "heads is showing on coin 1."
H1 and T2 means that heads is visible on coin1 and tails is visible on coin2.
T1 and H2 means that tails is visible on coin1 and heads is visible on coin2.
T1 and T2 means that tails is visible on both coin1 and coin2.

We want to be able to calculate the probability of at least one head showing after tossing two coins. From the figure we could simply count the outcomes: there are four possible, and three of them have at least one head showing, so the probability is 3/4 that at least one head is showing. However, not all situations are as easily drawn, and some involve a great many possible outcomes. A simple formula would be good to have.

With this in mind, look at the outcomes again. The event **H1**, which is heads showing on coin 1, is 1/2, and arises through the either of the outcomes **(H1 and H2)** or **(H1 and T2)**. The probability of this is:

$$P(H_1) = P(H_1 \, and \, H_2) + P(H_1 \, and \, T_2) = 1/4 + 1/4 = 1/2$$

which is as we would expect. In the same way, the event **H2** arises through either **(H1 and H2)** or **(T1 and H2)**. This probability is

$$P(H_2) = P(H_1 \, and \, H_2) + (T_1 \, and \, H_2) = 1/4 + 1/4 = 1/2$$

The formula for the probability of either **H1** or **H2** occurring in a two-coin toss starts with **P(H1) + P(H2)**, which would correspond to the events:

(H1 and H2) or (H1 and T2) or (H1 and H2) or (H1 and T2) and has probability **P(H1 and H2) + P(H1 and T2) + P(H1 and H2) + (T1 and H2).**

This is wrong, but now notice that **(H1 and H2)** appears twice! Subtracting gives us the correct formula:

$$P(H_1 \; or \; H_2) = P(H_1) + P(H_2) - (H_1 \; and \; H_2)$$

This formula is correct for all independent events, that is, events that do not affect one another. We now have a basic knowledge of how events and their probabilities are calculated and combined. To be sure, this knowledge is essential in gambling, and it will come in handy when thinking about randomness in general and simulation in particular.

GENERATING RANDOM VALUES

The need for a practical source of random numbers dates back to a physicist named Enrico Fermi in the 1930s in the context of problems in particle physics that could not be calculated analytically. It was suggested that a simulation involving random numbers be created and made to run on an electronic computer. This was actually done in the 1940s, and one result was the hydrogen bomb. At that time there was no convenient source of random numbers. Electronic and physical devices were used to create events having measurable random properties, and those measurements were in turn used to create tables of random numbers that could be used repeatedly. The most famous of these was created by the Rand Corporation using an electronically simulated roulette wheel. The table was sold as a book, the relatively famous *A Million Random Digits* (Rand Corporation, 1955).

Using this book, when you wanted a random number, you would flip to a page (any page) and read off a set of numbers from any line or column. The numbers had been tested to assure randomness and were a reliable source for a long time. The problem was that access to the numbers was slow, needing a copy of the book and human intervention. Of course, computers were much slower then too, but even considering that the procedure was arduous.

Of course, people who owned computers in the 1940s and 1950s had a lot of money at their disposal, so if they really needed a random number, then they could have their own electronic random number generator built and connected to their machine. What was used as the basis for these devices was the essential unpredictability of noise signals obtained from radio or radioactive sources. If you connect a radio to a device that measures voltages and tune the radio to a place where no station is broadcasting, the human ear would hear a hissing sound from the radio. This is what random signals sound like, and the voltmeter will display this as random electrical voltage levels. These can then be converted into digital form and used by the computer as random numbers. Similarly, noise can be created using a vacuum tube or solid-state device and sampled in the same way as was the radio to produce random numbers.

Pseudorandom Numbers

Numbers that satisfy tests of randomness can be generated mathematically. Starting at a particular value called the *seed*, a sequence is created that will be the same each time, but that is random with respect to each other. Changing the seed changes the sequence of numbers.

When using Python, the module named *random* provides a set of methods that will generate such numbers, and in a variety of ways. The simplest call is to the method **random**:

```
random.random()
```

This returns a random number between 0 and 1, a real number. This can be used to implement any of the methods that will be discussed here. For example, a coin flip could be implemented as:

```
flip = int(random.random () * 2)
```

If the value of a flip is 0, then "heads" has appeared, otherwise "tails." Another way to accomplish this is to use the method **randint (a,b)**, which returns a random integer between a and b inclusive. The coin toss would be:

```
flip = random.randint (0,1)
```

A die roll would be **random.randint (1,6)**, and so on.

The method **choice(s)** returns a random selection from a tuple or a list. Thus:

```
print (random.choice ((1,2,3,4,5,6)))
```

returns a random element of the tuple (1,2,3,4,5,6), which would amount to a die roll. The method **random.sample(s,k)** returns a list of **k** unique members of the sequence **s**. As an example, the call

```
random.sample ([1,2,3,4,5,6], 3)
```
might result in [3,1,5] or [5,6,2], but never [2,1,2].

A very useful method for card games is **random.shuffle(x)**, where x is a list. It returns a permutation of the items in the list x. Consider:

```
cards = ["a","k","q","j","10","9","8","7","6","5","4","3","2"]
random.shuffle (cards)
```

The order of the values in **x** is now random, and could be ["8", "10", "k", "3", "4", "6", "7", "9", "q", "a", "2", "5", "j"] as one example.

Setting the seed for the random number generator can be an important starting point, because otherwise the sequence generated will be the same each time. The **random** module does this automatically when it is started, but it can also be done by the programmer. For example:

```
random.seed (431)
```

will set the set to the number 421. Setting the seed to a known value can be important when debugging. It is hard enough to analyze a program in the first place, but if it behaves randomly it is much harder. When developing code it can be useful to set the seed to the same values each time.

SIMULATING REALITY AND INTELLIGENCE

Almost all computer games are a type of simulation. They may not simulate a real situation, but they certainly have realistic elements. Reality has certain characteristics that are hard to represent convincingly, and humans have a knack for seeing these situations and evaluating their realism. It has been said that no two snowflakes are alike. They have random characteristics caused by the complex, chaotic way they are formed. Trees are like that too. All spruce trees seem very similar from a distance, but they are all very different at a finer scale, having different heights, number and shapes of branches, colors, bark variations, and so on. People see situations as real if their assessment of the randomness of the situation corresponds with that seen in the real world.

If a realistic tree is to be created on a computer, it could be done by using a detailed and complex simulation of the process of plant growth. Starting from a seed, the forces of moisture, light, temperature, and chemical gradients could be applied to the biological processes in the young tree. Over a great deal of simulated time, a tree could be "grown." Or, as an alternative to this process, the number and shape of branches for each tree could be selected at random using knowledge gained by examining a large number of real trees. This latter method would be much faster and would not require a detailed knowledge of how trees grow.

Games and simulations use randomness to simulate reality for two main purposes: as a modifiable abstraction of the objects being simulated; and as a way to represent complex processes that are not essential to the simulation, but that lend a sense of reality, complexity, or presence. The latter aspect is used in games. We can use randomness to provide accurate ambiance. As a pedestrian in the game, the way the traffic *looks* is an essential part of the background, but it may not be a primary component. If the traffic flow is too regular, too perfect, it does not seem real, and this detracts from the focus of the player/user of the game itself.

This use of random numbers gives the appearance of reality in a game or simulation. When the scenario involves human responses, it is important for the people involved to feel that the situation is normal, and it is also important that subjects or participants are not distracted by oddities in the simulated environment. Complex situations have some random properties that human observers come to see as "realistic," and so random behaviors created artificially can lead an observer to see a simulated situation as more realistic than it is.

This seems obvious, but there are many video games in which, like an old Bugs Bunny cartoon, the same car passes the same point repeatedly. The same is often true of computer-controlled characters in some games, who wander in exactly the same loop forever. These unnatural visuals detract from the main activity of the game or simulation.

It is not only visuals or intervals that matter, but it is the entire effect that should convey the illusion of complexity. Consider rain falling on a window. The time at which the next drop strikes the glass will be random. The location at which it strikes will be random. The size of the drop will be random. Even the sound that the impact makes will vary from drop to drop. This sounds complicated but is really about making things *look* or *seem* right. Looking at Figure 3.7, we see a pair of renderings of a window with rain on it; which one looks real? The rendering on the left has drops in random positions and sizes, much as would be seen in a real scene. The rendering on the right looks artificial. It shows the same droplet appearing many times in an ordered formation and would be the cause of some surprise if observed from your apartment window.

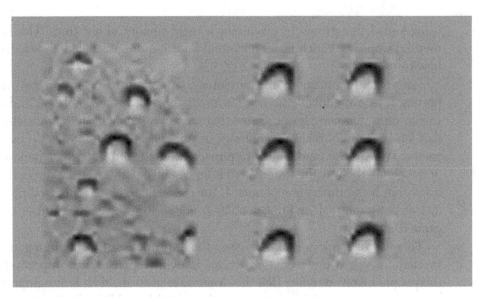

FIGURE 3.7 **Random and non-random rain drops on a window.**

EXERCISES

The following exercises will test your knowledge of the material in this chapter and sometimes require that you do more research before you are able to complete them.

1. Modify the basic button code, which was used to create Figure 3.3, so that the text "Change color" appears within the button, and so that only a click of the left button will cause the color to change. Also change it so that the right button causes the color to change back (to black) and the middle button causes the program to end.

2. Create a rendering of a four-lane road with vehicles placed in random positions. It should be a top view and should use at least four different vehicle images.

3. Modify the bouncing ball program so that the color of the ball changes with each bounce, as does the speed.

4. Modify the bouncing ball program so that the speed of the ball increases when the "w" key is pressed and decreases when the "s" key is pressed.

5. Find an image of a television set and make a copy in a file. Create random noise that will fill the screen and that changes each frame, so it looks like the TV is not tuned to a working channel.

6. Draw a rectangle on the drawing area. Have it rotate counterclockwise when the "a" key is pressed and clockwise when "d" is pressed.

7. Add code to Exercise 7 so that when the "w" key is pressed, the rectangle moves in its forward direction (i.e., where it is pointed), and have it slow and stop if the key is released.

RESOURCES

2D Game graphics tutorial: *http://gamebanana.com/tuts/11225*.
Intro to 2D Graphics: *http://rbwhitaker.wikidot.com/introduction-to-2d-graphics*.
Processing documentation: *http://processing.org/reference/*.
Techniques for fancy and lightweight 2d graphics (game producer blog): *http://www.gameproducer.net/2008/03/03/techniques-for-fancy-and-lightweight-2d-graphics/*.
Sprite Database: *http://spritedatabase.net/*. Useful information and downloads.
Open Game Art: *http://opengameart.org/*. Downloadable sprites and 2D art.

REFERENCES

1. T. M. Cover and J. A. Thomas. *Elements of Information Theory*. New York, NY: Wiley & Sons.

   This describes some of the basic mathematics involved in randomness and probability.

2. J. Dwyer. (1995). "Quick and Portable Random Number Generators." *C/C++ Users Journal* 13, no. 6 (June): 33–44.

   A discussion of how to implement random number generators in programming languages.

3. J. Dwyer and K. B. Williams. (1996). "Testing Random Number Generators." *Dr. Dobb's Journal* (June 1).

   An accessible discussion of how to test numbers for randomness.

4. G. S. Fishman and L. R. Moore. (1982). "A Statistical Evaluation of Multiplicative Random Number Generators with Modulus 231-1." *Journal of the American Statistical Association* 77: 129–136.

   An interesting look at a common type of random number generator and how "good" it is. This is valuable from the perspective of a user of the generator, and as an example of how to test these generators.

5. T. R. Hopkins. (1983). "A Revised Algorithm for the Spectral Test [in Fortran]." *Applied Statistics* 32, no. 3: 328–335.

   A discussion of one of the tests of randomness.

6. F. James. (1990). "A Review of Pseudorandom Number Generators." *Computer Physics Communications* 60: 329–344.

    A general discussion of random number generators from the perspective of people using them.

7. C. Kenny. (2005, April). "Random Number Generators: An Evaluation and Comparison of Random.org and Some Commonly Used Generators." Dublin, Ireland: The Distributed Systems Group, Computer Science Department, Trinity College. *http://www.random.org/analysis/* Analysis2005.pdf.

    A comparison of some of the common random number generators, based on experiments.

8. D. E. Knuth. (1981). *The Art of Computer Programming: Volume 2, Seminumerical Algorithms*, 2nd edition. Reading, PA: Addison Wesley.

    The seminal work on random number generation and their evaluation.

9. W. L. Maier. (1991). "A Fast Pseudo Random Number Generator." *Dr. Dobb's Journal* 16 no. 5 (May): 152–ff.

    A description of the R250 random number generator.

10. W. Palubicki, K. Horel, S. Longay, A. Runions, B. Lane, R. Mech, and P. Przemyslaw Prusinkiewicz. (2009). "Self-Organizing Tree Models for Image Synthesis." *ACM Transactions on Graphics* 28, no. 3: 1–10.

    A discussion of the simulation of tree growth as a means to creating tree images.

11. Rand Corporation. (1955). *A Million Random Digits with 100,000 Normal Deviates*. Glencoe, IL: The Free Press.

    The original Rand corporation source for random numbers in the 1950s and 1960s.

12. D. Stirzaker. (1999). *Probability and Random Variables: A Beginner's Guide.* Cambridge University Press. Cambridge, U.K.

    A good book from which to learn more about probability.

13. J. von Neumann. (1963). "Various Techniques for Use in Connection with Random Digits." *von Neumann's Collected Works*, Vol. 5, 768–770. Pergamon, Oxford.

    An early discussion of randomness written by a giant in the world of computing. Of great historical interest.

14. B. Wichmann and D. Hill. (1987). "Building a Random-Number Generator." *BYTE Magazine* (March), 127–128.

A beginners guide to building (i.e., programming) your own random number generator.

4

GAME AI: COLLISIONS

The words "artificial intelligence" bring to mind a host of advanced technology. Often our first exposure to AI, as it has come to be known, is through science fiction; the computers on Star Trek can speak fluent English, and the robots on Star Wars can serve drinks and pilot spacecraft. In truth, AI has not advanced nearly this far, and although computers can now defeat humans at chess and checkers, this is a far cry from the scenes we see on television and movies.

So what is AI really? Historically this subject has been called ***cognitive simulation***, and that is probably a more descriptive phrase for what is happening. AI is an effort to simulate the actions and responses of an intelligent creature. Why would a game wish to have simulated intelligent creatures? To simulate other intelligent creatures, allies and opponents, of course. At a high level, AI is used in games to implement other people performing intelligent tasks. These simulated persons, sometimes called ***bots*** or simply ***opponents***, are expected to behave in a manner that would be normal for a person. They do not have to be actually intelligent, and a discussion of the difference would be interesting but not profitable here.

At a lower, more practical level, the AI in a game keeps track of things: cars, people, trees, roads, and such. One of the most important tasks of the AI system is to determine when two things collide. This is because collisions are often key points in a game. A missile collides with its target, and the target is destroyed. A hockey player collides with another player and loses the puck. A car collides with a concrete bridge support and takes damage and changes direction. All of these require that collisions be detected, and that the location of the impact and its exact time be known.

It is also true that a good portion of the game AI system can be occupied with performing physics calculations. After a collision takes place, the result is that something breaks, or changes direction, or falls down. A good approximation of real-world physics is essential for a realistic looking game, especially a sports or driving game, and accurately determining the properties of collisions is a crucial first step in correctly simulating physics.

A professional programmer or engineering student would have some knowledge of "academic" AI, which can be a very exciting subject. However, there is very rarely enough time to use those methods in a computer game. Yes, there may be time to *use* a neural network that has been trained in advance to accomplish a particular task; there will not be time to train such a network to handle changing situations. A game programmer must have a practical view of AI, and in a game this means speed and simplicity. Most decisions in a game are made using simple look-up tables or decision trees.

All of the parts of the AI system will be discussed here sooner or later, and that includes opponents, collisions, plans, and physics simulation. However, we'll start with collision detection, because it is the basic thing that we must get right. If a game includes collisions, then collision detection must be fast and accurate if that game is to be playable, and we can't add it on at the last minute—it will be an integral part of the game from the start. There are packages that will do the hard work for us, but it is always dangerous to have code in your program that you don't understand at least somewhat, so please—at least skim this part before downloading someone else's code. Having said this, there are entire books written on the subject, and this chapter is merely a start on some of the basic ideas. You should use an existing collision detection system until you feel you want to do it from scratch.

COLLISION DETECTION

At the outset, the nature of the problem needs to be understood. In the real world, when two objects collide the result is a physical response: sound, heat, energy transfer, and so on. In a game, objects are not real; they are numbers representing how an object looks and where it is in a virtual space. When they collide, it is a virtual collision with no effect unless we detect that collision and simulate an effect. This is one way in which computer games are in fact simulations.

There are two major problems associated with collision detection in computer games. The first is complexity. A small game may have 100 or so objects active at a time. If they are all moving, we have to look at each pair to see if they will hit each other, which means about 100 x 100, or 10,000 tests. We do this each time interval, which is usually the time between two frames—say 24 times per second. This implies a quarter of a million tests for collision per second in a small game, and over a million in a fair-sized one. Any solution we implement must be fast.

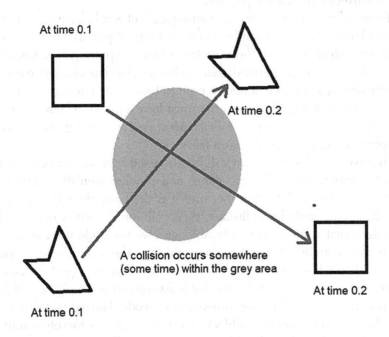

At time 0.1

At time 0.2

A collision occurs somewhere
(some time) within the grey area

At time 0.2

At time 0.1

FIGURE 4.1 Collisions between moving objects. They can occur between frames.

The second problem is that time in a game is **quantized**. Let's say we again have 24 images per second displayed on the screen, which is the speed of a motion picture. It is possible, even likely, that two objects approaching each other fast enough will pass each other in the time between two frames, 1/24 of a second. So they would have collided, but at time **T=0.1** they were some distance apart, and at **T=0.2** they had crossed paths and did not overlap at the new time. We can do two things in this case: look ahead (predict the time at which they will collide) or look back (to the past time when they did collide). Even a game can't easily roll time backward, so the former solution is best. We must figure out when they would collide, figure out the results of that collision, and draw only the **result** at time T=0.2. Figure 4.1 shows an example of this situation.

Just because two objects have changed places does not mean that they collided. Each occupies an area, and they collide only if the areas would also overlap at some time. This suggests a two-step test: first determine whether collision was possible, then determine whether it actually happened. In a real game, most objects will not be involved in collisions during any particular time period, so a fast test that rejects most potential collisions would be a good thing.

Polygonal Objects

In some cases we are concerned with moving polygons on a plane, and in detecting collisions between these. Let's name two polygons **A** and **B**, and give them positions and velocities at time **T**. A position is a 2D vector, and so is a velocity, and each component of a velocity vector is the speed in a direction, X or Y. Since a polygon contains N vertices and all of them are moving at the same speed and direction, we can easily define a straight line that corresponds to the path taken by each vertex in the time between T and T+1. We can also easily compute the position of all of these vertices at both times. A simple rule that excludes a collision between A and B is: ***If we compute a line L that represents the path of a vertex of A, then a collision cannot have taken place between that vertex of A and polygon B if B is on the same side of that line at both time T and T+1.***

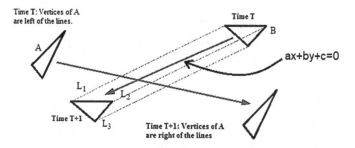

The start and end position of each vertex defines a line.
If any vertex in A changes sides of any of the lines defined by polygon B then a collision is possible.
This is indicated if the sign of ax+by+c changes.

FIGURE 4.2 Polygons A and B move in the direction of the arrows between times T and T+1. If any of the vertices of polygon A are on one side of any of the lines L1, L2, or L3 at time T and are on the opposite side of the same line at time T+1 then a collision is possible.

That doesn't sound all that simple, does it? So, take a look at Figure 4.2. Here we see a couple of polygons at two points in time, and with any luck at all the previous explanation will make sense in the context of the figure.

Basically, if any of the vertices of polygon **A** cross any of the lines L_1 to L_3, then a collision ***may*** have taken place. This is the same basic method we used for the 1D situation, and it has a similar solution.

The line called L_1 in Figure 4.2 is crossed by the triangle **A** if any vertex is on one side of the line at time **T** and on the other side at **T+1**. Every line has an equation that defines it, and this can take one of many mathematical forms. Let's use the ***standard normal*** form

$$ax + by + c = 0$$

A point (x,y) that satisfies this equation is **on** the line, and there are two other possibilities: **ax+by+c** is greater than zero, in which case the point (x,y) is ***above*** the line, and **ax+by+c** is less than zero, meaning that the point is ***below*** the line. Thus, if any vertex is above L_1 at time **T** and below it at **T+1**, then there could be a collision; otherwise there cannot be.

This is an example of ***broad phase*** collision detection, the elimination of objects that cannot possibly collide. The idea is to do this quickly, without using up too much CPU time. The next step, or the ***narrow phase***, is about accurately detecting collision events and determining the time and position of the collision. Breaking the problem into these two parts is about performance. The idea is to do the detailed and time-consuming narrow phase only if there is a chance the objects could collide in the first place. This has the effect of making the whole process more flexible too. There are many ways to solve each problem, and the solutions that are decided upon can be combined almost arbitrarily.

An Example

Imagine two triangular objects, as in Figure 4.2. Triangle A is defined by the points (100,130), (110,150), (130, 95) and has a velocity of (200, 30). Triangle B is defined by (300,65), (320,80), (330, 65) and has velocity vector (-190, 200). Question: could they collide?

Step 1: select a polygon (in this case we select A) and determine the equation of the lines defined by each vertex and the respective motion.

Let's take the first point in triangle A. The line it defines will begin at (100,130) and end at (100+200, 130+30) = (300,230) after adding the motion vector. The ***slope*** of the line is found directly from the velocity vector as dy/dx, or in this case 30/200 = .15.

The point-slope form of the line equation is y = mx + b, and we can solve for b:

$b = y - m * x$ for the point (100,130) is $130 - 0.15 * 100 = 130 - 15 = 115$

This makes the equation $y = 0.15x + 115$

and the standard form is $15x - y + 115 = 0$
and $a = .15, b = 1, c = 115$

Step 2: For each vertex in triangle B, plug in the x and y coordinate to the line equation we just found, before and after the motion of the triangle. If the sign of the result changes for any vertex, then a collision is possible.

Point 1: before $=$ (300,65) and after $=$ (110, 265)
Before: $.15(300) - (65) + 115 = 45 - 65 + 115 = 95$
After: $.15(110) - (265) + 115 = 16.5 - 265 + 115 = -133.5$

The sign changes, so a collision is possible. None of the other vertices need to be checked after it is found that a collision could take place.

Note: When finding the coefficients for the standard equation, if the line is vertical then the slope will be infinite, and that will cause an exception in the program. This is a special case, and the coefficients are:

$$a = 1 \qquad b = 0 \qquad c = -x$$

BROAD PHASE COLLISION DETECTION

It is in this phase where the greatest saving of time can be created by carefully selecting an algorithm and implementing it efficiently. This phase is about rejecting objects that cannot collide, eliminating collision tests that cost time but cannot yield fruit.

"Operational" Methods

The phrase operational has been used in a similar context with respect to security. It represents an examination of how the system operates at a general, perhaps even superficial level, to see if efficiencies can be created or obvious flaws found. In operational security, for example, they may determine that a computer operator's screen can be seen through a window, and so the first thing to do in improving system security is to move the monitor away from the window.

In a game, there are many objects that can be colliding or collided with, and the general collision problem takes an amount of time to execute that is in proportion to the square of the number of objects (which a computer scientist would call $O(n^2)$). However, consider that many objects do not move, as has been pointed out before. If there are four cars, a hundred trees, and twenty buildings, that is 124 objects and up to 15,376 collision tests.

However, testing A for collision with B is the same as testing B for collision with A, and we never need to test A for collision with A. This reduces to a total of $(N^2-N)/2$ tests, which is a lot fewer than N^2. It is, in fact, 7,626 tests in the previous example.

Now consider that the trees do not move and so cannot collide with one another. Same for the buildings—they are static and cannot collide with trees or other buildings. So the cars need to be tested against all other objects, but that is all we need to do! This represents 4*3/2 tests between cars (=6) and 4*120 = 480 tests with static objects, for a grand total of 486 tests. Any further efforts at broad phase detection will almost certainly not yield such significant savings but could still find more savings. Similarly, objects that are moving away from each other can't collide with each other, nor can objects that are very far apart relative to their speeds.

Most games have many classes of objects, and computation time can be reduced significantly this way. Alien missiles, for example, need not be checked against alien spacecraft, and sometimes asteroids or meteors need not be checked against each other. It's not as sexy as advanced code optimization, but a little good sense gives a much greater benefit than almost anything else we can do.

So, you should always look very carefully to make certain that you are not making any tests that aren't needed. Then you do the more difficult things and combine the two methods for a joint time savings.

Geometric Tests

When we checked to see which side of the line the start and end point of a polygon vertex was on at times T and T+1, we were using geometry to eliminate possible collisions. This is a pretty efficient process, and we can do it in three dimensions too. In 3D, a line becomes a plane, and the test becomes: is a particular polygon or node on one side of a plane at time **T** and on the other at time **T+1**? If so, a collision is possible, and if not, one has been eliminated.

In more detail, let us imagine that two objects in our game are to be tested to see if they collide with each other. We know that we're going to draw objects as collections of polygons, since that's how modeling programs define them, and it's how graphics cards draw things. So the question is: ***do any of the polygons in set A*** (i.e., object **A**) ***collide with any of those in set B*** (object **B**)? Each polygon is, in fact, a part of a plane. A mathematical plane is infinite in extent and a polygon is not, but in the broad phase we extend a polygon in one object to become the plane in which it is embedded and ask whether any of the vertices or polygons in another object are on opposite sides at times **T** and **T+1**. If so, a collision is possible, otherwise one has been eliminated.

This can be done quickly, in a manner similar to that already described in the previous section of 2D collisions. Two triangles A and B have vertices A0, A1, A2 and B0, B1, and B2. Both belong to different moving objects, and the question of collision is at issue. Instead of just plugging coordinates into the equation of a plane, it is possible to use vector math to do the equivalent thing, but in a manner that is faster.

First, close your eyes and picture a plane—or a triangle or rectangle—floating about in 3D space. Three points determine this plane; that is, any three points must belong to a plane in the same way that any two points are on a line and can be used to define it. However, consider any point on that plane and a line not passing through that point; this, too, defines a plane. Most importantly, so does a point and the ***normal*** to the plane. Normal means perpendicular, or 90 degrees to the surface of the plane, and if we can quickly find a vector that is normal to a polygon, and if we have a point on that polygon, we have the equation of the plane.

It turns out that a simple-to-calculate operation known as the ***cross product*** takes any two vectors and creates a vector that is perpendicular, or normal, to the plane on which the two input vectors lie. For two vectors **h** and **j**, the cross product **h X j** is a vector:

$$h \times j = \begin{bmatrix} h_y j_z - h_z j_y \\ -(h_x j_z - h_z j_x) \\ h_x j_y - h_y j_x \end{bmatrix}$$

If we have a triangle (or a quad, or course) then we have two such vectors—any edges will do.

The ***dot product***, another simple operation on vectors, computes the length of the projection of one vector onto another; for vector **a**, **a·a** = the length of a, and if **a** and **b** are perpendicular then **a·b = 0**. The dot product is defined as:

$$a \cdot b = \sum_{i=1}^{n} a_i b_i$$

in **n** dimensions, and it looks like a simple distance calculation. The usual form of the equation of a plane is:

$$c_0 x + c_1 y + c_2 z = d$$

Going back to the triangles A and B, note that each vertex of **A** (i.e., A_i) has three coordinates, and is therefore a 3D vector. Thus, $\mathbf{A_0} \times \mathbf{A_1} = \mathbf{N}$ is a vector cross product that is a normal to the triangle (plane) **A**. The dot product between N and any point in the plane of A, say any vertex, is the equation of the plane. So, $\mathbf{A_2} \cdot \mathbf{N}$ is:

$$d = N_x A2_x + N_y A2_y + N_z A2_z$$

which has the same form as the equation of plane. That's because it is, of course, and it is the equation of the plane that the triangle **A** lies in. This is what we want. We can store the plane as **N** and **d**, which are really just the constants for the equation of the plane, and we do this for every polygon we may want to test for collision. Testing is a matter of plugging in the **(x,y,z)** values of the target (i.e., what we are testing for collision, like another polygon vertex) before and after motion, and seeing if the target is on opposite sides of the plane. If so we need to look further, and if not we can ignore this target.

Using Enclosing Circles

Two objects, let's say cars, may consist of multiple polygons each. If one of them is *Enzo's* car, and he is clever enough to pass yours in our race, it is possible that many of the polygons in his car will be candidates for collision with polygons in your car. This could cost a lot of time in detailed tests that are not needed. One way to avoid this is to process collisions at a higher level at first, looking at all of the polygons in your car as belonging to a single object that has a virtual shape—how about a circle? So, if the circle that encloses *Enzo's* car never intersects with the circle that encloses yours, then they can't have collided. We could save hundreds of polygon-polygon collision tests!

Better yet, the enclosing circle can be defined along with the car, or whatever object we're looking at, once, when the game is created. All we need to do is find the center of the circle, which would be the ***centroid*** of the object, and the radius, the distance to the most distant vertex. The centroid of the car will be what we actually move; the car is drawn on the screen relative to that point, and the collision tests are initially performed on the circle centered on that point too.

The centroid, or center of mass, can be approximated by finding the mean coordinate of all polygons in each dimension. So, in 2D the X coordinate of the center of mass is the sum of all polygon X coordinates for the object divided by the number of polygons, and in the same way the Y coordinate of the centroid is computed. The distance to the most distant vertex can be calculated at the same time as we calculate the centroid, which is to say at some time after the object is created but before the game is distributed.

So now each object has a center of mass and a radius associated with it, in addition to a set of polygons. The question that faces us now is: for each pair of objects that could possibly collide, is it possible for the enclosing circles to collide? If not, we can ignore all of the polygons that are part of those objects, and that will save us a large amount of time. Of course, if it *is* possible then we have a lot more checking to do. Sometimes it is more useful to keep the object as polygons, as in the case of walls and buildings. Covering them with a circle would be a waste of time, because it's easier to keep their relatively few planar faces as lines or planes.

Sphere vs. Plane Collision (Circle – Line)

The first step is to see if the circle changes sides of the line during the time interval. The situation is diagrammed in Figure 4.3: the circle at time **T** is labeled S_T, and its center **S** = (**Sx,Sy**) is a distance D_T from the line and the positive side. At time **T+1** the center of the circle is at D_{T+1}, and the figure is on the opposite (negative) side of the line. We must make sure that $D_T > r$, or the sphere is intersecting the line at the beginning.

A sphere is not a point; it has volume. For this reason the test concerning whether a sphere may have collided with a polygon is a little different from before: if $D_T > r$, where r is the sphere's radius, and $D_{T+1} < r$, then a collision is possible. A simple way of computing this is

$$d_T = (S_T - Z) \cdot N$$

for some point on the plane **Z** and plane normal N.

If a collision with the plane occurs, when does it happen? We know it is sometime between **T** and **T+1**, but *exactly* when? We can parameterize time between **T** and **T+1** to be one unit using a new variable τ:

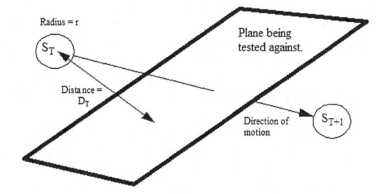

Radius = r

S_T

Plane being tested against.

Distance = D_T

Direction of motion

S_{T+1}

FIGURE 4.3 Given the position of the sphere at time T and T+1, did the sphere pass through the plane?

$$\tau = \frac{d_T - r}{d_T - d_{T+1}}$$

where τ is between 0 and 1. This ratio is the fraction of the distance difference between **T** and **T+1** that is represented by the sphere's radius, and it is the fraction of the distance traveled in that time by the sphere. So, the location of the center of the sphere at the time of the collision is

$$x = S_{xT} + \tau(S_{xT+1} - S_{xT})$$
$$y = S_{yT} + \tau(S_{yT+1} - S_{yT})$$
$$z = S_{zT} + \tau(S_{zT+1} - S_{zT})$$

where, as a reminder, S_{xT} is the X coordinate of the center of the sphere at time **T**, and similarly for the **Y** and **Z** coordinates and time **T+1**.

Circle-Circle Collisions

It is common for objects in a game to consist of polygons, but it is not universal. A sprite could be a small raster image, representing a car or a boat or an Italian plumber. In those cases, a collision would involve any pixel in the sprite colliding with any other pixel in another object. There could be a lot of pixel-pixel tests. One way to accommodate this would be to enclose the image in a polygon, and then test the polygons for collisions. The **bounding box** or minimally enclosing rectangle would work; so would a circle, and circles are easier to implement.

The idea is simple: find the smallest circle that will enclose all of the pixels. The test for a static collision is now whether the center of the circles for the two objects is within a distance of the sum of the radii of the circles. Given that both objects may be moving, the test has to be a bit more complicated.

The problem is diagrammed in Figure 4.4. Temporarily simplify the problem to assume that one object (A) is moving and the other (B) is stationary; now use the movement vector for A, using the center of the circle around A, to find the point on the path of travel that is nearest the center of the circle surrounding B. This point is labeled **c** in Figure 4.4. If the distance of this point to the center

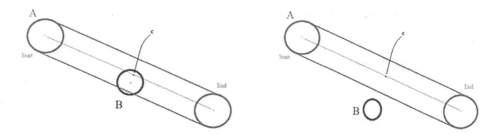

FIGURE 4.4 Collisions between two circles. The point c is nearest to the stationary object B. In this case there is no collision.

of B is greater than (or equal to) the sum of the radii of the two circles, then a collision can't happen; otherwise, it can.

To do this, it is necessary to calculate the point on a line that is nearest to a specified point. By nearest, we mean "what is the length of the line that is perpendicular to a given line and passes through a specific point."

Finding the Closest Point on a Line to a Specified Point

This is really an extension of the algorithm that finds the point of intersection of two lines. Begin with a given point **(px, py)** and a given line segment, described by endpoints **(x1, y1)** and **(x2, y2)**.

1. Take the endpoints of the line segment and turn it into an equation of the form ax + by + c = 0. This we have done before in the previous section.
2. The equation of the line perpendicular to the initial line segment is given by the negative slope to the original line. Have it pass through the specified point: Specifically, `-b x + a y - d = 0`.
3. Solve these two equations simultaneously; that is, find an x and y value that satisfies both. There are many ways to do this, and any one will do. The result is:

$$X = (ac - bd) / (a^2 + b^2)$$
$$Y = (ad - bc) / (a^2 + b^2)$$

If $(a^2 + b^2) = 0$, then the point is on the line, and thus the closest point on the line to the point is the point itself.

If the point (X,Y) found is within a distance of the sum of the radii of the two enclosing circles, then a collision is possible. If B is stationary then a collision **will** happen.

Using Bounding Boxes

A bounding box is a rectangle or prism that completely encloses all of the polygons of an object. The sides are planes, and the volume is relatively close to that of the object—generally a better approximation than is a sphere. An ***Axis Aligned Bounding Box (AABB)*** has faces that are parallel to the three coordinate axes. This has the advantage of being very simple to calculate: run a plane through the most distant point in each coordinate axis direction. That is, find the minimum and maximum X coordinates in the object and construct a plane though these points that is parallel to the YZ plane; do this for the Y coordinate (XZ plane) and the Z coordinate (XY plane), thus building a rectangular prism. This is the AABB.

A really complex calculation is not needed to find the AABB. We simply scan through all of the polygons for the object and note the minimum and maximum value found in each dimension—six values in all. Of course, this must be done using the polygon coordinates in the ***world domain***—that is, as drawn in place in the scene. Once we have minimum and maximum values, it is a simple task to use these to detect whether a given point is inside or outside of the box, and whether two boxes are overlapping. A point is inside the AABB ***if its coordinates are greater than the minimum and less than the maximum in each dimension***. Two AABBs overlap ***if any of the vertices of either one lies inside of the other***. Another similar test of overlap is: ***two AABBs overlap if their extents overlap in each of the axes.*** This is quite fast and simple to compute.

This is, of course, not good enough. The two boxes may pass completely though each other and not touch either at the beginning or the end.

How do we, as before, determine if a collision has occurred in between the start and end of the time interval? First consider a one-dimensional problem. A moving 1D box can be represented as two real numbers, s (start) and e (end), that describe the position of the box at two times. The set of all intervals can be represented as a list **L** of (s_i, e_i) values. It would be best to keep this list sorted in ascending order. What we need to do is find all values of (s_i, e_i) and (s_j, e_j) that overlap.

We create a fresh list, initially empty, that will contain entries for all objects currently "active"; call this the ***active*** list. As we scan the sorted list of intervals **L**, a new s_i being encountered results in the active list being output as a poten-

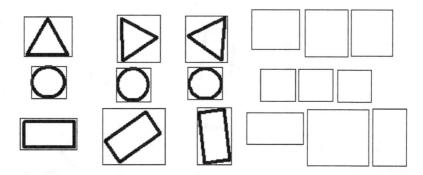

FIGURE 4.5 Axis oriented bounding boxes for three simple shapes in three orientations. On the right you can see the boxes alone and compare their sizes.

tial collision in interval **i**, and the interval **i** is added to the active list. When a new e_i is seen while scanning **L**, interval **i** is removed from the active list.

The great thing about AABBs is this: to expand this to the three-dimensional case, we simply have a list for each dimension. If all three dimensions report an intersection between $AABB_i$ and $AABB_j$, they intersect, and a collision may have occurred.

A new AABB must be determined each time the object changes direction. This is an expense not incurred by using spheres, but we shall see if there is a compensating trade-off. Another, more minor, problem is that the AABB can sometimes be a poor fit to the object. Consider a triangle, circle, and rectangle as in Figure 4.5. As the objects rotate the AABBs fit more or less well in the box. The closer the fit the more accurately the collision between boxes will predict an actual collision.

Object Oriented Bounding Boxes

An object oriented bounding box (OOBB) is always aligned along the primary axes of the object. This box is defined when the object is first created and is read in along with the polygon coordinates or computed as it is read in. The box is translated and rotated along with the object, and so it should be clear that the edges of the OOBB will not necessarily align with any axis.

Why use these? Well, they hug an object better than an AABB or a sphere, in general, as seen in Figure 4.6.

This means that a collision can be more accurately determined. On the other hand, it takes a lot more code and time to determine whether two OOBBs collide or not.

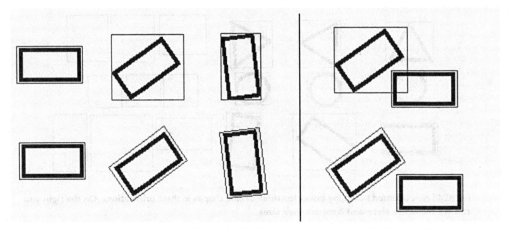

FIGURE 4.6 Object oriented bounding boxes. (left) As a rectangle is rotated, the bounding box has more empty space. Orienting to the object's orientation reduces the error. (right) An axis oriented box indicates a collision is possible where an object oriented box does not.

In the boat race game that is the principal example in this book, there is a need to detect collisions between boats.

There is an interesting thing here. It is true that a new AABB must be computed each time the object changes direction, and this can be time consuming. However, a nifty idea is to construct the OOBB at the outset and rotate and translate the box with the object. This will be done in the boat race game.

Space Subdivision

The process of looking at every pair of objects to see if a collision has happened is slow, but if the objects are spread out over a large area, we can break up the entire playing volume into small pieces, each large enough so that moving objects won't pass completely through one, but small enough to contain only a few objects that could possibly collide. The basic idea is to check for collisions only among objects that are within the same piece of space.

The data structure is simple, like the concept. Space is divided into equal-sized blocks, and an array can be used to represent each. A block contains a list of objects that reside in it, and at the beginning of each frame these are all cleared out. The list of objects is run through and each object is placed into the appropriate list. The blocks that contain objects also have a count of how many objects are in that block. Now, and finally, we look though the list of all blocks for those with more than one object—those are tested for collisions.

If a game has a lot of 3D interactions, this method could require a lot of storage. A game mostly takes place on the ground and on a flat-ish surface, which is what we could call 2 1/2 dimensional. By this it is meant that we will consider squares on the terrain surface and a small volume above and ignore the rest of the playing volume, which can't be driven on.

There are a variety of uses and implementations of the **block map** method, but in the context of a typical game it can be restricted in the following ways:

1. An object will be in one block, as a general rule. This will be the block in which resides the center of mass, or the center of the enclosing sphere.

2. The size of the block will be such that the object, and any other object with which it can collide, cannot pass through a whole block in one time interval. This means we only have to check the starting block and the ending block in the worst case, and in most cases the object will stay in one block.

3. We want a reasonable number of blocks, so they must be big enough that there are fewer blocks than objects.

4. There must not be more than a few (4–5 max) objects in any block.

So, let's say that the playing area is 2 x 2 kilometers. Let the maximum speed of any object be a highly reasonable 100 km/hr. At 24 frames per second a frame takes 1/24 second, or about 42 milliseconds. 100 km/hr is 28 meters/second, or 0.28 meters per millisecond, or 1.176 meters/frame. The previous rules give us the following limits:

1. The block should be at least the size of the object. A car is rarely more than 3 meters long, and a person is only 1 meter. Let's say the block must be at least 3 m.

2. In one frame an object will pass through 1.176 m, so 3 m is large enough that it cannot pass through a block in one frame at 24 fps. If we get to 60 fps, we'll have to make it 2.94 m. 3m is still big enough.

3. There will be about 250 objects in the game at most. 3m is too small—at this size there will be over 100,000 blocks. At 250 objects, the block size will be about 125 meters.

4. At a block size of 125 meters, we still want there to be fewer than 4–5 objects per block that can be interacted with. In some games an opponent will sometimes be very close. If we are careful about how we place objects, a block size of 100 meters should be fine. This size gives us a little less room, and it lets us put objects closer together.

At a block size of 100 x 100 meters, a fast object can pass though in about 4 seconds, but objects can be placed far enough apart that it takes a while to get to one. How many blocks are there then? 10 blocks per km is 20 x 20 blocks, or 400 blocks all together. This is a bit large but small enough to be reasonable to search. Most, after all, will be empty.

Another advantage of using a block map is that only the moving objects need to be updated every frame. Everything else is placed in its block at the beginning of the game and it will remain there. A moving object can be quickly placed in a block by mapping the coordinates of the object center onto block map grid coordinates. For the previous 2 x 2 km map, we first map the object's (x, y, z) coordinates onto block indices. An easy way: X coordinate in Kilometers/100 = column index = J and the same for the Y coordinate, which we will call I.

Each block is represented by a structure stored in a 2D array, indexed by (I,J). Each structure contains the number of objects in that block and indicators that allow access to each object. These could be pointers or indices to an array of objects. If a complex structure is used to store them, it would be no worse than a simple linear list. Let's have a maximum of six (6) objects per block and have a fixed-size array of indices of objects within each block structure. To speed things up even more, create a global list of all blocks containing more than one object. This, too, could be a fixed-size array. Whenever an object moves, we check to see if it stays in the same block. If not, decrease the object count for the old block and increase the count for the new one. Remove the old block from the global list if it has less than two objects, and add the new one if it has more than one.

Before starting collision detection, add the blocks at which objects will end up after motion to the global list. Next, looking only at the global list, check for collisions between objects within every block in that list. Finally, update the global list to remove the blocks no longer having more than one object.

NARROW PHASE COLLISION DETECTION

Once we determine that a collision is possible, the next stage answers "*does a collision occur?*" If one does, at what point on the surface and in which polygon on the model? This question can rarely be answered as fast as we'd like, and never as fast as the broad phase question. And, as always, the more accurately we need the answer, the more expensive it will be. The hope is that this detailed and expensive calculation will not have to be done very often.

There is a wide variety of narrow phase algorithms, and an entire book could be written on this alone. However, we must restrict what is discussed here, so only the most obvious methods will be examined. When a narrow phase algorithm is invoked, it is because a collision could occur between two objects that consist of polygons. These objects were enclosed by spheres or boxes, but now we must look at the details. Let's assume that the polygons are triangles—each has three vertices, and if the object consists of 1,000 triangles, then there will be 300 vertices, right?

No, because in an object most of the vertices are shared. An estimate would be 1,000 *distinct* vertices in this object. Each vertex will move in a known direction by a known amount, the so-called movement vector. This means that there are 1,000 *rays*, or directed line segments, that we need to examine. It can be assumed that the second object is still, because if it were moving then we'd subtract its movement vector from both objects to give a net movement vector on the object being tested, as previously described where we checked for collisions using spheres.

So we have 1,000 rays and a similar number of polygons in the other object we are testing against. This would be a million tests, each ray against each polygon. It's possible to eliminate some rays and some polygons though. Only polygons that are on the side of the object facing the other object need to be tested, so we have perhaps 500 x 500 tests. This is still a significant number, but 1/4 of the previous value.

Ignoring the back-facing polygons can be done using something called *back-face culling.* Each polygon (triangle) has a normal associated with it, or we could compute one every time we need it. Now, back-face culling is really a visibility algorithm. The question is: *can you see that polygon from where you are now?* We use the dot product between the normal to the triangle and a vector from the viewer's position to get the angle between these vectors; if it is between 90 and 270 degrees, then the polygon is facing the viewer; otherwise, it is not and can be ignored. In this case, replace the viewer with the centroid of the object being tested against, and the method is the same. Of course this must be done from both objects involved in the collision, each taking turns being the viewpoint. There are tricky ways to speed this method up too.

Ray/Triangle Intersection

The meat of the collision test is determining which polygons intersect, where, and when. From the previous discussion, we have selected some polygons (perhaps all of them) to test against each other, we have determined what the movement vector is, and we know that object **A** is moving while **B** remains still, or at least has been made still by computing a relative movement vector. Now we will select vertices in **A** and determine their positions before and after movement, then see if that line segment or *ray* intersects a polygon in **B**. If so, it is simple to determine when and where this happens. So, step by step here is what we must do.

1. The movement vector expresses relative movement, so by adding it to a point we find where the point moves. Vertices in **A** will be named V_A. They are numbered from 0 to n, so they are V_{A0} to V_{An}; finally they have **x**, **y**, and **z** coordinates named V_{A0x}, V_{A0y}, V_{A0z}, and so on. The point **V'** is the same point as **V**, but it is a position after the motion is complete.

The ray associated with a vertex V_{Ai}, given the movement vector **M**, would be a vector **R** from V_{Ai} to $V_{Ai}+M$. This is to say that

$$R_x = V_{Aix} + M_x$$
$$R_y = V_{Aiy} + M_y$$
$$R_z = V_{Aiz} + M_z$$

The line that needs to be tested runs from V_{Ai} to **R**. Call this line **L**, and it is:

$$L_x = V_{Aix} + (tR_x)$$
$$L_y = V_{Aiy} + (tR_y)$$
$$L_z = V_{Aiz} + (tR_z)$$

where **t** runs from 0 to 1 to give any point on the line segment.

2. Now compute the equation of the plane in which the selected triangle in object B resides. Recall that we need the normal **N** and a point in the plane **P** to get the plane:

$$N_x(x-P_{0x}) + N_y(y-P_{0y}) + N_z(z-P_{0z}) = 0$$

3. Substitute the line **L** into the plane equation for (x,y,z) to solve for **t**, the time at which the collision will occur.

4. Use the value of **t** found in 3 to plug into the line equations to find the point **(x,y,z)** at which the collision will occur.

5. Finally, determine whether the point found in 4 resides inside the triangle. This can be done in a few simple ways.

The interior angle test: compute the angle between the point and all three triangle vertices, in order. The sum of the angles should be 360 degrees, within rounding error, if the point is inside the triangle.

The odd intersections test: draw a line from the point being tested to a faraway point. If this line intersects exactly one edge exactly once, then it is inside the triangle. If through some bad luck the intersection is a vertex, then select a new direction and draw another line—a vertex is part of two edges and can't be used in this test.

Area test: Make all triangles between the point being tested and consecutive points on the triangle—there are three. If the sum of the areas of these triangles equals the area of the big triangle, the point is inside. This test is approximate, partly again due to vagaries of floating point arithmetic.

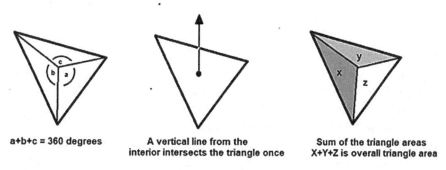

a+b+c = 360 degrees   A vertical line from the   Sum of the triangle areas
                             interior intersects the triangle once   X+Y+Z is overall triangle area

FIGURE 4.7 The three tests for determining whether a point is inside a polygon.

All of the five previous steps can be accomplished in a remarkably small time period and are actually done in many games. You can implement any or all of the collision detection schemes that have been described using what has been said here, combined with a few details found on the Web.

Or, you could use someone else's code. There are quite a few packages that can be downloaded from the Internet in a few minutes, and almost any of them will save you a huge amount of time, but they will require a degree of adaptation. A particular game might not be able to use just any such package.

COLLISION DETECTION IN THE BOAT RACE

The *Jet Boat Race* presents a few difficulties that have not been discussed, the main one being that the boats are raster sprites and not polygonal objects. Imagine two small images of boats moving at known angles—the object oriented bounding box can be created by knowing the size of the image and drawing lines around it. These lines must be drawn at an angle that is related to the orientation of the boat.

Consider that the boats are raster images that are *NxM* pixels in size, and that the angle that the boat is facing is (to the horizontal, which is 0 degrees, facing right). Then the boat and the associated bounding box has to be rotated by degrees. The bounding box for the basic image is easy to find, starting from the upper left as (0,0), then to (width,0), (width, height), and (0, height). When this box is rotated by degrees, it can be seen as four line segments that are not necessarily oriented in the X or Y axis. Each boat has such an object oriented bounding box.

Now every boat has a velocity vector, which is added to the current position to yield the next position. This vector, when extended in length, gives a ray (a line segment) in the direction that the boat is facing. If that ray intersects with another boat's bounding box, then a collision could occur. It means that the boat should change direction to avoid a collision.

If any of the sides of the bounding boxes of any two boats intersect, then those boats have collided. This means checking each of the line segments of the bounding box of boat A against each of the line segments of the bounding box of boat B. An intersection means a collision (Figure 4.8). This means testing sixteen line segments to see if they intersect.

The bounding boxes are found by locating the corners of the boat image and then rotating those to correspond with the orientation of the boat. The upper left (ul), upper right (ur), lower right (lr), and lower left (ll) corners for boats are:

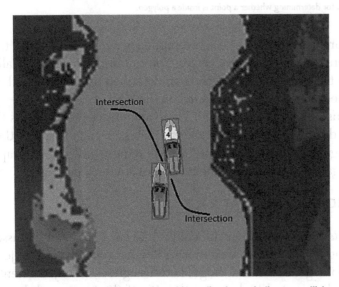

FIGURE 4.8 Intersecting axis-oriented bounding boxes indicate a collision.

```
ul = rotate((boats[i].x, boats[i].y),
   (boats[i].x - 42, boats[i].y - 13), -boats[i].angle)
ur = rotate((boats[i].x, boats[i].y),
   (boats[i].x + 42, boats[i].y - 13), -boats[i].angle)
lr = rotate((boats[i].x, boats[i].y),
   (boats[i].x + 42, boats[i].y + 13), -boats[i].angle)
ll = rotate((boats[i].x, boats[i].y),
   (boats[i].x - 42, boats[i].y + 13), -boats[i].angle)
```

These points (each is a point having an X and a Y component as a tuple) now have to be converted to screen coordinates:

```
ul = terrain_to_screen (ul)
ur = terrain_to_screen (ur)
lr = terrain_to_screen (lr)
ll = terrain_to_screen (ll)
```

A box consists of four points, specifically these points:

```
box.append([ul,ur,lr,ll,ul])
```

A function named **box_intersect (b1, b2)** checks for the intersection of the two boxes passed as parameters. It does so by doing the sixteen intersection tests, each of which is determined by the function **line_intersect (a,b,c,d)**, where each parameter is a point and **(a,b)** and **(c,d)** are lines specified by endpoints. A fast method for determining whether two segments intersect has been devised that warrants exposure [1].

The segments **(a,b)** and **(c,d)** intersect if the points a and b are separated by the segment cd and also c and d are separated by the segment ab. If that is true, then the three points acd should have a different orientation than the points bcd, where orientation is defined as clockwise or counterclockwise. This is shown in Figure 4.9. Thus, determining the intersection is a matter of:

```
def line_intersect (p1, p2, p3, p4):
    r1 = ccw(p1, p3, p4) != ccw (p2, p3, p4)
    r2 = ccw(p1, p2, p3) != ccw (p1, p2, p4)
    if r1 and r2:
        return True
    return False
```

where the **ccw** function returns **True** if the points passed as parameters have a counterclockwise orientation with respect to each other. This is remarkably fast. By the way, the function ccw is:

```
def ccw(a, b, c):
    return (c[1]-a[1])*(b[0]-a[0]) > (b[1]-a[1])*(c[0]-a[0])
```

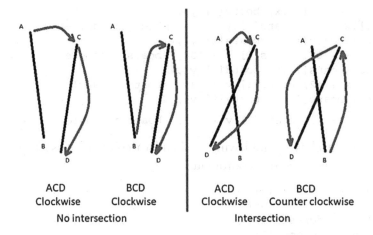

ACD	BCD	ACD	BCD
Clockwise	Clockwise	Clockwise	Counter clockwise
No intersection		Intersection	

FIGURE 4.9 The idea behind the fast line segment intersection method ([1]).

Ray Casting

If it can be assumed that each object that moves is associated with a movement vector (dx, dy), then this vector can be used to project motion into the future. A vector or ray can be drawn from the object's center forward, and the greater the length of this ray, the greater the amount of time that is being examined. The ray looks into the future to where the object might be. If it happens that this ray intersects some other object, then it would seem a collision is possible, and perhaps the object should alter its trajectory to avoid the obstacle.

Given a movement vector **V**, the first step in building a ray that points in the movement direction is normalizing it, which means scaling it so its length is 1. The length of **V** is $L = \sqrt{v_x^2 \times v_y^2}$ so the normalized vector **V'** is $\left(\frac{v_x}{\sqrt{v_x^2 \times v_y^2}}, \frac{v_y}{\sqrt{v_x^2 \times v_y^2}} \right)$. Given that we want to look ahead by a distance D, now multiply this vector by D, giving the vector $R = \left(\frac{Dv_x}{\sqrt{v_x^2 \times v_y^2}}, \frac{Dv_y}{\sqrt{v_x^2 \times v_y^2}} \right)$. The ray is (x, y) to R, where (x,y) is the position of the object concerned. If this ray intersects any object's bounding box, then a collision is possible in the future and action should be taken, such as steering away from the obstacle involved.

If the object is located at **P= (x,y)**, then the ray is the line segment from P to P+R. The function **line_intersect** defined in the previous section can be used to determine whether the ray intersects with some other object, like the bounding box of an NPC.

Rays can be used for more things than this though. It is common to use ray casting to ensure that an object is in contact with the ground, for example. Cast a ray that is 1/2 of the height of the target object down from the object's center. It should intersect with the ground or a supporting platform. In driving games, a vehicle could leave the ground for a few moments, rendering it unable to brake or steer; in platformers, characters leap from platform to platform. Ray casting can be a simple way to deal with these issues.

EXERCISES

The following problems will exercise your knowledge of the material in this chapter, and they will sometimes require that you do more research before you are able to complete them.

1. In circle-circle collision detection, the distance between the two circles is calculated, and if it is less than the sum of the radii, then a collision is in progress. Simple code would be:

```
d = sqrt((x1-x0)*(x1-x0)+(y1-y0)*(y1-y0))
if (d < (radius1+radius))   // Collision
```

where (x0,y0) and (x1,y1) are the coordinates of the sphere centers. A square root calculation is expensive—what is the code that does this without a call to **sqrt**?

2. Write a program that has two balls (circles) bouncing in a box. Use the code in exercise 1 to determine when the balls collide with each other, and have them react to the collision.

3. Write code that will check for a collision between two moving cubes in a 3D space.

4. Use the code in Exercise 3 to create a stack of four cubes and hurl a fifth cube at the stack. The sketch should detect collisions between the cubes and have them respond. Approximate bounces are OK.

5. Some games, like snooker, are all about collisions. Write a sketch that allows a white (cue) ball to be shot in any direction on a table and collide with one of a set of (at least) two other balls. The collisions should result in correct-seeming bounces.

Idea: When the mouse is pressed, draw a line from the cue ball to the mouse coordinates. When released, the cue ball will follow the line at a fixed speed until it collides with a cushion or another ball.

6. Using a circle for a ball and a line for a bat, construct a bat and ball simulation. The bat will be rotating, not moving linearly, and the ball will move toward the bat. You need only determine the point of collision and time and need not determine the line along which the ball will move.

Note: The point to line distance is key here, but the line is a segment, and a bounds test is important.

REFERENCES

1. Bryce Boe. (2006). Line Segment Intersection Algorithm. *http://bryceboe. com/2006/10/23/line-segment-intersection-algorithm/*.

2. A. Bowyer and J. Woodwark. (1983). *A Programmer's Geometry*. Newton, MA: Butterworth-Heinemann. *https://www.amazon.com/Programmers-Geometry-Adrian-Bowyer/dp/0408012420*.

3. E. G. Gilbert, D. W. Johnson, and S. S. Keerthi. (1988). "A Fast Procedure for Computing the Distance between Complex Objects in Three-Dimensional Space." *IEEE Journal of Robotics and Automation* 4: 193–203.

4. Gino van den Bergen. (2004). *Collision Detection in Interactive 3D Environments*. Morgan-Kaufman /Elsevier.

5. M. Lin and J. Canny. (1992). *Efficient Collision Detection for Animation*. Third Eurographics Workshop.

6. Brian Mirtich. (1998). "V-Clip: Fast and Robust Polyhedral Collision Detection." *ACM Trans. Graph.* 17, no. 3 (July): 177–208.

7. Jeff Erickson, Leonidas J. Guibas, Jorge Stolfi, and Li Zhang. (1999). *Separation-Sensitive Collision Detection for Convex Objects*. Proceedings of the Tenth Annual ACM-SIAM Symposium on Discrete Algorithms, 327–336.

8. Julien Basch, Jeff Erickson, Leonidas J. Guibas, John Hershberger, and Li Zhang. (1999). *Kinetic Collision Detection between Two Simple Polygons*. Proceedings of the Tenth Annual ACM-SIAM Symposium on Discrete Algorithms, 102–111.

9. Joe van den Heuvel and Miles Jackson. (2002). "Pool Hall Lessons: Fast, Accurate Collisions between Circles or Spheres." *Gamasutra*, January 18, 2002.

10. Wolfram Research. (n.d.). *Point-Line Distance, 3-Dimensional*. *http:// mathworld.wolfram.com/Point-LineDistance3-Dimensional.html*.

5

Navigation and Control

For the purposes of this discussion, navigation will be defined as the process of getting from one location in a game to another. There are many differences between navigating the real world versus a virtual world, but a basic rule of game AI programming is: *cheat*! Remember that it is only important that the simulated characters (we'll call them *non-player characters* or *NPCs*) appear to behave more or less like a real person. The program that controls the opponents does not have to navigate using vision, and it has advance knowledge of everything that is in the game. In addition, there are markers that can be placed all through the terrain that the AI can use to guide the NPCs. These markers are not visible to the players because they are not rendered as objects—they are merely points in 3D space that are used to create a path.

The opponents will, in fact, either take the same path at the same speed each time through a course or will at most have a finite number of variations, each one taken with a particular probability when encountered. We can even change those probabilities each time a choice is made, but that too is programmed and well defined. Most opponents do not act in an intelligent way but are guided by quite simple and quick algorithms.

BASIC AUTONOMOUS CONTROL

The word *autonomous* implies independent or alone. Autonomous control of opponent characters in a game is essential for making the game fun and exciting, partly because it gives a sense of competition, and partly because other characters or objects are obstacles and have to be avoided, thus creating a more complex problem to solve. If the opponents are autonomous, then they are controlled by software, and so we treat the problem as one of software design. The first question is: *what is the problem?*

Another way of asking this is *what is the goal?* This is a question we can answer in general, at least partly. The goal of a player in a game is to have fun, and this means winning, doesn't it? Oddly, the answer is "no." Winning a game regularly amounts to beating it, which frequently means that it is time to purchase another game! The entertainment value is in the game play, the puzzle, or the contest; beating a game too easily is the kiss of death, at least for a commercial game. Word will get out, and the game will not sell.

On the other hand, if a game is impossible to beat, then it is just as bad. Players simply give up, and again word gets out that the game is impossible. We start to find them in garage sales.

Thus, we will state a carefully worded high-level goal for the opponent in a game:

> Goal 1- Since a main goal of a game is to provide entertainment and engagement, the opponents should provide a challenge to the player without being impossible to defeat.

This goal is vague enough to be a guide for any game, but too vague to implement as is. However, it leads to a logical set of sub-goals that *can* be implemented:

> Goal 1.a If at all possible, the human player should beat some opponents if there are many. The player should not be humiliated by a computer if they are still actually playing.
>
> Goal 1.b Some opponents should decrease their skill level as they get a distance ahead of the player, allowing a chance to catch up.
>
> Goal 1.c The goal of an opponent is not to win, but to provide entertaining competition. If the game involves objects, like weapons, the opponent must be able to use them. It should play the game much as a human would.

Goal 1.d When there are many opponents, they should not all be the same. They should have variable skill levels and should in some sense respond to the displayed skill of the player.

Goal 1.e The player should be offered a choice of difficulty when starting the game, so that easy opponents are available as well as hard ones. They can find their skill level and strive to improve it.

Most of these rules or goals are probably not a big surprise. You may not know that the AI system actually "dumbs down" to let you have a better chance, but you probably suspected as much. We will add to this set of goals, but for now we have enough to get started. Since the precise nature of the game we are discussing is unknown, we'll keep things at a high level for the moment.

How to Control a Car

Let's use the example of a car in the discussion. There are similar movement controls and navigation features for cars and other NPCs, but vehicles have navigation as one of the principal issues. The user controls a car using the keyboard or mouse or game pad. Basically, there is something that can be treated as character input and that can be interpreted by the game as a command; left arrow means turn left, forward arrow means go forward faster, for instance. We could control an opponent in the same basic way, except that we don't need input. So, we could have a function

```
def turnLeft (CHARACTER x)
```

that would turn the opponent represented by **x** left by the standard turn angle, in the same way that the player's car would turn by angular increments. Or, we could enhance the opponents by allowing arbitrary relative angles

```
def turnRelative (CHARACTER x, float delta)
```

and even absolute angles, for instance:

```
def turnAbsolute (CHARACTER x, float angle)
```

The idea is that a car is controlled using a set of very obvious primitive operations that can be combined into higher and higher level operations. We also need accessor functions that return key values to the AI system, like a car's current speed, position, and direction, so that a high-level goal can be specified in terms of low-level operations and current parameters.

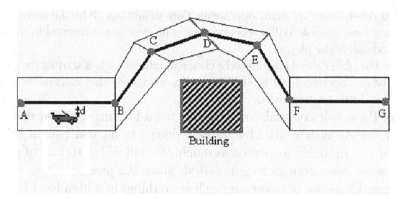

FIGURE 5.1 **The simple set track and a set of line segments that allow driving behaviors to be defined.**

The high-level goals will be expressed in terms of minor goals, which may in turn be expressed in terms of local goals, and so on until at some level the goal is "go left," which can be done with a primitive. The design would be from the high level downward, keeping in mind that the lowest level is pretty much defined at the outset. Let's take a detailed look at one of the possible intermediate goals: something called *cruising behavior*.

Cruising Behavior

The goal of this behavior is to maintain a set speed, more or less, while following a set track towards a geometric goal. It may also be important to avoid collisions too. The "set track" mentioned is a piecewise linear path drawn along the game's terrain, perhaps along the middle of the road or racetrack. Figure 5.1 shows an example of this and labels a couple of interesting objects and locations.

The track can be identified as a connected sequence of straight line segments, AB, BC, CD ... FG. Points A and B are points in 3D space (A_x, A_y, A_z) and (B_x, B_y, B_z) that define the ends of a line segment. The vehicle being controlled is at a known position P=(x,y,z). It is, in the figure, the vehicle is moving toward the point B; it is at a distance **d** from the track and has a known speed **S** and desired speed S_{AB}. How do we keep the car on track?

So long as the vehicle is moving in a straight line, things are relatively simple. The program must try to keep the car as near to the line as possible, and it will attempt to keep the speed as near to S_{AB} as possible.

```
s = getSpeed (THISCHARACTER)
if (s < Sab):                    #  vehicle going too slow
    a = fmin(amax, k*(Sab-S))
elif (s > Sab):                  #  vehicle going too fast
```

```
    a = fmax (amin, k*(Sab-S))
else:
    a = 0.0
s = a*dt + s

d = linePointDist (A, B, P)
if (d < RIGHTTHESHOLD):
    turnLeft (THISCAR)
elif (d > LEFTTHRESHOLD)
turnRight(THISCAR)
```

This code does the following: there is a maximum and minimum acceleration, and if we are going too slow, we increase the acceleration a little, up to the max; if we are going too fast, we decrease the acceleration (increase the deceleration) with the limit being the minimum. We then compute a new velocity based on the calculated acceleration and the time since we last did this. The constant k is used to apportion acceleration between time frames, and it should be determined by experiment.

Then we pay attention to the steering. If we are right of the center line by a large enough distance, the car is turned by one unit to the left. If we are left of the center line by a large enough distance, we turn to the right by a unit. The system will straighten the steering angle automatically over the next few frames, but there is a risk of oversteer. We could fix that by only adjusting the steering angle every few frames.

Avoidance Behavior

While cruising it is possible to encounter an obstacle. In a race it would not usually be a wall or tree or the like, because the set track would not be placed where there were natural hazards like this, but in an urban driving game or when using characters who are walking it would be common. An obstacle on the track will usually be another vehicle on the track ahead, presumably not moving as quickly. *Avoidance behavior* is what the AI vehicle does when it comes upon this situation.

The first thing to note is that other AI vehicles will be following the track, more or less. That's a reason that there's one in your way. So, the first solution is to create another set track to be followed in order to pass a car on the existing track—let's call the original set track the *A-track* and the new one the *B-track*. Some game developers would call the A-track the *driving line* and the B-track the *overtaking line*. Figure 5.2 shows this arrangement.

So, as a vehicle V_1 approaches another vehicle V_0 from behind, it detects the potential collision, not by traditional collision detection, but by noting another vehicle ahead on the driving line. V_1 switches to the overtaking line and steers toward that line, thus avoiding the vehicle V_0. If another AI vehicle is already on the B-track, then we simply slow down until it is gone. In a game like Mario Kart we could also simply speed up and hit the other car, letting the collision sort things out—unless V_0 is the player's car, of course.

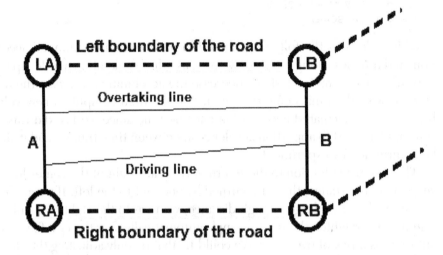

FIGURE 5.2 Section AB of the road defined in Figure 5.1, showing the driving line and the overtaking line.

If V_0 is the player's car, then its behavior is not predictable. If V_1 changes to the overtaking line, the player may just move over to block, but it could speed up, slow down, or hit something. Rather than having a fixed overtaking line in this case, we could create a new line by placing a target point in the middle of the largest gap, either left or right, between the player's car and the boundaries of the road. This point will move from frame to frame, but it does present a target to steer at until V_1 gets very close.

The speed of V_1 needs to be controlled too. In principle V_1 must slow down a bit until a gap opens up that is big enough to take advantage of. The AI could compute the trajectory of the player based on the current parameters and figure out where the player would be in 3–5 frames. If the gap is big enough at that time, V_1 could speed up to fill that gap and force the player to decide whether to collide with it or to avoid it.

This is partly illustrated in Figure 5.3.

The use of the nodes or points that connect to create a path is generally referred to as *waypoint pathfinding*. The waypoints can be saved as coordinates in

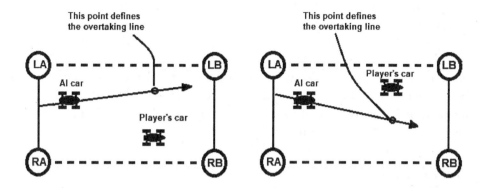

FIGURE 5.3 How to react if you come up on the player's car from behind. (a) The new overtaking line uses the largest gap between the player and the side of the road. (b) If the player moves over to block, it merely changes where the overtaking line is.

a special structure, in which there is a next and a previous waypoint. Every vehicle saves the current waypoint that it is using, the one immediately ahead, in its own structure so that we don't have to search for the point closest to it. When the vehicle passes that waypoint, the next one becomes current. The use of waypoints eliminates the need for pathfinding algorithms in general, and it simplifies the task of keeping the AI cars on the road and moving in the right direction.

In fact, there are a few ways to determine the path that an autonomous vehicle will use to traverse the race course. One is to create a driving and an overtaking line as we have described. The other is to create a different line for each AI car that can be on the track at the same time. Each car then has a relatively simple task—to keep as near to its driving line as possible. If another car is in its way, they simply collide, and the collision resolves the problem. The creation of many driving lines requires some effort up front, but it simplifies the game as it plays; the cars just don't have to be as smart, because the designers have done the work. Most game players don't recognize that there is only one line per car, especially if the lines are assigned at random at the beginning of the race.

Also, the driving lines can be associated with other information, like speed at each point. As a result, the line that is assigned to a car determines how well the car will do in the race. This practically eliminates the need for advanced computations while the game is going on.

Waypoint Representation and Implementation

The first thing to remember about waypoints is that they are, basically, points in 3D space. So the first thing we need to keep track of is their X, Y, and

Z coordinates. We also need a previous and next point, which can be stored as waypoints. Oh, and in general we may have multiple previous and next points. Let's assume that we will have at most two of each; this will be explained later.

It has been pointed out that we may want to specify a speed. This will be the desired speed at that specific waypoint. If the point is approaching a turn, it will be in a decreasing sequence, and it will increase on straight sections. It should be mentioned that the actual AI vehicle may not travel at that exact speed when passing though that waypoint. The specified speed is a goal.

A class structure that could hold this information is:

```
class waypoint:
    floating point variables x, y, z, 3D position
    float point variable speed
    list of waypoints next
    list of waypoints previous
    list of floats Dnext holding the desired speed at the
waypoints.
```

The simplest way to use waypoints is to direct the vehicles toward straight lines that run through them. If we do, then the cars will always pass through the waypoints, and will turn sharply whenever each one is encountered.

A different way to manage waypoint traffic is to approximate a path between them and to look ahead more than one point.

FINITE STATE MACHINES

The idea that an NPC can be cruising, chasing, or avoiding is not especially profound, and clearly different behavior can be assigned to each mode or *state*. It is also convenient from the perspective of design to be able to break up the different behaviors into distinct parts, which can then be implemented independently. The use of the traditional computer science tool, the finite state machine, is a pretty natural way to deal with this kind of situation. Finite state machines, also called FSAs, are used in programming languages, computability, control systems, and artificial intelligence, and because they have been widely used, their properties are well known and efficient implementations abound.

We have seen the basic idea of an FSA when implementing the game states in Hockey Pong, for example. The basic idea of an FSA is a collection of states and of transitions between these states upon some input or calculation. The states have numbers, used in the implementation, and names, used by the designers and programmers as meanings of the states. In the situation described in the previous section, the AI vehicle starts out in the *cruising* state. If it encounters another AI car on the road ahead, it enters the *overtake_AI* state, and if it encounters the player's car, it enters the *overtake_player* state. The behavior of the AI is quite different in each state, and its goals and methods of achieving them are distinct. Figure 5.4 shows a diagrammatic representation of an FSA, specifically one for the previous three states. It is essential to have a clear mechanism for moving between states and a clear plan for what to do while in each state.

Mathematically, an FSA is a simulated machine or mathematical construction consisting of a set of states, which are usually integers, a special state called the *start* state, a collection of input symbols or events, and a transition function that takes an input symbol and the current state and decides what the *next* state will be. The FSA begins a computation in the start state and enters states based on input symbols/events and the transition function. There can be a special state called the *accept* state that can be used to decide when the calculation is complete.

So, if we are in the *cruising* state (state 0) and an AI vehicle appears in front of us, we enter the *overtake_AI* state (1); if we are in the *cruising* state and the player's car appears in front of us we enter the *overtake_player* state (2). These are the only state transitions out of state 0 in Figure 5.4.

While in the *overtake_AI* state, there are a couple of events that could take place. We could pass the AI car, or we could be blocked further. If we pass the car, we can go back to the *cruising* state again. If we are blocked—well, perhaps we need another state called *delay* in which we slow down and look for a change in the situation. The delay state will be state 3.

The delay state can mean different things to different vehicles, if we choose. Some cars will in fact slow down and look for a gap through which they can sneak. Other instances of cars might aggressively try to push their way through, colliding with their opponents if they refuse to move. Still others might leave the road, if that were allowed, to try to find a way around. Any of these options could be associated with the same state, depending on the actual vehicle.

FSA In Practice

Implementing a Finite State Machine is a simple matter, so here are some good ideas about style and convention. Figure 5.4 will be used as an example, as it is simple and on the topic.

First thing to notice is that the states are integers, from zero to some maximum. They also have meanings and so can be given names. Thus, one generally defines states as integer values. For example:

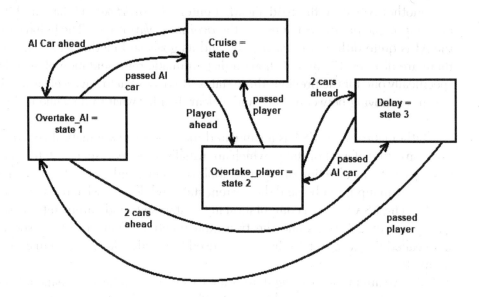

FIGURE 5.4 **A finite state machine for AI vehicles.**

```
STATE_CRUISE            = 0
STATE_OVERTAKE_AI       = 1
STATE_OVERTAKE_PLAYER       = 2
STATE_DELAY             = 3
```

Now we can define a state transition function. This function takes two parameters: the current state and a state transition event. It results in the current state changing as defined by this particular FSA. This normally means that state transition events, however complex detecting one might be, need to be assigned integer labels and names, just like states:

```
TE_AI_CAR_AHEAD         = 0
TE_PASSED_AI_CAR        = 1
TE_2_CARS_AHEAD         = 2
TE_PASSED_PLAYER        = 3
TE_PLAYER_AHEAD         = 4
TE_ERROR_XXX            = 9
```

The error state `TE_ERROR_XXX` is representative of many possible error states, for example `TE_ERROR_103`, which means that some transitions are actually illegal and result in some remedial action on the part of the program. Also notice that the transitions are context sensitive; the event `TE_PASSED_AI_CAR` does different things depending on what state you are in.

The actual machine can be implemented in a number of ways. A particularly good way, from the point of view of efficiency, modularity, and portability, is to use a table. Transitions are integers, and these can be used to index into an array. States are integers too and can also be used as indices. So, a state transition table for the FSA in Figure 5.4 could be:

		State			
		0	1	2	3
	0	1			
	1		0		2
Transition	2		3	3	
Event	3			0	1
	4	2			

This table contains state numbers, and it is indexed by both the current state and a transition event. So if we are in state 1 (Overtake_AI) and we pass the AI car (event 1=PASS_AI_CAR), then we enter state 0 (Cruise), that is, an assignment of the form:

```
new_state = transition_ table[TE_PASSED_AI_CAR][STATE_OVERTAKE_
AI]
```

The missing entries in the table would be filled with either error states or a null transition meaning "don't change the state."

This is an effective implementation of an FSA, but it relies on a correct initialization of the table. If the table is read in from a file, it consists of integers that have no symbolic form, and this is somewhat error prone. If the table is initialized from a declaration, it is less simple to modify, but we can now use the declared state names. Either way we do it, the code is less clear than some options and needs good documentation.

Another way to implement an FSA is to do so in discrete code. The usual situation is to just use if and switch statements. The first two columns of the previous transition table could be implemented in the following way:

```
    switch (state)
    {
if state == STATE_CRUISE:
        if (transition_event == TE_AI_CAR_AHEAD) :
            new_state = TE_PASSED_AI_CAR
        elif (transition_event == TE_PLAYER_AHEAD) :
            new_state = STATE_OVERTAKE_PLAYER
elif state == STATE   _OVERTAKE_AI:
        if (transition_event == TE_PASSED_AI_CAR:
            new_state = STATE_CRUISE
        elif (transition_event == TE_2_CARS_AHEAD)
```

```
                new_state = STATE_DELAY
    elif state == STATE_OVERTAKE_PLAYER:
            if (transition_event == TE_2_CARS_AHEAD:
                new_state = STATE_DELAY
            elif (transition_event == TE_PASSED_PLAYER):
                new_state = STATE_CRUISE
    elif state == STATE_DELAY:
            if (transition_event == TE_PASSED_AI_CAR):
                new_state = STATE_OVERTAKE_PLAYER
            elif (transition_event == TE_PASSED_PLAYER):
                new_state = TE_PASSED_AI_CAR
else:
    error()
```

In this case there are no anonymous integers being used. All names are symbolic, and it is a simple matter to read through the code to see what the transitions are. This improves the maintainability of the code and allows it to be more easily checked for correctness on a casual basis.

Both of the previous implementations could be encapsulated within a simple function like:

```
def transition (int state, int event)
```

which would return the next (new) state given the current state and the nature of the last event that occurred. The implicit assumption is, by the way, that two events cannot occur within the relatively small time interval between two consecutive frames. This is pretty standard, and what happens in practice is that we sometimes get two state transitions in quick succession if two events happen more or less at the same time.

State and the "What Do We Do Now" Problem

We now know how to move from one state to another, how to implement this, and what the states mean. What do we do when in a particular state? Well, this is not a matter for the FSA to deal with. What needs to be done is to determine what kinds of activities are associated with each state and then execute code that performs those activities when in the correct state. Oh, and we need also to execute code that determines whether any of the transition events has occurred.

Here is a general sketch of how the FSA-based AI would function:

```
if state == STATE_CRUISE:
    cruise ()
elif state == STATE_OVERTAKE_AI:
```

```
    overtake_AI ()
elif state == STATE_OVERTAKE_PLAYER:
    overtake_player ()
elif state == STATE_DELAY:
    delay ()
event = test_all_transition_events(state)
state = transition (state, event)
```

This program causes the game to change between the feasible states as controlled by the events that have been defined by the designers and tested for in the function `test_all_transition_events`. By the way, this function can be quite complex, and it would probably be a good idea to test only for those events that are significant from the current state. This is why the state is a parameter.

Other Useful States

It is impossible to describe the states that a driving game can be in without knowing the detailed context of the game being discussed. However, there are certain options that can be seen to be commonly useful. This includes the following states:

Start:

In driving games, it is common to have a race begin with all of the cars in predetermined start positions. The cars are not moving, and in fact may not move until the starter fires a gun or waves a flag. They then accelerate to the desired speed and select a driving track. This describes a state we could call the **Start** state.

In some games there is an actual countdown to the start, and if the player starts within a specified time of the actual start time, he gets a speed boost for a few moments. This can be done for AI cars as well, but because the AI system knows exactly when the start will take place it could easily cheat—actually, it's hard not to. So, a random time is generated at the start, and any AI vehicle with a start time below the threshold is given a boost.

Normally the `Start` state would change to `Cruise` when a certain speed had been achieved or a specific time interval had expired and the car had been assigned a track.

Air:

A car that hits a big bump or crests a hill at a high speed may actually leave the ground for a few seconds. This has a few consequences: the engine usually revs up to a high value, causing the engine sound to change. The accelerator pedal has no practical effect—the car cannot accelerate forward nor brake. The car cannot change direction, as the wheels are not in contact with the ground, and it cannot be steered. This could be described as the `Air` state.

There should be a specific sound that is played when leaving the `Air` state, that of the wheels hitting the pavement while spinning—a combination bump and screech. Then we enter the state we were in before entering the `Air` state.

Damaged:

Vehicles can become damaged in many ways. The simplest way is to collide with another car or with a stationary object, but some games involve weapons that can inflict damage or processes that can cause the vehicle to deteriorate. Damage can result in an inability to perform normal tasks, like steering or braking. It can reduce the top speed or the ability to switch tracks. So there may be many damaged states, perhaps even one for every other "undamaged" state. That is, there should in some cases be a `cruise` state and a `cruise_damaged` state, an `Air` and an `Air_damaged` state, and so on. In the `cruise_damaged` state the car may not be able to reach the prescribed speed, but it should still behave in the same basic way as in the `cruise` state.

Being damaged may also restrict the states that the vehicle can change into. For example, from `cruise_damaged` it may not be possible to move into the `overtake_ai` or `overtake_player` states or their damaged equivalents. Perhaps a damaged car should not try to pass another vehicle in the race or at least one that is not also damaged.

From a `damaged` state the car should change into the equivalent non-damaged state when it is repaired; so, we go from `cruise_damaged` to `cruise`, for example.

Attacking:

In combat or combat driving games, an attack can take a number of forms, from simply firing missiles to an intentional collision or an attempt to push another car off of the road. The attacking state corresponds to the AI's effort to damage another car, perhaps another AI car or the player. The difference in behavior between `attacking` and `cruise` can be profound, since the attacking car has a quite specific goal—to destroy an opponent.

The `attacking` state may require that a vehicle actually *chase* a car, be it the player or another AI car. This is quite a distinct change from the usual `cruise` or `Overtake_AI` state in which the goals are simply to make geometric progress.

Defending:

If an AI realizes that it is being attacked or chased, and there must be a carefully defined set of circumstances that determine when that is, then its car can adopt a strategy of avoidance, hiding, and perhaps high-speed escape. These actions characterize `defending` mode in those games where such conflicts are possible. The goal is obviously to hide from or destroy the attacker, and the previous goal indicated by the previous state is temporarily forgotten.

So, when the conflict is resolved, the vehicle should return to its previous state. Unfortunately, the chase could result in the vehicle being quite a large distance from where the chase began, moving in the wrong direction for the original goal. So, it may be best to move from `defending` to `cruise` and then have the system move between states based on the new local conditions.

Searching:

Some games have objects that must be retrieved during the course of the game, and in other cases the opponents are moving about and you must find them. `Searching` behavior is like that of the cruise state, but the goals are a bit different. There is often no geographic goal in the `searching` state, only an objective one—to locate something. Thus, the driving behavior would result in large areas being covered and a minimum of backtracking or revisiting.

It would be reasonable to define searching tracks as a design feature of the game. Like a driving track, these would be defined by waypoints and would have the goals of the search built into the layout of those waypoints. The AI would then have less "thinking" to do, needing only to follow the waypoints blindly.

Patrolling:

Patrolling behavior is very much like searching; indeed, patrolling can be called *searching for trouble*. Think of a police car on watch, driving the city at night. This is patrolling, an organized random route through an area. It should be random in practice so that bad guys cannot predict where you will be, of course. Whether it is truly random in the game is up to you, the game creator.

The nature of what is being sought is also a bit different from that seen in `searching` behavior. It is possible that a patrol is seeking a particular person, in which case it may be the same as searching. It may also be that the patrol seeks complex behaviors that indicate a crime in progress or some form of enemy activity. This is harder to identify, and it requires some careful definition of the goals in advance. For example, speeding is simple to spot since the AI always knows how fast all objects are moving. An illegal lane change by the player may be more difficult to spot.

Skidding:

When a car tries to turn a corner too fast, the wheels slide on the road. They try to keep moving in their original direction as indicated by Newton's law. We call this a skid, and it may be useful to define a `skidding` state. This state is characterized by a lack of control, so steering will work differently than in other states. Turning into the skid may tend to align the axis of the car with the direction of motion, but the car continues in much the same direction as before. Turning away from the direction of the skid will tend to give the car a rotational velocity about its center, again without changing the direction of motion of the car very much. Braking may make the skid worse, but slowing down would permit the wheels to grab the pavement and give control back. It is a complex situation, but anyone who has been in a skid knows one thing—the original driving plan, be it going to the store or getting to work, goes out the window in favor of just staying out of the ditch and getting control back.

Stopping:

The AI might need to stop the car from time to time, perhaps to pick up passengers or to collect an object. A car cannot stop instantly, and it may be necessary to pull over to the side of the road to avoid being smashed into. This `stopping` behavior is certainly needed in some games, including the one we are going to discuss and build later.

It is necessary to enter the `stopping` state well ahead of the point where the car wishes to stop. The goal is to stop at a particular place to conduct an activity, and so that place must be identified in advance, and the car needs time and space in which to slow down. Again, we'll need rules to dictate how far away to change states given the current velocity and direction.

PATHFINDING

Until this point the assumption has been that an NPC exhibits a specific behavior based on what is happening in the game, but sometimes an NPC has a specific destination, and sometimes the NPC behavior is expressed in terms of a destination. Patrolling behavior, for example, may well consist of a set of waypoints to be visited in sequence. In static situations this can be handled by fixed waypoints, but if obstacles can be placed in the way, then the situation becomes more complex.

A full AI solution would be to discover a path to the next waypoint on the NPC's path. There are many such path-finding algorithms, including the famous A* algorithm that we'll mention soon. If the NPC is blocked by a movable object but is still relatively near its path, it might be possible to simply move to a nearby location and then back to the path. A* attempts to find the "best" route according to some heuristic, usually based on the shortest distance. As a result, A* can be more time-consuming than we might like, given that a game executes in real time and has rather a lot to do. What would be acceptable is a less than optimal but still feasible route that takes less time.

One practical idea is to use a predefined grid of directions, indexed by using the vehicle's current position. This grid could be relatively coarse, containing perhaps a few thousand entries, and it should map onto the terrain of the game. Entries in this grid, easily implemented as a two-dimensional array, would be directions: either vectors or simply compass angles. The game designer would have to fill in the values at each location in the grid with the direction to steer to get back to the road or path. This is the usual trade-off: to make the machine seem clever, a person has to do a lot of work in advance, just as we did with waypoints. The other traditional trade-off in computer work is that of space versus time, and that can be seen here too. In order to speed up the pathfinding in this situation, a bunch of extra storage space is used (the grid).

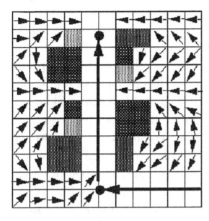

Squares with arrows show the direction that the car should move to get back to the path. The path is the route between the black circles, marked with the long thick arrow tipped lines. If the car is not pointing in the right direction then it must at least steer that way.

FIGURE 5.5 Use of a directional grid to find a route back to a road.

If this method is used, the sequence of steps is:

1. Find the grid element that corresponds to the current location of the vehicle. If the playing area is 1000 x 1000 yards, for example, we could break up this area into 25 x 25 grid elements, each being 40 yards square. Locating the grid is a matter of dividing the (x, z) coordinates by 40 and truncating.

2. Steer in the direction saved in the grid entry. This could be a byte value to save space and could be in fairly crude terms, since we simply have to get back to the path, not find the best route.

3. Use a low speed, since we're out of the race for the moment anyhow. The only obstacles that are a problem are moving ones, since the grid will be designed to avoid stationary objects. We could store a suggested speed along with the direction, again crudely quantized.

4. Grid elements that are near a path could contain a special value to indicate to the AI that the car should now be allowed to continue in its usual mode.

Figure 5.5 shows such a grid in a small example, and this example actually has obstacles so that it is easy to see how the grid is built—directions are chosen to steer the car toward the path, not always directly at it, but sometimes around static objects. As the car moves from one grid to another, it adjusts its steering direction to the new grid direction.

Thus, anywhere that the vehicle ends up after a collision will have a grid entry that directs the AI how to control the car.

A* SEARCH

The A* algorithm is a method for searching through a set of states for a good one, one that should lead to the solution of a problem. This is a pretty vague statement, but A* can be used for quite a few distinct kinds of problem in AI, so it makes sense to be vague. In terms of finding a path, a *state* will be a situation that has a position identified that is unique and is associated with a positional goal, a target position we are trying to get to. We also need a way to determine a *cost* associated with positions; in terms of paths, a cost may be how long it will take to get to the goal, or how much fuel it will take. The cost of moving from one position to another may well be connected to the terrain. Mud will cost more, and so will steep inclines, while paved roads will probably cost the least. The idea behind A* is to create a method for determining which route costs least without exploring all of the possibilities, which could be quite expensive.

It is important to realize that in order to use the A* algorithm, the playing area must be divided up into a grid, like we did before when using the directional grid. Each grid element corresponds to a discrete state and has a value that is related to the start and goal states. Each of these grid elements is called a *node* in A* terms. Each node has a *cost* associated with it, which is related to how far it is from the goal or how expensive the route is from that point.

There are a couple of obvious things to notice before we get too far into the description of the method. The first thing is that it is logical to reduce the amount of computation that is done by remembering the cost associated with each node, and not re-computing it. Next, we wish to keep a collection of nodes that are candidates for the next one in a path. A good way to do this is to have a set of nodes which are possible next ones: this is the open list or open set. We will also have a list of nodes that do not need to be considered, possibly because they have already been examined. This is the closed set.

The A* algorithm is important enough in games and AI to spend a few pages on, and a picture can be very valuable in explaining how things work. So, let's walk through an example that illustrates the method. Here is the grid that gives the situation:

The first thing to do is to add the node **S** to the open list, since we need to consider it as the 0th step in the path to the goal. The open list should be sorted so that the node with the smallest value of the total cost function (which we will call **F**) is first. The function F is a score traditionally composed of the sum of the

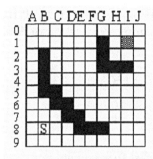

The starting point is marked 'S', and is at the node indexed as B8. The goal is a shaded node/square at I1.

Open list   Closed list

Empty   Empty

FIGURE 5.6 Initial situation in the A* example.

function G, which is how much it cost to get to this node, and H, the estimated cost for the remaining nodes between here and the goal. So **F = G+H**, and it seems as if **H** is impossible to calculate.

G is easy—each time we move horizontally or vertically to get to a node we add 1 to the value of H for that route, and we add the square root of 2 for diagonal steps if they are allowed. To make the calculations a bit faster, we multiply by 10 and convert to integers, since integer math is much faster than floating point math—so horizontal or vertical steps cost 10 and diagonal steps cost 14.

How do we determine **H**? A common way is to use the *4-distance* or *Manhattan* distance between that node and the goal. This is simply the number of rows between the nodes added to the number of columns between them.

After S has been added to the open list and F is computed, here is the result:

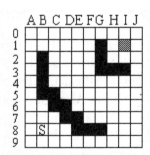

The distance between S and the goal at I2 is $10*((8-1) + I-B) = 70 + 70 = 140$.

Open list   Closed list

B8 F=0+140   Empty

FIGURE 5.7 Initialization for step 1 of A*.

Next: we take one of the nodes from the *open* list—the one with the smallest **F** value. Right now there's only one node in the *open* list, S, so no problem. Now add all of the nodes that neighbor S to the *open* list and move S to the *closed* list. Compute F for all of the new *open* list entries.

Remember, left-right and up-down neighbors are a distance of 10 from S, and diagonal neighbors are a distance of 14. A sample calculation of **F** for the node at B7 is:

$$H = distance\ to\ goal = 10 * (6 + 7) = 130$$

$$G = accumulated\ distance\ from\ S = 10$$

$$F = G + H = 130 + 10 = 140$$

We do this for all eight neighbors in the *open* list to arrive at:

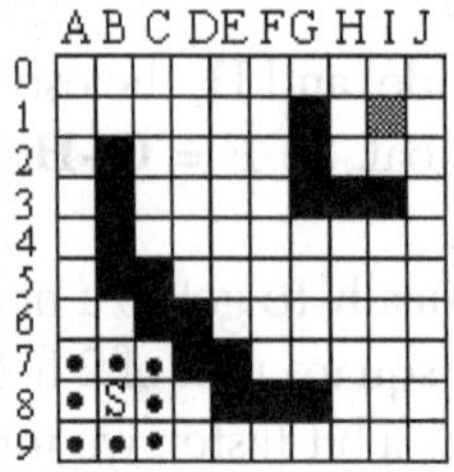

Open list	Parent	Closed list
B7 F=140	B8	B8=140
B9 F=160	B8	
A8 F=160	B8	
C8 F=140	B8	
C7 F=134	B8	
C9 F=154	B8	
A7 F=154	B8	
A9 F=174	B8	

FIGURE 5.8 After step 1 of A*.

One more thing. Whenever a node is added to the open list, we make a note of how we got there—it is the neighbor of a node that was on the path, and that node is the parent. We always remember the parent of a node, because that's how we trace the route back to the start when the method is done.

Let's do the next step. We pick the node in the *open* list that has the smallest value of **F**—in this case the C7 node—and put it into the closed list. The we start examining its neighbors. We must ignore squares that can't be traveled on, so the black ones that represent an obstacle are ignored. Also ignore nodes in the closed list. Clearly there are just four nodes that are legal neighbors of C7: C8, B7, B6, and D8. Add these to the *open* list if they are not already there. C8 and B7 are already there, so we don't add then, but we do check to see if the value of F for these nodes is smaller than it was before; that is, is the path that goes through the node C7 better than the one that has been computed already? If so, change their parent to C7 and their F value to the new one; otherwise, do nothing. For the new nodes B6 and D8, add them to the open list and compute F values.

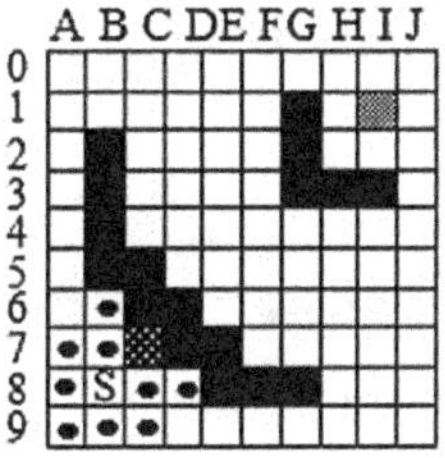

Open list	Parent	Closed list
B7 F=140	B8	B8 140 ◂
B9 F=160	B8	C7 134 B8
A8 F=160	B8	
C8 F=140	B8	
B6 F=148	C7	
C9 F=154	B8	
A7 F=154	B8	
D8 F=148	C7	

FIGURE 5.9 Step 2 of A*.

Now do it again. The node in the *open* list with the smallest F is B7. Move it to the *closed* list and place its eligible neighbors into the *open* list. There are only two nodes of interest here: node A6 is new and is added to the *open* list. The node at B6 is one that is already in the *open* list, but the exciting thing about it is that the value of F computed through the new parent is smaller than the old. Therefore, we change parents to B7 and adjust its F value to the new one, 140. The new situation is:

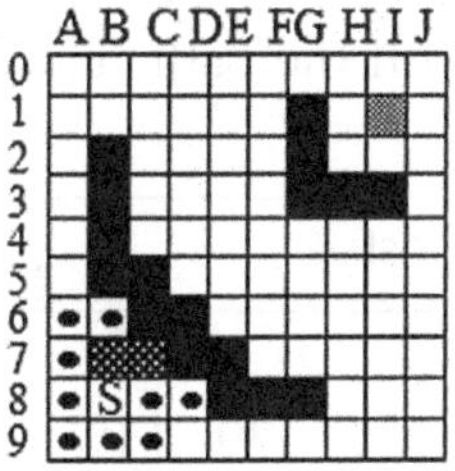

Open list	Parent	Closed list
C8 F=140	B8	B8 140 ◂
B9 F=160	B8	C7 134 B8
A8 F=160	B8	B7 140 B8
B6 F=140	B7	
C9 F=154	B8	
A7 F=154	B8	
D8 F=148	C7	
A6 F=140	B7	

FIGURE 5.10 Step 3.

And so we continue, pulling out the *open* node with the smallest F, putting it into the *closed* list, and putting its neighbors into the *open* list.

When do we stop? First, when the *open* list is empty. This means that the goal cannot be reached. The other termination condition is that we add the goal node to the *open* list. We trace the path of parents back from the goal node to read off the sequence of nodes in the "optimal" route.

The algorithm, in summary, is:

1. Create **start** and **goal** nodes.
2. Place the **start** node into the *open* list.

3. Repeat while there are nodes in the *open* list.
4. Select the node **P** from the *open* list with smallest **F** value.
    Place P in the *closed* list.
5. if **P**=**goal** then we quit with the solution.
6. for each neighbor **N**$_i$ of **P**
7. if **N**$_i$ is unusable or in the closed list then continue from 6.
8. Let the cost of **N**$_i$ = **H**(**N**$_i$)+ distance to **P**.
9. If **N**$_i$ is not in the open list then add it
10. else if **N**$_i$ is on the open list and the path has a lower **F**
11. then change **F** to the new value, change the parent of **N**$_i$ to **P**.
12. end of FOR
13. end of repeat
14. If the open list is empty, there is no path to the goal.

Did you forget what we were doing? Now we have a path from the AI vehicle that was knocked far off of its path by a collision to a waypoint that is on the original path the car was following. In other words, we have a way to get back to the "normal" situation after being knocked off the path. The path found in the example is:

Path	Costs									
`..........`	100	96	100	110	120	130	140	.	.	.
`......#.S.`	82	86	96	106	116	126	#	162	158	162
`.#....#.^.`	72	#	100	110	120	130	#	158	148	144
`.#....###^`	62	#	.	.	.	.	#	#	#	134
`.#......^.`	52	#	.	.	.	.	128	124	120	124
`.##.....^.`	42	#	#	.	.	.	118	114	110	114
`..##....^.`	24	28	#	#	.	.	100	104	100	104
`..^##...^.`	14	10	14	#	#	.	90	86	90	100
`.E.^###^..`	10	0	10	28	#	#	#	76	86	10
`....^^^...`	14	10	14	24	42	52	62	72	90	100

The cells marked "." were never used. The path runs from the cell marked 0 to the one marked 158 and follows the lighter grey values.

STOCHASTIC NAVIGATION

The word "stochastic" means "having a random component or element," and that's really what is wanted from ambient traffic. If you look at traffic from the top of a building, the individual vehicles behave both predictably and randomly—they predictably obey traffic rules but follow what looks like a random route. That's because we don't know where the cars are going. They all have a destination, but without knowing what it is we don't really know what a car will do at the next intersection, and especially at the intersection three blocks down. We want the traffic to look natural, and we do not want all cars to turn left at 5th street or have the same cars go around the same block for the whole game.

So, each car should have a plan for at least the next choice. If a car is going to turn left, it makes sense that it should get into the left lane before the intersection. Each vehicle in traffic should have a short-term plan which is updated every time it executes a planned move like a turn. The plan is random, so it is based on the drawing of random numbers. The most likely event is to drive straight through an intersection, but left or right turns have a finite non-zero probability. For example, we could have:

Straight through	80% chance
Left turn	9 % chance
Right turn	9 % chance
Right next alley	1 % chance
Turn into next access	1 % chance

Now draw a random number x between 0.0 and 1.0. The code for the previous is:

```
if (x < 0.8):
    plan = GO_STRAIGHT
elif (x<0.89):
    plan = TURN_LEFT
elif (x<0.98):
    plan = TURN_LEFT
elif (x < 0.99):
    plan = NEXT_ALLEY
else:
    plan = NEXT_ACCESS
```

If the car enters a parking lot, it should park. This activity is likely initiated by a finite machine state change.

It is important to realize that the traffic needs only to behave properly so long as the player is watching. Indeed, it takes time for the AI to move the vehicles sensibly, and if we can avoid taking this time it would be good. Should we create traffic when it becomes visible? That is, when the player's car turns a corner, do we need to invent some cars and plans for them?

That is certainly an option, but it would cause a problem in cases where the player chooses to explore the environment, especially if he does so by following ambient traffic. Imagine turning a corner to find that the cars you just saw have vanished. No, it is probably better to have more of the traffic be inactive (not moving) until is within a specific radius of the player. Naturally, if the player stays in one place too long, the traffic in his neighborhood could vanish—as it leaves the active radius it stops, and nothing can start up until the player moves closer.

Things are getting complicated. So, what may work is to give some CPU time to moving ambient traffic once in a while, each few frames. If the player is idle, there is going to be a lot of free time to give to this task. So, if traffic is within a radius of, say, five blocks of the player's car, it will get a "turn" (a few cycles) each frame for movement control. Otherwise, it will get a turn based on its position in a queue and the number of free cycles. As the frame rate increases, we have extra time to give to the traffic, unless the player is engaged in combat or something. So, the distant vehicles are places in a queue, and the front few are given movement control each frame and are then placed at the end of the queue. This is fair, and it will automatically give as much spare time as possible to traffic motion.

Navigation is the process of getting from one location to another. Sometimes there is a final destination which is arrived at in stages, and sometimes there are predefined routes to known destinations that are defined by the game developer. A *waypoint* is an intermediate destination along a route, and it is defined by a set of 3D coordinates and actions to take upon arriving. A character moves from one waypoint to another on its way to its final destination. For characters that don't have predefined destinations, we use *pathfinding* methods like the A* algorithm.

Characters may have a set of states that control their movement and navigational behavior as a function of what is going on at the moment (current state). It is also common to have characters simply moving around to create some form of traffic, essentially providing ambiance.

EXERCISES

The following problems will exercise your knowledge of the material in this chapter, and they will sometimes require that you do more research before you are able to complete them.

1. Create a simple elliptical track on an 800 x 600 image and use it to implement a basic driving simulation. One car should drive around the track completing at least five laps before stopping. Use no fewer than eight waypoints to guide the vehicle.

For the next exercises use Figure 5.11, which shows an 800 x 600 image that is to be used in pathfinding. Presume that a character's avatar, represented by a small blue circle, is to move from the small house in the upper right of the image to the larger house in the lower left. Presume also that this dot may not pass through the river or through the brick barriers.

2. Mark possible and impassible squares on the image, creating what we call a *mask*. Have the avatar move toward the destination when possible and back up and try a new path when not. Turn at random when a decision has to be made, toward the destination when possible. Does the avatar find a path? If so, how long does it take?

3. Find a set of paths to the destination manually and mark them either in a same-sized image or as arrays of individual pixel x and y movements. Create at least four paths that branch from the starting point and are selected at random. Does the behavior look realistic?

Idea: A program has been written that allows the developer to use the *wasd* keys to move from the source to destination and record the path. The path was written to a file and read in and used by the problem solution. You could write such a program too or use the one provided.

4. Repeat Exercise 3 using waypoints. In what ways is this solution better and in what ways is it not better than the ones previously tried?

5. Add a new NPC avatar to the solution of Exercise 4, a red circle, which will try to prevent the player's blue avatar from reaching the destination. It will start in the upper left and move toward the blue avatar when it "sees" it; that is, when there is a clear line of sight between the red and blue circles that does not pass through a brick wall. If the red avatar gets to within 12 pixels of the blue one, then it succeeds and red wins. If the blue avatar gets to the destination, then blue wins. Who wins this game and under what circumstances?

6. Navigation is not only connected with existing paths and physical obstacles but sometimes by more abstract things like traffic rules. Describe the rules for behavior when a car arrives at a stop sign on a typical city street. Sketch a plan for the behavior of a vehicle from the approach to a stop sign until the moment that it is decided the vehicle can proceed.

7. Streetwise navigation can be complicated by road closures, one-way streets, and other features of modern life. In computer science terms, street intersections can be considered to be nodes on a *graph*. An entity called an

adjacency matrix is used to represent which nodes are connected to which others. An element j in row i of the matrix is a 1 if there is a way to get to node j from i in one step. Here is an example:

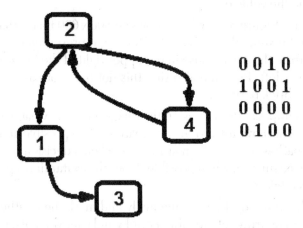

```
0 0 1 0
1 0 0 1
0 0 0 0
0 1 0 0
```

There is an algorithm to determine if a path exists between any two nodes and how long that path is—it is referred to variously as Warshall's algorithm, the Floyd-Warshall algorithm, or the WFI algorithm. Look up this algorithm and describe it; then discuss its usefulness in finding routes in urban contexts. How is a one-way street represented?

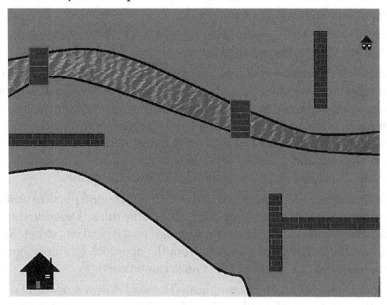

FIGURE 5.11 Sample 2D pathfinding image for the exercises.

RESOURCES

Path Finding Tutorial: *http://wiki.gamegardens.com/Path_Finding_Tutorial.*
Useful tutorial description of A*.

Gamasutra tutorial on realistic pathfinding: *http://www.gamasutra.com/view/feature/3096/toward_more_realistic_pathfinding.php.*
Very good video game context.

Video demonstration of Dijkstra's algorithm: *http://www.youtube.com/watch?v=8Ls-1RqHCOPw.*

Pathfinding concept, the basics (Michael Grenier): *http://mgrenier.me/2011/06/pathfinding-concept-the-basics/.*

REFERENCES

1. E. G. Gilbert, D. W. Johnson, and S. S. Keerthi. (1988). "A Fast Procedure for Computing the Distance between Complex Objects in Three-Dimensional Space." *IEEE Journal of Robotics and Automation* 4: 193–203.

2. Dan Higgins. (2002). *Generic A* Pathfinding*. AI Game Programming Wisdom, Charles River Media. Hingham, Mass

3. James Matthews. (2002). *Basic A* Pathfinding Made Simple*. AI Game Programming Wisdom, Charles River Media. AI Game Programming Wisdom, Charles River Media. Hingham, Mass

4. J. Pearl. (1984). *Heuristics: Intelligent Search Strategies for Computer Problem Solving*. Addison & Wesley, Boston, MA, USA.

5. Anthony Stentz. (1996). *Map-Based Strategies for Robot Navigation in Unknown Environments*. Proceedings of the AAAI Spring Symposium on Planning with Incomplete Information for Robot Problems. *http://www.aaai.org/Press/Reports/Symposia/Spring/ss-96-04.php.*

## CHAPTER 6

SOUND

Here is an interesting experiment: play a first-person shooter, such as *Halo* or *Half-Life*, with the sound off. It is amazing how much of the energy and emotional content is contained in the audio part of a game. The tempo of the music gets the blood racing, and the sounds of weapon fire and nearby explosions can guide you away from trouble or into situations where points can be won. It's not just shooters: play any of your favorite games with the sound off if you need convincing.

1. Computer games use sound for four basic things:
2. Music. A great deal of emotional content is contained in the music alone. Alfred Hitchcock knew this very well.
3. Sound effects. If a car crashes or a gun fires, we expect to hear that.
4. Speech. Many games tell a story by allowing you to listen in on conversations or even participate. Your side is often typed in and is not really understood, but the characters in the game speak and expect to be heard.
5. Ambient sound. This is background noise, such as a river, or rain, or even the sound of coffee shop.

It is interesting that many programmers, even those with many years of experience and who know graphics and event-based programming, know almost nothing about how to manipulate and play sounds on a computer. It is especially interesting because sound programming is in many ways much like graphics programming: the goal is to display something, there is object positioning and rendering to be done, the listener's (viewer) position affects the result, there are colors (frequencies) to be handled, and a special device is at the heart of everything (sound card/video card).

So it is with some excitement that we begin a trek into the dark, unknown world of computer audio. Like graphics, there can be a lot of math associated with sound; unlike graphics, some of it is not necessary to perform simple reproduction of sound using a computer. You see, most games do not create sounds on the fly, but merely read sounds from files and play them at an appropriate moment. Games would be very dull indeed if the approach to graphics was the same. Graphical objects need to be moved, rotated, transformed, and tested for visibility and collisions. Audio objects basically turn on and off, get louder or softer, and perhaps move from the left to the right stereo channel. Display of sounds is in fact simpler than display of graphics. Expect this to change as more options present themselves.

Processing has no built-in scheme for audio display; that is done by a downloadable add-on. The fact that *Processing* is based on Java means that the add-on is coded in *Java* and uses the *JavaSound* API, and could be used with other purely *Java* code. This also means that later on, when we discuss HTML5, we'll have to revise the audio display scheme. Additionally, there are a few choices for audio systems, and you might be interested in trying some of them. For the purposes of this book we're going to use *Minim*, the most common option.

BASIC AUDIO CONCEPTS

Although there are similarities between our sense of vision and our sense of hearing, the differences are significant. Most important is the concept that objects that are seen normally reflect light from another source, rather than generating light on their own. Thus, we see by reflected light. Audio, on the other hand, is usually produced by the object that is being sensed; that is, an object that we hear is generating the sound, not reflecting it.

Of course sound reflections can be important, and they contribute to the ambiance of the sounds. The idea that sound sources are spatially localized is key to positional audio generation, but it is less important in stereo and web-based games. In graphics, what would it look like if we could only observe light sources and not reflections? Things would be much simpler and vastly less interesting. Also, we don't really have an audio image, a two-dimensional pattern that can be interpreted. Instead, we have two sound receptors (ears), each of which perceives the sum of the sounds that reach them at any particular moment.

This can also be thought of as another way that audio is simpler than graphics.

Sounds are essentially vibrations of the air. The intensity of the vibrations is called the *volume* or *loudness* of the sound. The duration between two consecutive peaks of the vibratory motion is called the *period*, and the number of peaks that occur in a second is called the *frequency* or *pitch*[1] (Figure 6.1).

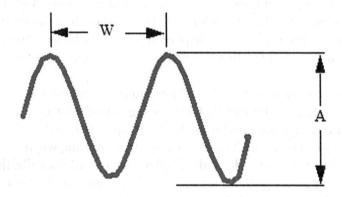

FIGURE 6.1 A sound wave viewed as a graph of intensity VS time. The wavelength W is the distance between two peaks; the period is the time between two peaks. The amplitude A is the distance between the peak and the trough (lowest point). The frequency is the number of peaks that pass by a stationary point in one second. High-pitched sounds have a higher frequency than do lower pitched ones.

The unit of frequency is Hertz (shortened as Hz), which was named after a person. This name will sound familiar; your computer has an execution speed that is also measured in Hertz—well, megahertz (MHz = million cycles) or gigahertz (GHz = Billion cycles)—and this refers to the number of clock cycles per second.

A typical human can hear sounds that have frequencies between 40 Hz and 15,000 Hz (1,000 = 1 kiloHertz or KHz). Some people can hear 20 KHz sounds and even higher, but as we get older our ability to hear high-pitched sounds declines. In any case, frequencies above 15 KHz are not as important as the lower ones in computer games, as computer speakers are generally not able to reproduce these sounds, and many people cannot hear them.

---

1   Frequency and pitch are not precisely the same thing. Pitch is a subjective psychoacoustic characteristic of sound, or how a frequency is perceived by the auditory system and brain.

We have two ears, and normally any sound presents itself at both of them. There will normally be a slight time difference between the arrival at the left and right ears caused by the distance to the object and the distance between your ears. Essentially, it takes time for the sound to travel the short distance represented by the width of your skull. This is how you locate a sound. Most people can determine a fairly precise location for a sound even with their eyes closed, but only if both ears function properly. This fact is important in a game, because an object that looks like it is at the left side of the screen should also sound like it is to our left.

In day-to-day life we are surrounded by sound, and we can actually detect much of it. What we hear is really the sum of all of the sounds that reach us at each moment in time. This makes audio rendering simpler than graphical rendering, because the screen requires that we compute the intensity and/or color of at least 640 x 480 pixels (places). For audio, we need to compute only two audio "pixels," one for each ear. However, we need to compute these audio points more often than graphical ones. Twenty-four frames per second is usually enough to realistically represent moving objects on a screen. To render audio realistically, we need to generate a new intensity value at a rate that is at least twice the frequency being created, or up to 30,000 times per second! Fortunately, the sound card can do a lot of the work.

In order to store a sound on a computer, it has to be digitized, or *sampled*. A standard sound card can do this if you plug a microphone or other sound source into it. Sound is represented as electrical signals, which can actually look like Figure 6.1 when viewed on an oscilloscope. Sampling a signal involves making a measurement at a regular and frequent interval. An electrical signal can be measured as voltages, for example, so to store a sound we could measure the voltage being sent to the speakers every millisecond and store this measurement as a binary number on a file. Playing the sound back requires that we can convert binary numbers into voltages again and send them to an output device.

Without getting into too much detail, because signal processing is a whole subject unto itself, we need to sample a sound at a rate that is at least twice the highest frequency that we want to reproduce. For example, if we want to be able to hear 15KHz sounds, we have to sample the signal 30,000 times per second. If a sample is an integer (16 bits), this means that a four-minute song requires 4 * 60 * 30000 *4 bytes to store (28 MB), and 56 MB if the song is stereo. Of course, there are compression schemes and such to reduce the size as saved on disk. In any case, what we need is to store these samples as numbers, either integers or floats, and have a means to send them to the sound card.

A standard PC sound card can perform sampling at a high rate, and it does so from both the line input and the microphone input. The device that does this is called an *analog to digital (A to D) converter* or *ADC*, and the sound card has some of these. The way the ADC works is much less relevant than is the result and the implications. Figure 6.2 shows an example of the sampling process for the sine wave of Figure 6.1. After each sample interval the sound is converted into a voltage measurement and converted into a binary number for storage. Since these numbers are digital, they can't be saved perfectly and so are rounded to the nearest integer, which necessarily creates a small error in each sample (sampling error).

The sound card can reverse the process too, taking a sequence of digital samples and converting them into voltages that can be sent to speakers or an amplifier for playback. Sounds in numeric form can be, and most often are, stored on files, retrieved, and played back as needed. The sound card is a complex and clumsy thing to program directly, and so a software library that does this is essential when developing a game.

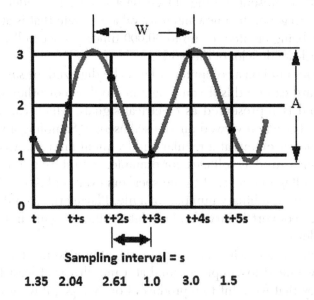

FIGURE 6.2 Sampling of a sine wave by an analog to digital converter. After each fixed interval s the sound is measured as a voltage and converted into a number for storage. Numbers at the bottom show the numeric values of the sound at each sample point.

This is where Pygame comes in. We can create reasonable sounds for a typical game without needing to know too much of the math or physics of sound. We also won't need to know too much about our sound card. What we do need to do is understand the paradigm used by the developers of Pygame.

INTRODUCTION TO SOUND IN PYGAME

The key module in Pygame for displaying audio is *mixer*. It defines objects that represent sounds and allows the programmer to load them and play them. Within the mixer module is a class named *Sound*, which is an essential audio interface for Pygame, and another called *channel* which is equally important. The *mixer* module is designed to allow multiple sound sources to be mixed (combined at various levels of intensity) into a stereo or mono output, possibly for real-time playback. By default, it permits eight channels, but complicated code can create more sophisticated output. The *Sound* class is the sound object in Pygame, associating a sound with a file and allowing it to be loaded and played, and controlling volume, pan, and other properties.

The simplest thing to do with sounds is to load and play them. A program that does this would first initialize Pygame and create a display. This must be done even if the display will not be used for displaying anything. Then the Sound class is used to create an object, specifying the name of the sound file to be associated with the object:

```
m = pygame.mixer.Sound("song.wav")
```

The variable **m** is a handle or access variable to the sound. To play it, use the *play* method:

```
m.play()
```

Now the standard Pygame loop must be entered or the sound will not play:

```
while True:
        pygame.display.update()
```

This program is a basic WAV file player. Pygame does not play MP3 files by default, but it is possible using other modules. The entire previously described program is (**sound.py**):

```
import pygame
pygame.init()
canvas = pygame.display.set_mode( (200, 100) )
m = pygame.mixer.Sound("song.wav")
m.play()
```

```
while True:
    pygame.display.update()
```

Sound Options

In the real audio world, a *mixer* is a device that accepts some number of input sounds and combines them into a single sound that is a combination of all of the inputs (Figure 6.3). The input sounds could be from microphones or CDs, tapes, or vinyl. The degree to which each sound will be a part of the final mixture is set by using a volume control, sometimes a sliding one or sometimes a rotating one. Each sound is assigned to a *channel*, which is a single path the sound takes from the input to the output. A channel can be mono or stereo, with stereo channels counting as two. The mixer in Figure 6.3 has eight channels, two mono and three stereo.

Pygame has a mixer class that simulates a real mixer to some degree. Within that class there is a Sound class that represents a sound, as stored on a file, and Pygame has a channel class. When using the mixer class, there are some controls for the overall sound, and in addition each channel and Sound have controls that apply to them. By default, a Pygame mixer has eight channels. The previous example did not explicitly use channels, and that is completely acceptable if there are only a few sounds and control of them is simple. The sound being played was assigned a channel by default. If a programmer states m.play() where m is a sound object, then the mixer can perform the following operations:

FIGURE 6.3 A ten-channel audio mixer.

m.play() – Start playing the sound

m.stop() – Stop playing the sound
m.pause() – Temporarily stop playback of all channels

There are other controls, but what should be understood is that the previous operations are not normally available on a real mixer. Assume that the actual sound being played is a song from a CD player. The player can be started, stopped, paused, and so on. The mixer does not do these things; it accepts sound into it when the sound is playing and manipulates it. Each sound has a volume, which in the example is the volume of the CD player. The Pygame mixer class does have a global stop operation that stops all sounds entering the mixer.

Sounds are assigned to channels, and the channel has a volume control too, which is the relative level of the specific sound within the overall mixer output (usually just called the *mix*).

Sound Volume

Each sound can have its volume set to a value between 0 (off) to 1.0 (Full volume). Moreover, the volume setting on each sound can be retrieved, and the length of the sound in seconds can be found. The length is known because the sound is actually a sound file, and the length can be calculated from the size of the file and the sample rate.

The essential methods from Sound are:

```
set_volume (v)      Set the volume level, between 0 and 1
get_volume ()       Return the current volume setting
get_length ()       Return the length of the sound in seconds.
```

A program that plays a sound and allows the user to control the volume spends most of the code handling the keyboard events. Let's say that the up arrow key turns the volume louder and the down arrow key turns the volume lower. The initialization is the same as before, but the main loop is more complicated because the key presses need to be captured and parsed. Let the volume be set to a level controlled by the variable v, which can take a value between 0.0 and 1.0. The program (sound0.py) is:

```
# Volume set

import pygame

pygame.init()                                    # Initialization
canvas = pygame.display.set_mode( (200, 100) )
m = pygame.mixer.Sound("song.wav")               # Read the sound
file
m.play()                                         # Begin playing
```

```
the sound

v = 1.0                 # Initial volume is maximum (1.0)
while True:
   for event in pygame.event.get():
      if event.type == pygame.KEYUP:
         if event.key == pygame.K_DOWN:  # Down key lowers the volume
            v = v - 0.1                   # Decrease the volume by the
standard amount
            if v < 0:                     # Check bounds
               v = 0
            m.set_volume (v)              # Set the volume to v

         if event.key == pygame.K_UP:    # The Up key increases the
volume
            v = v + 0.1                   # Increase the volume by the
standard amount
            if v > 1:                     # Check bounds
               v = 1
            m.set_volume(v)               # Set the volume to v
print (v, m.get_volume(), m.get_length())
   pygame.display.update()
```

Each time a key is pressed, this program also prints the volume level and the length of the sound.

Channels

A channel is assigned using a call to the **find_channel()** method of the *mixer* object. This locates a free (unassigned) channel and returns it. When using channels, instead of playing the *Sound*, one assigns a *Sound* to a *channel* and plays the *channel*. So, if m represents a *Sound* then:

```
chan = pygame.mixer.find_channel()    # Get a channel that's
not being used
   chan.play(m)                       # Play the Sound m on the
channel chan
```

Each channel has a volume control too. A channel can be mono or stereo though. If it is stereo then it is really two channels, and setting the volume would mean setting the volume of each channel. This allows the idea of panning the sound, setting a different volume level on each of the left and right stereo channels, thus positioning it in space. Setting the volume is done using the channel:

```
chan.set_volume(1, 1)
```

This call sets the volume to the maximum on both the left and right. Panning is a little more complicated. Assuming that, as before, the variable **v** holds the current overall volume (between 0 and 1), let's add a new variable **a** that is 1.0 for full volume on the right channel and 0 for no volume on the right. The left channel volume will be **1-a**, and a is a positioning of the sound between channels: 1 for full right and 0 for full left. A function **pan(a)** can be written as follows:

```
def pan (a):
  global leftAmp, rightAmp, chan, v

  if a < 0:  a = 0
  if a > 1:  a = 1
  leftAmp = (1 - a)*v
  rightAmp =  a*v
  chan.set_volume(leftAmp, rightAmp)
```

Now the program sound0.py can be modified to also allow the user to change the pan value using the left and right keys. The main loop would be (sound1.py):

```
while True:
  for event in pygame.event.get():
    if event.type == pygame.KEYUP:
      if event.key == pygame.K_DOWN:
        v = v - 0.1
        if v < 0:  v = 0
        pan(p)
      if event.key == pygame.K_UP:
        v = v + 0.1
        if v > 1:  v = 1
        pan(p)
      if event.key == pygame.K_LEFT:
        p = p - .1
        if p<0: p = 0
        pan(p)
      if event.key == pygame.K_RIGHT:
        p = p + .1
        if (p>1):  p = 1
        pan(p)

    print (leftAmp, rightAmp, p)
  pygame.display.update()</CODE>
```

Creating Your Own Sounds

Sounds, especially pieces of music, are protected information. If you wish to use the property of someone else, you are generally expected to pay for it.

That's perfectly reasonable. After all, people are expected to pay for games, right? As is the case with art, sounds that someone else creates and posts on the Internet would have a value, and a game developer is expected to pay for such resources.

On the other hand, it is possible to create your own sound effects, voices, and ambient sounds in many instances. Music may be a more significant problem, as it requires composition and playing skills that not everyone has. It's important to understand that music used in a game must attribute and pay both the composer and the artist. The only exceptions are music that has been placed into the public domain by the artist and music that is old enough that the copyright has expired. One must make quite certain that the assets being used, music in this instance, have been given the proper legal consideration.

Having said that, many sound effects can be recorded using equipment that many people already possess. In that case the sounds are your property, unless you record someone singing a proprietary song, of course. Recording is very simple using a PC, with some very good software available for free or little cost. Recordings can be done using cellular phones and most mp3 players. Of course, there are dedicated high-quality recording devices available for professional quality work.

Recording Using Cell Phones and MP3 Devices

Android	IPhone
Use the voice recorder app in the Tools folder. Open the app and press the red button to record and the blue square to stop recording.	Use the voice memos app.
Sound files will be saved in the My Files/Audio folder.	Open the app and begin recording by pressing the red button. Press the same button to stop recording.

The quality achieved by a cell phone is good enough for most sound effects, but not for voice or music. The problem is the microphone, which is tiny and cheap. It's possible to connect a better mic to some phones, and that is to be recommended.

MP3 players usually have a record mode, which is intended for voice memos. They suffer from the same problem as telephones with respect to the microphone. For iPods or Sony players, select the *settings* mode and then *record*.

A Small Studio

The small mixer shown in Figure 6.3 is sufficient for many small game developers and costs around $100. A sound studio would require four microphones, and decent (but not brilliant) mics can be purchased for $100 each. Stands for the microphones are $35, and cables are $12–$20. The computer will be the recording device, and a laptop will work, but to properly record outdoor sounds, a portable recorder is valuable. The Zoom H1 and similar recorders run about $100.

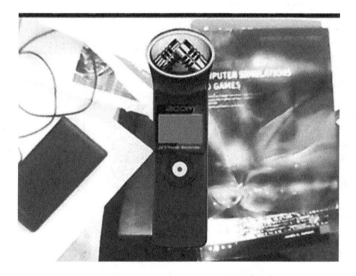

FIGURE 6.4 **The Zoom H1 recorder.**

The total cost of the sound studio described here would be about $700. Do not skimp on quality; many audio enthusiasts would claim that you can't get a good microphone for $100, and while that's not really true and technology has gotten a lot better in the past twenty years, it's better to have fewer good mics than a lot of bad ones.

There may be other bits and pieces that would be useful—a CD or DVD player, maybe a turntable, and other sources of sound. All of these are connected to their own channel of the mixer, and the main outputs of the mixer are connected to the computer line input. You can monitor the mix from the mixer or the computer using headphones.

Some special purpose software is needed now to capture the sound and store it.

Audio Software

 The CD that comes with this book provides a copy of the music editor named Audacity. For most small games this is the only software that is needed to record and edit sounds for a game.

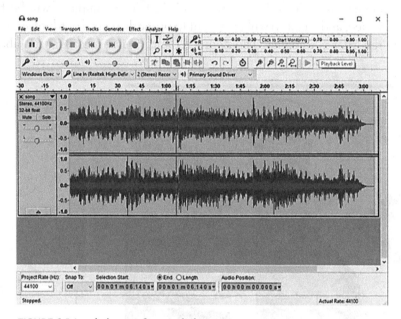

FIGURE 6.5 A typical screen from Audacity.

Like most sound editors, Audacity shows the sound as a graphic. In most cases a left and right channel are shown, one atop the other. Simple editing is done using the mouse, where sections of the sound can be selected with a click and drag. The section selected will appear in a different color, and can be deleted, copied, or both. Once copied it can be inserted in another location.

Audacity has an impressive set of operations it can perform on a sound. It can change volume, filter by frequency, fade in and out, crossfade, reverb and tremolo, reduce noise, echo, and perform dozens of other operations. It can also load multiple tracks and mix them as desired.

Rather than simply describe this program, let's use it to create a sound effect. Consider that the boat race game will need an engine noise sound for each boat. An engine is a constant low-frequency noise that has some variation in volume.

It can't be too regular though. A sine wave would not sound right. But it may be a start.

Using Audacity with no tracks present, select "Generate" and then "Tone." Select 75 Hz and "OK." A new stereo track will appear containing a 75 Hz sine wave. Audacity looks like this:

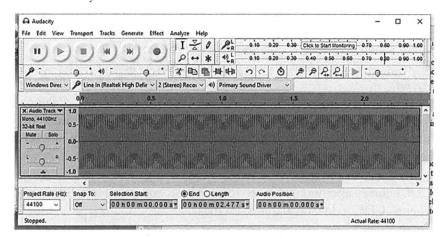

FIGURE 6.6 Audacity showing a generated 75 Hz tone.

When played (the green triangle button) it sounds like a low musical note. Now we need to add some random changes. Select "Generate" and "Noise." The drop-down menu will offer a noise type (select "Pink") and amplitude (select 0.8). Click on "OK" and a second stereo track will appear containing the noise. The Audacity window will look like this:

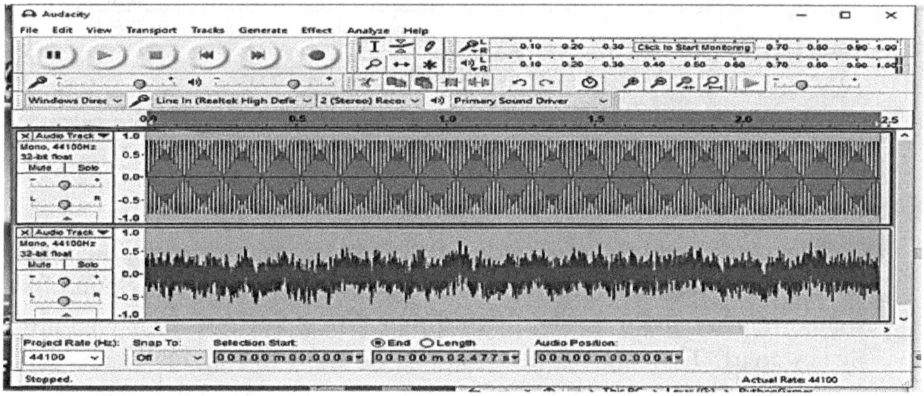

FIGURE 6.7 The 75 Hz tone on one track and a pink noise sound on a second track.

Playing these two together now sounds more like an engine. Select both tracks (Shift and click) and then choose "Tracks" and "Mix and Render to New Track." The two tracks will be combined into a third. You can now delete the other two tracks (click on the "x" in the upper left of the track display). We can now see the mixed track.

As a last step, select "Effect" and "Tremolo." Choose the parameters: sine, Wet level = 30%, frequency = 8.7, then OK. We now have a passable boat engine sound. Obviously, one should experiment with the parameters of the effects so as to get a feel for what they do, and to permit better effects to be created.

This activity is very much like creating art from scratch with Paint or Photoshop. It is also possible to record sounds and incorporate them into the effects. For example, one could record the sound of a flowing water tap into the engine sound. A finger snap or thump on a table could be recorded and slowed down to sound like an explosion.

Of course, another option is to purchase sound effects from producers, either as CDs or downloadable MP3 files.

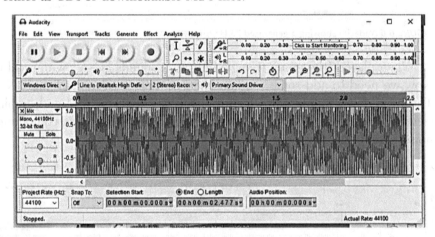

FIGURE 6.8 The tone and the noise track mixed to one stereo track.

Positional Audio

The concept of positional audio is relatively simple, although the implementation is not. You, as a human, almost certainly have two ears. Sound from any source reaches them at slightly different times, because your ears are a few inches apart. That time differential can be used to roughly locate the sound source in space: if the source is to your left, then the sound reaches your left ear first, for example. This can be simulated in systems that have stereo sound display capability.

It's also true that a sound that occurs nearby seems louder than one occurring a distance away, all other things being equal. We use this fact instinctively when judging the distances in real life, and it should be true in games as well. This is a basic aspect of positional audio, one that everyone perceives on a daily basis, and it requires only distance to the source and not the precise position.

What is needed for positional sound to be possible is the position of the sound event, which is to say the location within the game space of the thing that generates the sound. Collisions, for example, happen at a precise location. The position and facing direction of the player, or the avatar at least, is also known, and the relative intensities of the sound at each ear can be calculated and displayed at each speaker. It is clear that what's needed is the position of the sound, the position of the player (listener), and the direction the player is facing in the game.

We can assume that the player's position is known, since it is being updated by the game each frame. The sound position is also known, as most events have a known position within the game. The player's facing direction can be assumed to be the direction of motion, or if stationary then the last known direction of motion.

Example: Distance Attenuation

In computer graphics, clipping is the act of removing lines and polygons that are outside of the viewing volume. This includes lines that are too near the camera and lines that are too far away. The near and far clipping planes are defined as distances; we shall do the same with sounds. At some sufficiently far distance **d**, a sound can no longer be heard and will be *attenuated* (i.e., reduced in intensity) completely (100%). At some sufficiently near distance the sound will be attenuated not at all (0%), and at every distance in between the sound will be attenuated by some function of distance. In real life the function is related to $1/d^2$; that is, the sound gets fainter as the square of the distance to it. The important thing in a game is that things seem correct rather than being correct, and this degree of attenuation may be too great. A linear function may seem more realistic.

Let's define variables **maxSoundDistance** and **minSoundDistance** to be the 100% and the 0% attenuation distances respectively. Then, if **d** is the actual distance to the sound, the attenuation **a** can be calculated as:

where **a** will have a value between 0.0 and 1.0. Every sound will have a natural or intrinsic volume at which it is played, as well as a minimum and

$$a = (d - \min SoundDistance) / (\min SoundDistance - \min SoundDistance)$$

maximum, and this intrinsic volume will be modified by multiplying by the attenuation before it is played.

In Pygame, each Sound/channel has a predetermined volume setting that applies to it. The attenuation will be used to set the gain to the proper value between these two points. Volume has a minimum value of 0 and a maximum value of 1. The volume setting would be some value between 0 and 1 as determined by the distance between the listener and the sound-creating object. If a variable **maxSoundDistance** was the distance at which a sound could not be heard, then the volume setting for the channel displaying that sound would be:

```
g = distance/maxSoundDistance
```

Setting the volume could be done as follows for a listener at (lx,ly) and a source at (x,y):

```
# (x,y) is sound position; (lx, ly) is avatar position
def playDistance (int x, int y, int lx, int ly, channel player):
        global maxSoundDistance
        d = sqrt ((x-lx)*(x-lx) + (y-ly)*(y-ly))      # Distance
        a = d/maxSoundDistance                        #
Attenuation
        v = 1-a                                       # Volume
        if v > 1:
            v = 1
        player.setVolume (v)
```

Example: 2D Positional Sound

Humans have the ability to approximately locate the physical location of a sound. Most people know this and believe that it has something to do with the volume at each ear. It does, somewhat, but it's really more about the time at which the sound arrives at each ear—the time difference, that is. Your ears are about eight inches apart, or about 0.6 milliseconds at the speed of sound. Your brain combines the time difference between the two ears with any volume difference, takes into account the attenuation due to your head and the shape of the *pinnae* (the shaped part of your external ear), and calculates the position of the sound.

A computer game does not have to do that. The game knows where the sound source is, and what it attempts to calculate is how that should sound at your ears. It then sends those sounds to the left and right channels of a stereo sound system (or the N speakers of a 5 or 7 channel sound system, but we'll stick with stereo here). The game sound system depends on the spatial separation of the electronic sound system and the ability to set volume levels on the left and right channels to *simulate* how the event should sound. We have to calculate those two sound levels. It is not possible to use time as a positional factor, because it is not possible to know where the player is with respect to the speakers (unless headphones are used).

To figure out how to do a positional sound calculation, we need to decide how to tell where the sound location is relative to the player's avatar and the direction that it is facing. We will find the angle between the player and the sound and use that to adjust the pan control. The player's location is known; the facing direction must be known too, and it will be an angle in the same coordinate system. Recall that the Python *math* class uses a system that has 0 radians/degrees as screen right, and π/2 radians (90 degrees) as the screen *up* direction. With the player at position (**X, Y**), we'll define a point (**faceX, faceY**) that corresponds to an imaginary point to which the player is facing. This point will be:

$$faceX = (\text{int})(X + \cos(facingDirection) * d)$$
$$faceY = (\text{int})(Y + \sin(facingDirection) * d)$$

The value of **d** is a distance from the player, and it can be anything that provides a long distance; the value **d=1000** works pretty well.

Figure 6.9 shows something of the geometry of the situation. The left part of Figure 6.9 shows a diagram of a player in two extreme situations—one where the sound is precisely to the right, the other where the sound is directly ahead. In the first case the sound is at maximum loudness in the right ear and the minimum in the left, and in the second the loudness should be the same in both ears. As the sound moves along an imaginary curve from the first point to the second, the pan between the right and left channel also changes. This describes what we want to do. Figure 6.9 (right) shows a more abstract geometry, where the player and the facing direction are used to determine the relative angle to the sound.

The math and the programming is a bit complicated (See Appendix A for the relevant mathematics), but the basic steps for determining a pan value from the positions of the sound source and the listener are:

1. Calculate the angle between the facing point, the listener, and the source. In the code provided on the web site for this chapter, the function that does this is

```
float angle_3pt (x1, y1, x2,y2, x3, y3);
```

It is passed the coordinates of the three points that define the angle, with the listener being the center, and returns an angle in degrees.

2. Determine what side of the line is defined by the listener and the facing point the sound source is on. This is done using the line equation and plugging in the x,y values of the source: if the result is positive it's on one side, negative and it's on the other. The function that does this is called:

```
int whichSide (x1, y1, x2,y2, x3, y3);
```

It returns +1 if the source is on the left, -1 if on the right.

The product of these two values tells everything we need to know about the orientation of the listener with respect to the source. This value has to be mapped onto a pan value between -1 and +1; a **sourceAngle** value of -90 is a pan value of -1; a **sourceAngle** value of 0 is a pan of 0; **sourceAngle** value of 180 is a pan of 1; and **sourceAngle** value of 360 is a pan of 0 again. Values in between can be interpolated, but the use of a pre-computed table can eliminate repeated calculation (the computation is done many times a second).

The table of left and right channel volumes can be built by starting at 0 degrees, where both sides will be in balance (equal) with a value of 1. As the angle increases, the sound should move to the left channel until an angle of 90 degrees, where the left is at a medium volume (0.6) and the right is at minimum. Minimum should never be quite 0, as it is always possible to hear the sound from both ears. The table is indexed by angle and need not have a large number of elements. Breaking the angle between 0 and 90 degrees into 10 parts yields 20 volume levels for that range (10 per channel) and a total of 80 for the entire table. Interpolation is done to find the volume levels at any particular angle, assuming that the change in volume is linear. As an example:

Index	Angle	Left	Right		Index	Angle	Left	Right
0	0	0.6	0.6		11	99	0.96	0.15
1	9	0.64	0.55		12	108	0.92	0.20
2	18	0.68	0.50		13	117	0.88	0.25
3	27	0.72	0.45		14	126	0.84	0.30
4	36	0.76	0.40		15	135	0.80	0.35
5	45	0.80	0.35		16	144	0.76	0.40
6	54	0.84	0.30		17	153	0.72	0.45

Index	Angle	Left	Right		Index	Angle	Left	Right
7	63	0.88	0.25		18	162	0.68	0.50
8	72	0.92	0.20		19	171	0.64	0.55
9	81	0.96	0.15		20	180	0.6	0.6
10	90	1.0	0.1					

Note that the process reverses as we move from 90 degrees to 180 degrees (facing away). From 180 degrees back to 0, the left and right volume levels exchange places in the table, so the right channel becomes the loudest. The values change in the same ratio.

Index	Angle	Left	Right		Index	Angle	Left	Right
20	180	0.6	0.6		31	279	0.15	0.96
21	189	0.55	0.64		32	288	0.20	0.92
22	198	0.50	0.68		33	297	0.25	0.88
23	207	0.45	0.72		34	306	0.30	0.84
24	216	0.40	0.76		35	315	0.35	0.80
25	225	0.35	0.8		36	324	0.40	0.76
26	234	0.30	0.84		37	333	0.45	0.72
27	243	0.25	0.88		38	342	0.50	0.68
28	252	0.20	0.92		39	351	0.55	0.64
29	267	0.15	0.96		40	360	0.60	0.60
30	270	0.1	1.0					

Using the table involves first computing the angle between the source and the listener (using **angle_3pt()**). Make sure this angle is between 0 and 360 degrees, and change it into that range if need be. For example, if the angle is -40 degrees, then add 360 to give a positive angle of 320 within the range 0 to 360. Divide this angle by 9 to get the index into the table.

The program named **soundPositional.py** is an illustration of how this works. It displays a green circle, which is the source of a short jazz piano piece written for inclusion in this book by ***Nigel Gebert***. It also displays a white circle, indicating the position of the listener, and a blue line that shows the direction the listener is facing. Clicking the mouse in the window changes the listener's position, and pressing "a" or "d" rotates the listener to face a new direction. It is best

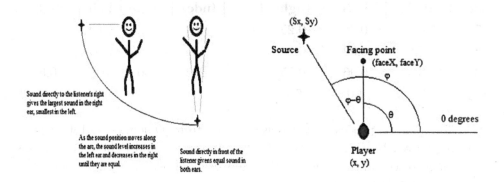

FIGURE 6.9 (left) The listener geometry of positional sound. The ear that faces the source most directly gets a larger fraction of the sound. (right) The more technical geometry of that situation. We need to determine the angle - and need to know what side (left or right) the source is on.

to listen to the sound displayed by this program using headphones. It clearly displays the sound positioned in 2D space as the graphic indicates. It also shows attenuation by distance.

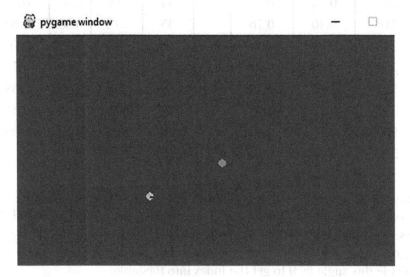

FIGURE 6.10 Demo program soundPositional.py.

EXERCISES

The following problems will exercise your knowledge of the material in this chapter, and they will sometimes require that you do more research before you are able to complete them.

1. You have 5 minutes of stereo recording, sampled at 11025 KHz and 16 bits per sample, uncompressed. How big is the file?

2. Given any mp3 file, Write a program that will read and play the file. Display the time played so far on the screen.

3. Implement a pan control for the solution to Exercise 2: when the mouse is on the left side of the screen, the sound will play only on the left speaker, and as the mouse is moved to the right, the sound is shared between the speakers and then moves right.

4. Create a simple keyboard that plays the basic notes starting at A (440 Hz). Each note will be played when an appropriate key is pressed: a, b, c, and so on. The note frequencies are: A (440) B(493.9) C(523.3) D(587.3) E(659.3) F(698.5) G(784.0).

5. Finish the sound recorder example. When the "r" key is pressed, begin recording, and when pressed again, stop recording. Save the recorded sound to a file when the "s" key is pressed. Indicate that recording is taking place with a message or other obvious sign.

6. Construct a visual/auditory demo of distance attenuation. Let the sound source be represented by a circle and the position of the listener be represented by a second circle, drawn at the current mouse position. The volume with which the sound will be played (any file you like) is to be a function of the distance between the two circles.

7. Construct build a sketch similar to that of exercise 6, but now have two sound sources indicated by two circles drawn a few hundred pixels apart. Both sounds are playing simultaneously, and the volume of each is a function of the distance between the mouse position and the circle representing that sound. You can "mix" the sound levels relative to each other by moving the mouse about.

8. (Sound editing) Locate a recording of a hockey game on the Internet or record the sound from your television. Using Audacity, GoldWave, or a similar sound editor, locate a clean instance of a puck hitting the boards. Extract this into its own file, and clean it up using whatever filters you choose so that you think it sounds good. Edit the beginning and end so that the sound clip plays immediately when the file is started. Save this file for the problems in the next chapter.

RESOURCES

Where to download Minim:
http://code.compartmental.net/tools/minim/
http://processing.org/reference/libraries/
Top-level *Minim* documentation:

http://code.compartmental.net/minim/javadoc/
Javasound Documentation:
*http://docs.oracle.com/javase/6/docs/technotes/guides/sound/programmer_guide/
    contents.html*
Minim audio signal documentation:
http://code.compartmental.net/minim/javadoc/ddf/minim/AudioSignal.html
    Audacity:
http://audacity.sourceforge.net/download/
    GoldWave:
http://www.goldwave.ca/
Free sound effects: *http://www.grsites.com/archive/sounds/*

REFERENCES

1. K. Collins. (2008). *Game Sound: An Introduction to the History, Theory, and Practice of Video Game Music and Sound Design.* Cambridge, MA: MIT Press.

2. C. Crawford. (1984). *The Art of Computer Game Design.* Berkeley, CA: McGraw-Hill/Osborne Media [out of print but available as an eBook or download at *http://www.vic20.vaxxine.com/wiki/images/9/96/Art_of_Game_Design.pdf*].

3. Johnny Friberg and Dan Gärdenfors. (2004). *Audio Games: New Perspectives on Game Audio.* ACE '04 Proceedings of the 2004 ACM SIGCHI International Conference on Advances in Computer Entertainment Technology.

4. 4. J. Heerema and J. R. Parker. (2013). *Music as a Game Controller.* IEEE International Games Innovation Conference 2013, Vancouver, BC, September 23–25.

5. Ben Long. *The Insiders Guide to Music and Sound for Mobile Games* [eBook].   *http://www.amazon.com/Insiders-Guide-Music-Sound-Mobile-ebook/dp/B0077QMKNU.*

6. J. R. Parker and John Heerema. (2008). "Audio Interaction in Computer Mediated Games." *International Journal of Computer Game Technology.* Pp 1-8

7. Richard Stevens and Dave Raybould. (2011). *The Game Audio Tutorial: A Practical Guide to Sound and Music for Interactive Games.* Burlington, MA: Focal Press (Elsevier).

8. Nigel Gebert (2018) **Keys for Jim,** musical composition. *https://soundcloud.com/seeking-satellites/keys-for-jim*

## CHAPTER 7

C2H6O Jet Boat Race

Having looked at the internal structure of a game, some basic graphics, and audio, we now have the tools at our disposal to build a complete 2D game. We began a game design document for the *Jet Boat Race* in Chapter 1, so let's complete that game as an example. One should never jump right into coding at the very onset of a project, because we don't know at that time where we are going. On the other hand, a degree of organization and discipline are needed, and iterative prototyping is a good way to structure a project in game development: create a playable game as soon as possible and then play it, taking note of deficiencies and exciting parts. Then use that information to make a second improved version and play it again, repeating until it is excellent or until you run out of time.

Game developers work from documents. The high concept was a sales device, not a working development document. The most important thing to have when building a game is the *game design document* (GDD), which is really a blueprint of what the proposed game will be. There are many forms of GDD but all have some basic things in common. It must describe the game in enough detail to implement it unambiguously. In most game development companies there is a team building a game, and that team will each work from the same GDD. It defines the goal.

So, we should now add to the GDD for *Jet Boat* and then stick to it when building the game, just as is done in real life. This is a simple game and the document will be short, but the GDD for a major game can be hundreds of pages long.

IMPLEMENTING THE GAME: PROTOTYPES

In traditional software development it is not uncommon to have a complete design document before starting the coding part of the project.

"Don't write any code until you have a spec" is what they teach at school. When developing a game, it can be very useful to have a malleable set of executable prototypes right at the very beginning. These are executable but not functional, if that makes sense; the game implemented is a primitive one that has only the main feature or two working. The purpose is manyfold, but first it allows the client, the person contracting for the game, to get a visual feel for what is being proposed. It's very well to say that we're building a *Mario Kart* variant in the style of a boat race, but it is quite another to see it on the screen.

Next, it gives us an idea of how complex the project is. Many developers have the ability, after decades of practice, to conceptualize this in their heads. However, seeing the game surface, the size of the parts, the speed of the objects, the colors—this can give new ideas, can identify places where things could get difficult, and generally helps get the project off to a good start. Later prototypes allow testing of new ideas, addressing efficiency matters, and trying out new art and music. Final versions are play tested so as to ensure that the final product is as much fun as possible.

Prototype 0

This first tentative version is mainly for an initial evaluation in-house. In this particular case the basic code only required about thirty minutes to create. It gives only a basic feel: the gameplay area is displayed,

Does this look like what we want? Is the window big enough? The boat, is it too small? There is no sound yet, no interaction.

This is pretty impressive, really. In *C* or even *Java* it would have been very difficult to create this in under an hour, and the number of lines of code would grow enormously. The things that *pygame* gives us are the things that are not interesting to code and that take a lot of time: window management, graphics, animation, and interaction.

Prototype 0 only displays the terrain and a boat. The terrain moves as the "wasd" keys are used, with the boat staying in the same relative position in the window. From this prototype, it was noticed that the background image was too small or the boats were too large (Figure 7.1). As a result, the background image was increased in size, and the rivers were widened.

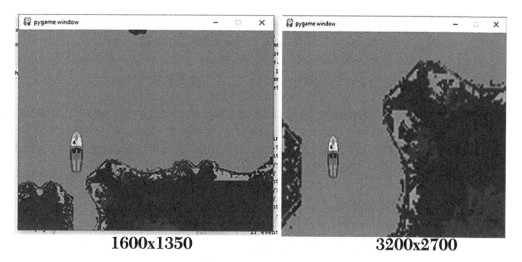

1600x1350   3200x2700

FIGURE 7.1 The first prototype game screen.

Prototype 1

This is the prototype that was first shown to the client. It has the suite of screens that will be used in the final game, if not the actual art that will be in place. It has boats that can be drawn and some intermediate graphics. This is a better example of how the game will look, and it can be given to someone outside of the development group for comments.

The art for the screens exists, even if it is preliminary. The buttons on the screens work, so transitions between screens can be illustrated. The game itself has not progressed much, but the entire system seems more finished. The amount of code needed to implement the screens and the buttons is significant: prototype 1 has about eleven times the amount of code as did the previous version. It took over eighteen hours to build, including the art. It turns out that the artwork and positioning buttons took the lion's share of the time involved.

Screens

According to the game design document, there are to be four different screens used in the game: a start screen, an options screen, a play screen, and an exit screen. The consequences for the code are that each screen corresponds to a different state in the display and enables distinct activities in the game code itself. The keyboard, for instance, has no effect on any of the screens except the play screen, where it controls the paddles. The mouse has no impact on the play screen, but it is used on the other screens to select an option or screen transition. And of course, quite different graphics are displayed in each screen.

A simple finite state machine can be used to keep track of things. The state is the screen being displayed, and the transitions are controlled by the mouse and the game play itself. The **start** screen takes you to the **options, end,** or **play** screen. From each of those you can return to the **start** screen.

So, the screens can be numbered: startState=0, optionState=1, playState=2, and endState =3. These are state numbers, and the function we use to draw the screen uses the state number to display the correct screen. Each screen will be displayed by a distinct function (**startScreen()**, **optionScreen()**, etc.) so the body of the main loop will look like this:

```
while True:
    for event in pygame.event.get():
        if screenState == STARTSTATE:
            startScreen (event)
        elif screenState == OPTIONSTATE:
            optionScreen (event)
        elif screenState == PLAYSTATE:
            playScreen (event)
        elif screenState == ENDSTATE:
            endScreen (event)
        else:
            print ("ERROR: Bad state in main loop.")
            exit()
    pygame.display.update()
```

In this way the state we're in is used to draw the screen each time a new frame is drawn. Screen transitions are done in the mouse handler **mouseReleased**, and the code looks very much like the previous code. If the mouse is clicked in a button on a screen, the value of **screenState** is changed.

Buttons

A "button" is not a thing that *pygame* gives us, so we have to implement it ourselves. It's really just a region, usually rectangular, that responds in a particular way to a mouse click. The button has a label that reflects its function, so we speak of "start" or "play" buttons. When the mouse is pressed or released, *pygame* calls a function named **mousePressed** or **mouseReleased** respectively, if those functions are defined. So, if **mouseReleased** is called and the coordinates of the mouse are within the bounds of the rectangle defined by the button, then the button was said to have been pressed.

The start screen has three buttons—"Options," "Play," and "Quit." The "Options" button has upper left window coordinates (300,250) and width and height (100, 30). The **Python/pygame** code that implements a button is best implemented as a class **button**, which can be used generally to create buttons on any game screen. This class has the description:

```
        class button:
    def __init__ (self, x, y, w, h):
        self.posx = x          # Coordinates of upper left
        self.posy = y
        self.width = w         # Width and height
        self.height = h
        self.text = ""         # Text displayed in the button
        self.size = 34         # Text size
        self.font = None       # Text font
        self.color = (255, 255, 0)     # Normal color (Yellow)
        self.col = self.color          # Current color
        self.armed = (255,0,0)         # Armed color
        self.family = None             # Font family

    def setText (self, t):
    def isArmed (self):
    def draw (self):
    def setfont(s):
    def textsize(self, n):
            def drawText(self, s, x, y):
    def setcolor(r, g=1000, b=1000, a=255):
    def setarmed(r, g=1000, b=1000, a=255):
```

Creating a button involves an initialization that mainly specifies the location and size of the rectangle the button contains. Creating a button is a matter of using the constructor. For the *Options* button on the start page:

```
    optionButton = button (300,250,100, 30)
```

This places the upper left corner of the button at (300, 250) and makes it 100 pixels wide by 30 pixels high. Next some text is placed in the button:

```
    optionButton.setText ("Options")
```

The default color for the text is **color** = (255,255,0), which is yellow. The color changes to the armed color of (255, 0,0) or red when the mouse is over the button region. Releasing the mouse button when the button is armed should cause the action indicated by the mouse to be performed.

Displaying the button is accomplished by calling the **draw** method of the button. The *Options* button is displayed only on the start screen, so in the function **startScreen** of the game program we place the code:

```
optionButton.draw()
if event.type == pygame.MOUSEBUTTONUP and optionButton.isArmed():
    screenState = OPTIONSTATE
    optionScreen(event)
    return
```

This draws the button and checks to see if the mouse button was released while the button was armed; if so, it changes the current screen to the *Options* screen. Then the *Options* screen is displayed. The method **isArmed** returns **True** if the button is currently armed. The **startScreen** function must also draw and activate the *Play* and *Quit* buttons. Setting the variable **screenState** to the value OPTIONSTATE means that the next time the main loop is executed, the *Options* screen will be redrawn.

Start Screen

When a player starts running the game, the *Start* screen appears. This screen is illustrated in Figure 7.2. It shows a graphic background and three "buttons" that allow transitions to the other screens. Many games and other interactive software that have buttons display when the button is *armed* (i.e., the mouse is over the button and a click will activate it) by changing the color or the font, or by showing the fact graphically somehow. In order to accomplish that, the buttons should be small images rather than simple text drawn on the screen. Each button has two images to represent it—one for

FIGURE 7.2 The Start screen. *https://commons.wikimedia.org/wiki/File:Shotover_Jet,_Jet_Boating_the_ Shotover_River_Canyons,_Queenstown,_New_Zealand.jpg.*

the normal button, and one for the armed button. In Figure 7.2, no button is armed.

When the mouse button is pressed while the coordinates of the cursor are inside of one of these buttons, a transition is made to another window simply by assigning a new value to the **screenState** variable.

Options Screen

When the player selects **Options**, the game makes the transition to the *Options* screen (**screenState == optionState**). This screen presents the player with the set of user selected parameters that can be chosen. This includes the ability to turn the sound off, but in other games there could be more options, such as a choice of a one- or two-player game, or the ability to select a home team or the avatar for the player.

Again, the buttons that allow a choice are small rectangular regions implemented as images. When the user clicks on the "Single Player" button, it is replaced by "2 Players" and back if clicked again, so that the current selection is visible on the screen at all times. This does not work in the case of the team selection, because all teams have to be visible to make a choice, so the selected team's logo will be the first one in the list. Clicking the button labeled "Back" takes the player back to the *Start* screen (**screenState == startState**).

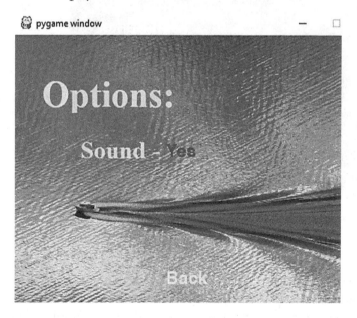

FIGURE 7.3 The Options screen. *https://commons.wikimedia.org/wiki/File:Fjordn_surface_wave_boat.jpg.*

When the sound is turned off, another flag is set (to false), which means that all calls to functions that play sounds are disabled. In this prototype there are no sounds yet, so no actual implementation details are available.

Play Screen

The *Play* screen is pretty much as shown in Figure 7.1. No visible change has been made to the play of the game as implemented even though the design has advanced, because the changes have taken place in the subsidiary aspects—art and screens for the most part. However, this is the screen that displays when the **Play** button is selected, where it was the only screen available in the initial prototype.

End Screen

The *End* screen is simply informative, giving game credits and contact information. A click anywhere in this window will terminate the game program (Figure 7.4).

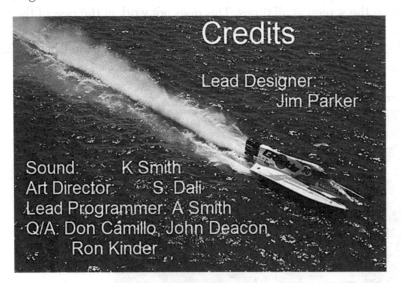

FIGURE 7.4 **The End screen, showing game credits.**

Prototype 2

After prototype 1 has been assessed and agreed to by the client or the design team, then next step is to develop the game features in detail. This means that the screen development is considered to be complete, and all changes will be seen on the game screen only. There are three major issues to be addressed in this prototype: user control, sound (including score), and the game AI.

Usually there will be intermediate benchmarks that the producer will insist on, and at those points in the development a play test or demo will be conducted to ensure that sufficient progress is being made. It is essential at all points in the development that a current working version of the game is always maintained, and that a demo of the more recent version can be conducted at any time.

The Play Screen

The play area is much larger than the viewing area, or the *display surface* in pygame terms. The play area is 3200 x 2700 pixels (see Figure 7.1) whereas the surface is 500 x 400. Think of the surface as a window into the complete play area. There are three important coordinate systems that have to be reconciled if we wish to only display the smaller window and always have the boat in the scene.

The first coordinate system involves the play area, the 3200 x 2700 pixel background image. The window and the boats will all have (x,y) coordinates within this area. Specifically, the player's boat will be at coordinate (bx, by). Simplistically this would seem to solve all of the other problems: the upper left corner of the viewing area is (x,y) = (bx-250, by-200) because the boat should be centered in this area. The background image must be translated by (-x,-y) so that the viewing area is drawn properly. That is, the code would be:

```
display.blit(background, (-x, -y))
```

where **display** is the display surface and **background** is the background image. Where is the boat drawn in this example? It's supposed to be in the center of the viewing area, or at (250, 200) in coordinates relative to that system. That is in ideal circumstances.

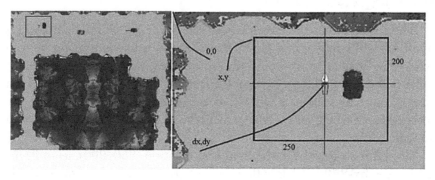

FIGURE 7.5 (Left) The entire playing area (terrain) showing the size of the display area. (Right) Close-up of the display area.

The values of x and y should never become smaller than zero; otherwise, there will be parts of the display area that do not have a terrain image covering them. These will be displayed in a background color, and it looks bad. It takes away from the fantasy of the game. There is a similar problem at the right side and bottom of the play area. The display is 500 pixels wide, so x must not be larger than 3200 – 500, or 2700; otherwise, it will exhaust the background image. In the y direction the limit is 2700 – 400 = 2300.

The code that does this is:

```
# (bx,by) are the game space coordinates of the boat
x = bx - 250 # Upper left x of window
if x<0: # Can't be less that 0
    x = 0
elif x > 2700: # Can't be larger than 2700
    x = 2699

y = by-200 # Upper left Y of window
if y < 0: # Again, must be positive
    y = 0
elif y > 2300: # y can't be larger than 2300
    y = 2299

xx = 250      # Boat will be draw at screen (250,200)
yy = 200      # Which is the center of the screen

# Draw terrain image, shifted so that upper left is at (x,y)
display.blit(background, (-x, -y))

# Draw the boat at (xx,yy) at approximately its centre
display.blit (pygame.transform.rotate(boat2, angle),
              (xx-boat2.get_width()/2, yy-
boat2.get_height()/2) )
```

The result is that the player's boat can never get closer than 250 pixels to a left or right boundary, or closer than 200 pixels to the top and bottom. This works fine if the terrain would also forbid this, that is, if there are no water areas in those boundary regions of the terrain. That's not true here. That means that in some cases the boat will either not be able to reach all of the reasonable locations on the map, or we'll have to modify the positioning of the boat in some specific cases.

Consider a case where the boat is at location (250, 200), as in Figure 7.6. Here, **x = bx-250**, which is 0. The background can't be drawn any further to the right, or down for that matter. Allowing the boat to be drawn in the correction position means repositioning it within the window. If it moves one more pixel to the left, the value of x must stay at 250, **bx** decreases by 1, and so the boat must be redrawn one pixel to the left (smaller x) within the window. The variable **xx** would be 250 – 1. Doing it again draws the boat at 250 – 2, and so on. In general, it is drawn at **250 –- dx** for **dx** equal to the number of pixels smaller **bx** is than 250, or in other words, **dx = 250-bx**. There is a global limit that **bx** can never be smaller than 0; otherwise, it would vanish off of the screen. The same scheme works for the y coordinate.

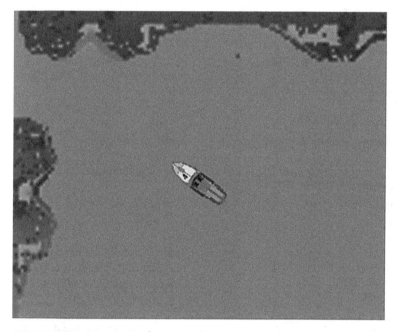

FIGURE 7.6 The boat cannot move any further to the upper left in this case because it is at (250,200).

As the boat moves to the right, the x coordinates increase until a value of 2700 is reached. This is the maximum value for **x**, since it is one window width to the left of the right edge, or 3200 – 500. In the y direction the maximum value is 2300. When **x** is 2700, because **x = bx-250**, it means that **bx** must be 2950. The boat will now move within the window to the right by 1 pixel each time bx increases, or **dx = 2900 – bx**. Similarly for y, **dy = 2500 – by** after **y** becomes greater than 2300.

Finally, a check is made to ensure that **(bx,by)** is within the play area. All of this can be encompassed within a function **move()**:

```
def move ():
    global speed, angle, x, y, xx, yy,

        bx, by, background, boat2
    speed = speed - 0.001  # Slow down
    if speed < 0:# Can't move backward
        speed = 0
        dx = 0
        dy = 0
    else:
        dx = speed * math.cos(math.radi-
ans(angle))
        dy = -speed * math.sin(math.radi-
ans(angle))

    bx = bx + dx   # New boat position

            # on map is(bx,by)
    if bx>3200:   # Keep the boat

            # on the play area
        bx = 3199
        speed = 0
    elif bx<0:
        bx = 1
        speed = 0
    by = by + dy
    if by>2700:
        by = 2699
        speed = 0
    elif by<0:
        by = 1

    speed = 0

    dx = 0
    dy = 0

    x = bx - 250    # Boat is far left.
    if x<0:
        x = 0
        dx = 250-bx # dx is offset from

            # centre of window
    elif x > 2700:   # 3200 - 500 is 2700
        x = 2700
        dx = 2950-bx
    y = by-200
    if y < 0:
        y = 0
        dy = 200-by
    elif y>2300:
        y = 2300
        dy = 2500-by

    xx = 250-dx
    yy = 200-dy

    display.blit(background, (-x, -y))
    display.blit (pygame.transform.
    rotate  (boat2, angle),
        (xx - boat2.get_width() / 2,

        yy - boat2.get_height() / 2) )
```

This will deal with any boat position specified by (bx, by). To generalize this for use with multiple boats, we can create two lists, boats_x and boats_y, that hold the coordinates of all boats, and always have the player's boat as the zero index. That means that bx = boats_x[0]. Now we'll look at how that position is controlled by the user.

User Control

User control involves making the software connection between the key presses and the position of the boat. It appears to be a simple matter, but there are important issues to resolve. Specifically: what do key presses mean, how fast can the boat move, and how quickly can it accelerate?

The motion is implemented using the event **pygame.KEYDOWN**. Pressing the "w" key, for instance, begins moving the user's boat forward, essentially increasing speed; the "s" key will slow the boat, but will not move it backward. The direction that amounts to *forward* is indicated by an angle, where 0 degrees is increasing x. Pressing the "a" key will increase the angle by 5 degrees, and pressing the "d" key will decrease the angle by the same amount.

Program control of the player's boat uses two variables: **speed** and **angle**. Each time the "w" key is pressed, the speed increases up to a limit, and when "s" is pressed it decreases. If the boat is moving and no key is being pressed, the boat will slow down and stop due to friction with the water. Thus:

```
if event.type == pygame.KEYDOWN:
    k = pygame.key.get_pressed()
    if k[pygame.K_s]:
        speeds[0] = speeds[0] - .1
    if k[pygame.K_w]:
        speeds[0] = speeds[0] + .1

Why not use:
if event.key == pygame.K_s:
                speed = speed - .1
```

because the player may wish to hold down the "w" and the "a" keys at the same time. The **get_pressed** method returns all of the keys that are being pressed.

The variable angle refers to the boat's direction of travel. Zero degrees is to the right, 90 degrees is up, and so on. Each time the "a" key is pressed, the angle increases by 5 degrees, and when the "d" key is pressed, the angle decreases by 5 degrees. This means that "a" rotates the boat counterclockwise. This angle-speed control scheme is typical of driving games, where "forward" always means "in the direction you are facing," and player control involves changing the facing direction and the speed of the avatar. The control of the angle is accomplished by:

```
if k[pygame.K_a]:
    angles[0] = angles[0] + 5
if k[pygame.K_d]:
    angles[0] = angles[0] - 5
```

Given the speed and the angle, a change is position is computed. The boat is now at **(bx, by)**. Its change in position is going to be **(dx, dy)**, so that the new position is simply **(bx+dx, by+dy)**. Some simple trigonometry gives the answer:

```
dx = speed * math.cos(math.radians(angle))
dy = -speed * math.sin(math.radians(angle))
```

The variable **dy** has a sign reversal because "up" is the -y direction, unlike on a mathematical coordinate axis. Displaying the boat in its rotated orientation uses the function **pygame.transform.rotate(boat, angle)**, where **boat** is an image of the boat pointing right (zero degrees). Hence the code for displaying the boat could be:

```
display.blit (pygame.transform.rotate(boat2, angle),
    (xx-boat2.get_width()/2, yy-boat2.get_height()/2) )
```

The Boat Class

There will be three boats in this game: the player's boat and two NPCs. It seemed clear from the outset that a boat should be implemented as a class, but until the user control and AI sections were designed, the structure of that class was fuzzy. Now it is fairly obvious. All boats, including the player's boat, have the same structure.

First, the important parameters of the boat upon creation are: the (x,y) position, the speed, and the course or angle. Variables local to each boat will include: the sound to be played for the engine, the current volume for the engine sound, the sprite to be drawn to represent this boat, the target speed, the target angle (i.e., when the boat changes course, these define the endpoint), the current destination on the map, and a name for the boat for debugging purposes.

```
class npc :
    def __init__(self, x, y, sprite, speed, angle):
        self.x = x
        self.y = y
        self.speed = speed
        self.angle = angle
        self.index = 1
        self.sound = False      # Engine sound.
        self.volume = 0
        self.targetSpeed = 0    # How fast does the boat want to
go?
        self.targetAngle = 90   # What is the course setting?
```

```
self.sprite = sprite    # The image of the boat
self.wpt = None         # Next waypoint
self.name = "NPC 1"</CODE>
```

The class has the following methods at this point in its development:

```
def setSpeed (self, s):     # Change the speed to s
def setCourse (self, a):    # Change the course (angle) to a
def setWaypoint (self, w):  # Change the current waypoint to w
                            # (see below - AI section
def setName (self, s):      # Change the name of the boat to s
def adjustAngle (self): # Make another step towards the target
angle
def adjustSpeed (self): # Make another step towards the target
speed
def distance (self, a, b):  # Distance between two points
def nextStep(self):         # Make one step: move the boat and
draw.
```

Note that the code written previously uses an array **speeds[i]**, **angles[i]**, and so on. Using a class this will be **boats[i].angle** and **boats[i]].speed**, where boats is a tuple of all boats. The item **boats[0]** is the player's boat. Where **bx** and **by** were used, the values are now **boats[0].x** and **boats[0].y**.

After each iteration of the game loop, the method **nextStep** for each boat is called. It moves the boat, and if a change of direction or speed has been called for, then a step is made to achieve that goal. Each change is broken into individual steps so that a boat cannot accelerate too quickly. Speed, for instance, can increase by 0.1 units per iteration and the angle by 1 degree. Changing the angle by 20 degrees will thus need 20 steps, as implemented by **adjustAngle**, which is called by **nextStep** if needed.

The boat class will be modified further as required, to add sound and animations and other new features.

Artificial Intelligence

The artificial intelligence portion of this game determines collisions and controls the non-player boats in a single player game.

Collisions

There are only two kinds of collision that can happen in this game so far, and both can be determined using simple geometry rather than needing more complex collision-detection methods. The boat can collide with the shore, which is the effective boundary of the game, or the boat can collide with a second boat.

Collisions with the shore involve an irregular collision surface that follows the shoreline, which can be difficult to deal with. One way to deal with this is to create a set of boundaries as connected line segments that follow the shorelines, beyond which the bounding box of any boat cannot pass through any of these line segments and should in fact bounce off of them. This is a very general solution, but it is pretty complex and may take a lot of time. For this game it should be sufficient to use the background to determine whether the boat is grounding or not.

If the boat is in the water, then the color beneath it will be blue; that is, the color on the terrain map at the boat location will be blue. The simple way to detect grounding is to see if the color at the front of the boat and on each side is the color of water. If so, no grounding has taken place; otherwise, it has. A function **shoreCollide** will do the work and will return True or False as the boat is grounded or not. It works as follows: obtain the the pixel (color) value at the four points that define the bounding box for the boat. Water has a red component of 33. If any of the three sampled points does not, then the boat has collided with something that is not water.

The method **nextStep** in the NPC class updates the screen position of the bounding box at each game step. These are stored in four tuples: **ul, ur, ll,** and **lr**. This is the object oriented bounding box, of course, and it is exactly what is needed for the purpose.

The **shoreCollide** function takes one parameter, the index of the boat being tested. It could have been a part of the NPC class, in which case the index parameter would not be needed. The first step is to convert the screen coordinates of the bounding box into terrain coordinates (function **screen_to_terrain**).

Now we use the corners of the box to retrieve the terrain pixel at those points. The red component must be 33 or that point is over a shore pixel. The function sets a corresponding Boolean variable to **True** each time such a pixel is found, and the function returns **True** if any of those variables are true. Otherwise, it returns **False**.

This seems like more work than needed, but it would be possible to define a new target angle for the boat knowing which of the four corners is grounded. The game does not do this right now, but it is on a list of improvements. The following code simply returns as soon as it becomes aware of any grounded point:

```python
def shoreCollide (i):
    global background
    boat = boats[i]
    ulx, uly = screen_to_terrain (boat.ul)
```

```
    lrx, lry = screen_to_terrain (boat.lr)
    urx, ury = screen_to_terrain (boat.ur)
    llx, lly = screen_to_terrain (boat.ll)

    pygame.draw.line(display, (0, 255, 0), (boat.ul[0], boat.
ul[1]),
                                          (boat.ur[0], boat.
ur[1]), 3)
    pygame.draw.line(display, (255, 0, 0), (boat.ur[0], boat.
ur[1]),
                                          (boat.lr[0], boat.
lr[1]), 3)

    c = background.get_at( (int(ulx), int(uly)) )
    if c[0] != 33:
        return True
    c = background.get_at( (int(llx), int(lly)) )
    if c[0] != 33:
        return True
    c = background.get_at( (int(urx), int(ury)) )
    if c[0] != 33:
        return True
    c = background.get_at( (int(lrx), int(lry)) )
    if c[0] != 33:
        return True
    return False
```

Note that two lines are drawn by this function. These correspond to the upper edge of the bounding box, drawn in green, and the right edge, which is

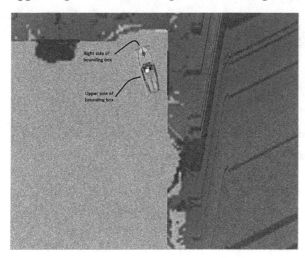

FIGURE 7.7 The upper edge of the bounding box is the long line on the left side of the boat (Green in the color image) and the right edge of the box is the short line near the front of the boat (Red in the color image).

drawn as red. It is interesting to see this because the boat image in the original file shows the boat facing right. This means that the left side of the boat is really the upper edge of the bounding box. This is clear from a screen capture of the boat in the test program.

Navigation

In this game there will be two other boats against which the player can race. If the game is to be entertaining, these boats have to put up a challenge to the player. They can't simply wander the lake aimlessly but must complete the same route as the player does, avoid the shore and other boats, and cross the finish line. Also, because the point of an NPC is to be entertaining, the NPC boats should not be so good that they always win. The player must have a chance.

The NPCs will use waypoint navigation, as explained in Chapter 5. This means building a system of waypoints and associated data manually, a time-consuming process. Only some of this process will be explained, because much of it is repetitive.

Boat 1, as shown in Figure 7.8, has 15 waypoints. Each specifies the location of the next waypoint and gives a speed and direction to maintain. The direction can change, of course, based on collisions and avoiding obstacles.

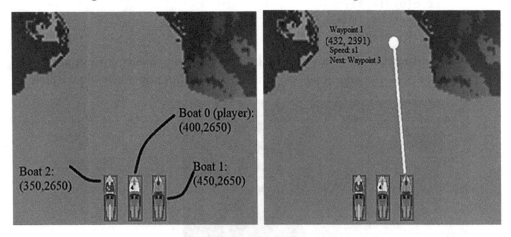

FIGURE 7.8 The initial positions of all boats, and the first waypoint.

Initially, boat 1 is destined for waypoint 1. When it arrives, it will be assigned waypoint 3 and a new speed. Boat 1 uses the odd-numbered waypoints only, and boat 2 uses the even-numbered ones. If a boat is knocked off course, it will try to reach its assigned waypoint. The waypoint paths assigned to boat 1 are shown in Figure 7.8.

A boat can change course (facing angle) by two means. First, a boat tries to avoid other boats. It will change angle to avoid either of the other two. In addition, if a boat collides with the shore, it will change angle again so as to get back on track.

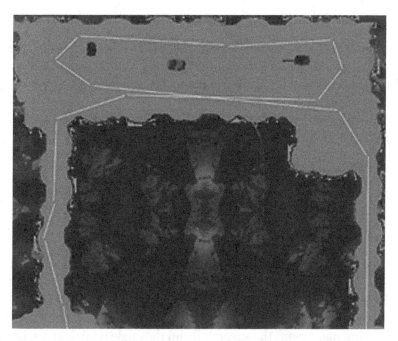

FIGURE 7.9 The course followed by a boat, connecting the waypoints.

Let's examine this navigation issue in a very practical and detailed manner.

Waypoints

As a data structure, a waypoint is a *tuple* holding the data needed to complete the next phase of the boat's journey. When the boat arrives at a waypoint, as indicated by the distance of the boat to the waypoint being sufficiently small, then the new waypoint becomes the next one. Each post has a next waypoint, which is an intermediate destination. Every waypoint holds the following data:

Coordinates of this waypoint (x,y).
The number (index) of the next waypoint.
The speed that the boat should try to maintain along this path.

In Python this *could* be a tuple:

```
(x, y, index, speed)
```

Each boat steers to the coordinates **(x,y)** of the next waypoint, whose angle is simple to calculate. The course (angle) to the next waypoint is a good start, and it is stored in the waypoint itself. Two consecutive waypoints define a course, and if nothing interferes it is all that's needed. The coordinates of the next waypoint can be used in the case where the boat collides with something or avoids another boat.

The waypoint data was created by using the terrain map and plotting courses on it as line segments, with each segment starting and ending at a waypoint. These data are stored in a file named ***params.txt***, which the program reads at the beginning of the game.

Within the program, a waypoint is implemented as a small class so as to avoid the use of a list of tuples, something some people find awkward:

```python
class waypoint:
        def __init__ (self, x, y, index, speed):
        self.posx = x
        self.posy = y
        self.index = index
        self.speed = speed
```

The collection of all waypoints is a tuple **waypoints** consisting of these class objects. Now consider an NPC boat as it executes from the start to the end of the race. Initially its waypoint is #1 if we're using boat 1. When the game begins this boat must be given a course (angle) that will take it to waypoint 1 at (432, 2391). When the race begins the speed is 0 and the angle is 90 degrees, because that is its initial state. The game loop calls the **move** function, which moves the player's bot and then ultimately calls **otherBoats**, which moves the NPC boats. It first calls the **nextStep** method of the **NPC** class, the one that moves the NPCs, and then draws the boats in their new locations. The **nextStep** function is the focus here.

A waypoint is a destination and specifies a speed. The method **nextStep** first adjusts its speed to account for friction. Then it determines what the new (x,y) position on the terrain will be, given its speed and course, and moves the boat to that location. It checks for a shore collision, as was done with the player's boat.

Now it checks to see if it has reached the waypoint. If so, it changes the target to the next waypoint in the path. The it adjusts the speed (**adjustSpeed**) and its course (**adjustAngle**) to make sure it is traveling at the correct speed and course for the waypoint. It steers to the next waypoint using the code:

```python
self.targetAngle = math.degrees (math.atan2
   (self.wpt.posy-self.y, self.x-self.wpt.posx) + math.pi)
```

It then draws the boat if it is located within the window.

Avoiding a Boat

Detecting collisions between boats is more critical, because such an event will destroy both boats. A broad phase detection could be done using enclosing circles. The boats are much longer than they are wide, though, and this will be misleading much of the time. Using bounding boxes is better, but they would have to be aligned with the axes of the boats.

The boat images are 84 x 26 pixels, and the base image has the boat facing right (0 degrees). Finding an axis-oriented bounding box starts with the bounding box of the base image, which consists of four points in the terrain image coordinate system. Now rotate these points by the same angle as the boat is facing. A function **rotate** is given that does this for a point and returns a new point. The rotation should be done about the center of the boat. Now convert these points from the terrain system to the screen coordinate system, for which a function **terrain_to_screen** has been provided. The bounding box is defined by the original four bounding box points, rotated and converted in this way.

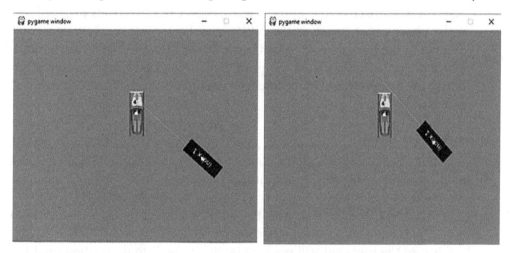

FIGURE 7.10 The ray projected by the black boat intersects the bounding box of the other (left) causing it to change course to avoid it, in this instance by rotating clockwise.

Two boats have collided if the ray projected by one of the boats intersects with the bounding box of the other. In Figure 7.10, the simulated black boat is showing the ray that is used to determine a potential collision, which is represented by the green line. The potential collision results in a movement by the black boat away from the other.

```
def avoid (self, i, ddx, ddy):
  self.state = self.AVOID
  zangle = math.degrees(math.atan2(ddy-self.y, ddx-self.x)-
       math.radians(180.0))
  if zangle < 0:
    zangle = zangle + 360.0
  elif zangle > 350:
    zangle = zangle - 360

  if self.angle < zangle*1.3:
    self.angle = self.angle + 1
  else:
    self.angle = self.angle - 1
  return
```

The variable **zangle** is the angle between the two boats. It is used to determine the direction in which the avoiding boat will turn. Also note that the boat that has decided to avoid the other is in a new state, **AVOID**. A boat in this state does not change its angle or speed in the usual way but lets the **avoid** function determine its course.

It is to be expected that in many cases one of the two boats involved will be the player's boat, because the NPCs have been given courses that avoid collisions in the first place. This particular strategy has the NPCs take a rather passive stance, and the player can push them around by being aggressive. Of course, this presents the risk of forcing a collision if the NPC cannot respond properly.

Colliding with the Shore

When a boat collides with the shore it must try to escape. Moving on land should not be possible. Its actions must be reasonable based on the situation in a real boat race.

So, if an NPC boat collides with the shore, it stops abruptly and must try to escape. This amounts to yet another state, which will be called **COLLIDED**. In this case the waypoint will cease to be the immediate destination until the boat steers away from the shore. The only way that an NPC can ground is if another boat pushes it, because in most cases it will move from waypoint to waypoint.

There are many ways the boat could try to escape, but an obvious one is to back up a bit and then turn. Then it will resume course. If it hits the shore again, it will repeat the process. The shoreline has been designed so that it should not be possible to get trapped in a loop while trying this maneuver. While in the

COLLIDED state, the boat will first attempt to back up. A count will be kept of the number of steps the boat has made doing this, and after a fixed number (20 in this game), it will then try to turn. Again, 20 steps are performed, and each one turns the boat by 2 degrees. At this point the boat attempts to resume course to the current waypoint.

The method that does this is called **escape** and looks like this:

```
def escape (self):
    if self.estate < 20:            # Back up
        ddx = self.speed * math.cos(math.radians(self.angle))
        ddy = -self.speed * math.sin(math.radians(self.angle))
        self.x -= ddx*2
        self.y -= ddy*2
    elif self.estate < 40:     # Change the angle by 2 degrees
            self.angle += 2.0
    else:                          # 40 steps. Exit COLLIDED state
        self.state = self.NORMAL
        self.speed = 1
    self.estate = self.estate + 1  #estate is the current
step number
```

There are other ways to accomplish this that take more effort but could be better:

1. Another set of waypoints running down the center of the track and closely spaced to be used as targets, and a nearby one would be selected when the boat grounded.

2. The path just followed could be stored, and the boat could back away along that path when it hits the shore.

3. The distance to the center of the water area for each point could be found, and the boat could move toward that point.

Sound

Now that the user control system is being implemented, it makes sense to assign audio events to events in the game. There are only a few audio events in this game, but it is important to give them sensible sound effects, ones that a boat racing fan would recognize. In particular:

-   There will be the sound of the boat engine(s) whenever the engine is running, that is to say, when the boat is moving in the forward direction.

- There could be sound effects of bounces against the shore.
- There will be sound effects of explosions when boats are destroyed.
- There is a gun that indicates the start of the game, and one that indicates the end.
- There could be extra audience sounds, like cheers, which can be played at random.

Engine Sounds

Some time was spent in Chapter 6 showing how engine sounds could be created using Audacity. The sounds created in this way have been saved as mp3 files named *engineBoat1.mp3* through *engineBoat5.mp3*. Each engine sound is distinct, and each should be assigned to a different boat in the game. The sound should play as long as the associated boat is under power. For example, the player's engine should play as long as the "w" key is pressed.

A simple modification to the previous control code will do this. Add a global variable **engine_on** that has the obvious meaning. Now if any of the "a," "s," "d," or "w" keys are pressed, a local variable **eon** will be set to **True**, indicating that the player wants to move the boat (turn the engine on). If it is already on, no problem. Otherwise, turn it on (start the sound):

```
if eon and not engine_on:
    start_engine()
elif not eon and engine_on:
    stop_engine()
```

Each check of the keys that are depressed now looks like this:

```
if k[pygame.K_s]:
    speeds[0] = speeds[0] - .1
    eon = True
```

Each time through the event loop, the variable **eon** is first set to **False** so that if the player releases the keys, the engine will shut off. The functions that do the work are:

def start_engine():
  global engine_on,sound_on,engine1
  engine1.play(1000)
  engine_on = **True**
	def stop_engine ():
	  global engine_on,sound_
	  on,engine1
	  engine1.stop()
	  engine_on = **False**

There are other sounds, and those will be implemented in more detail after we know more about animation and when more of the game rules have been implemented.

Collisions and Explosions

When a boat collides with another boat, an explosion takes place. The sound of the explosion has been created using Audacity, and there are three variants: *expl00.mp3*, *expl01.mp3*, and *expl02.mp3*. One of these should be selected at random and played when an explosion takes place. This reduces the repetitive nature of sound. The same event rarely sounds exactly the same twice in real life, but frequently a game uses only one sound file for a particular event. One should always have multiple sounds for any event that occurs frequently.

Starting Gun

This is only used at the beginning of the game, so there is only one file: *start.mp3*. This is played when all of the NPC boats are allowed to begin their motion, and it allows the player to manipulate their boat. It was created by recording a pencil pounding on a desk and extending the duration and adding a reverb. It would be better to record an actual gunshot or use a pre-recorded sound effect.

Finish

There is a sound that plays when the winning boat passes the finish line. This sound is *finish.mp3*.

TESTING

When testing any game, as with testing many human-built objects, there are really two aspects to be considered. The first is "does this object meet the criteria for being functional?" The second can be expressed as "is this object a good example of its type?" or in the words of a game designer, "is it art?" The former kind of testing for a game is often just called *game testing*, but it is largely about testing the software that implements the game. The latter is called *playtesting*, and it is intended to answer the question "is it fun?"

Software testing is a tedious process. The program is executed again and again in an attempt to execute every line of code and make certain that it executes as designed. Code is tested against the design document and against a set of standards. The design document answers questions about what the game should do at any particular point. The standards indicate correctness criteria:

does this code do the correct thing when a file is not found or when converting a real to an integer? Does it divide by zero? Are there any off by one errors in the loops? These are more technical questions, and ones that arise in any software.

Game testing is performed by the Q/A (Quality assurance) department in some development companies, and sometimes by people outside of the company hired as testers. You might think that being hired to play computer games is a great job, but it is mostly a grind. The tester must play through the game quite analytically, and when a problem is found, the nature of that problem must be carefully defined. The precise circumstances of the error have to be found by trial and error and given to the developer for correction. Then, after being fixed, the tester must make certain that the error is in fact gone, and that the process of correcting it did not create any new problems.

Playtesting is a different process. It is like other kinds of product testing, where people are hired to try the product and are then asked questions. In game testing, players are recruited to play the game. They are asked questions before play to characterize their demographic identity, they play the game, and they are later asked questions about it. Players are often recorded on video while playing to identify emotional reactions. All of the data collected goes to answer questions about whether the game is enjoyable, where it is fun, and where it is not. Iterations of this testing can be done, making design changes between each test, involving six to twelve people each time.

Beta testing is the final stage. Unlike beta testing for software systems, a game continues to have the code testing as something of a distinct process from that of the game play. The beta test involves a release of the game to the public, or a subset of the public, so many people can play it. They will find problems in the code if any remain, but the key element is play. Many people are playing and report on their experience. Final tweaking can be done before the ultimate release of the game, which we hope will be the best we can do.

Playtesting can and should be done from the early stages of development, from the first playable if possible. It can prevent the game from going too far in the wrong direction, which would cost a lot of time and money to fix. It is easier to fix a game in the early stages, of course.

Here's how you do it. First, select a small group of players to test your game. They must not be selected from the developer group or their families. The best choice is a group selected from the game's target group. Five or six is sufficient.

The testers are given instructions: they are to play the game according to the rules that are provided for a fixed time, usually fifteen or twenty minutes. Then they are allowed to proceed. The testers are observed carefully during the test to see what that are doing, which paths they select, where they have difficulty, and where they seem to be having fun. The observers should not be on the actual development team. It's common to record these sessions on video, and the team can watch those, but developers tend to have opinions and the players should not be exposed to them.

It is of special interest where they are looking on the screen and when they make any verbal utterance. Verbalization is an indication of an extreme reaction, one way or another. Growling and cursing are signs of frustration, whereas cheering and laughing are signs of fun. What is happening when utterances are made is very important.

The observers should not offer assistance unless asked for help. Obviously, any assistance given should be noted so that the game or the rules can be modified to fix the problem. Assistance must be limited to the questions asked; the observers should never volunteer information. Indeed, sometimes one should repeat the question back to the player. For example:

Player: How do I fire this gun?
Observer: How do you think you should fire the gun?

This not only indicates a possible problem but also suggests a solution. One should not do this *too* often or it will become irritating.

After the play session is complete, the players should rest and sometimes fill out a questionnaire. Some of these are long, some are brief, but one of the best is found on Schell Games' web site (*https://www.schellgames.com/blog/insights/the-definitive-guide-to-playtest-questions*):

1. What was the most frustrating moment or aspect of what you just played?
2. What was your favorite moment or aspect of what you just played?
3. Was there anything you wanted to do that you couldn't?
4. If you had a magic wand to wave, and you could change, add, or remove anything from the experience, what would it be?
5. What were you doing in the experience?
6. How would you describe this game to your friends and family?

This information is used to give feedback to the developers about what should be changed, and why. Such a test can be done at almost any phase of development once some of the basic mechanics are working. There is a tendency to wait until the art is in place, but that could be a mistake. It is critical to catch problems while they are still easy to fix.

There is a lot more to say about play testing, entire volumes in fact, but these are the key items.

SUMMARY

In this chapter, we almost finish the design and implementation of the boat race game. The player's boat moves under player control, NPC boats follow pre-defined paths, and collisions are identified.

EXERCISES

1. Select a web-based game of your choice and document the following aspects:
    a.   Identify all screens and transitions.
    b.   Characterize all interface actions (key presses and mouse clicks).
    c.   Does the game possess internal states? Identify them.
2. Discuss the pros and cons of using the mouse as an interaction mechanism instead of keys on the keyboard.
3. There are multiple sound effect files for many of the effects used in the game, and as described the system chooses one at random every time a sound is needed. This could result in the same sound being played many times in a row, defeating the purpose. Devise a scheme that makes it impossible for the same sound to be played twice in a row. Implement that scheme.
4. Create or download a sound effect that represents a typical audience sound, such as clapping, pounding, or a horn blowing. Edit the sound so that it is acceptable in the context of the game (i.e., adjust the pitch or duration, reduce noise). Then have this sound played at random moments during game play.
5. Write a short voiceover to begin the race—something like "Racers prepare for the start." Record using any equipment available, such as a VOIP microphone; then add ambiance such as echo. Play this at the beginning of the race.

RESOURCES

Sound Effects

The sounds from SoundBible.com *(http://soundbible.com/about.php)* that are labeled "public domain" or "creative commons" can be used without fee in games. Attribution should be given.

Some of the sound effects were downloaded from freesfx.co.uk or are based on those effects (*http://www.freesfx.co.uk*).

Sound Editing

Audacity – This is freely downloadable editing software with a high degree of functionality. If saving as an MP3 is needed, you'll have to download the LAME MP3 encoder and install it (*http://audacity.sourceforge.net/*).

Goldwave – Freely downloadable sound editor with a large set of audio formats in which sounds can be saved (*http://www.goldwave.com/*).

LAME – MP3 encoding software. (*http://lame.sourceforge.net/*).

Graphics Editing

Paint – Comes with Windows and is a highly underestimated tool for putting together 2D images.

LView – An image editor that is a valuable addition to Paint. It is especially useful for making backgrounds in GIF images transparent. Free download, but you should send them money if you like it (*http://www.lview.com/*).

REFERENCES

1. Fernando Bevilacqua. (2013). *Understanding Steering Behaviors: Collision Avoidance. https://gamedevelopment.tutsplus.com/tutorials/understanding-steering-behaviors-collision-avoidance--gamedev-7777.*

2. Jeremy Gibson Bond. (2014). *Introduction to Game Design, Prototyping, and Development.* Addison-Wesley Professional.

3. Bryce Boe. (2006). *Line Segment Intersection Algorithm. http://bryceboe.com/2006/10/23/line-segment-intersection-algorithm/.*

4. Tracy Fullerton, Chris Swain, and Steven Hoffman. (2004). *Game Design Workshop: Designing, Prototyping, & Playtesting Games.* CMP Books, San Francisco.

5. Zack Hiwiller. (2015). *Players Making Decisions: Game Design Essentials and the Art of Understanding Your Players.* New Riders.

6. Shawn Patton. (2017). *The Definitive Guide to Playtest Questions. https://www.schellgames.com/blog/insights/the-definitive-guide-to-playtest-questions.*

## CHAPTER 8

ANIMATION

Animation is a discrete art by necessity. There is no technology that permits the recording of the motion of real-world objects precisely; such motion is continuous. In between two positions of a moving object there is always another position, and recording all of them is impossible. Video recordings capture still pictures every 1/30 of a second, and when these are played back at the same speed, they look good enough to seem like they are moving. It is an illusion caused by *persistence of vision*. The human eye takes some time to process an image and keeps it for a fraction of a second while processing it. Still images displayed fast enough can give the appearance of motion because our eye-brain combination can't process the images any faster than that in real life.

Animation uses drawings, human or computer generated, to simulate a video scene. The objects in an animation don't exist except as renderings. Consecutive images in an animation, or *frames*, show motion as a change in position, size, and/or orientation of the drawn objects. With its main loop running at 30 frames per second, *Pygame* could have been designed specifically to display animations. A programmer could simply display the next frame in sequence each time it is called, a simple program of about two dozen lines including the reading of the image files. This program is **Animation01. py** on the accompanying disc. It reads eleven files of a person walking. It displays them in intervals of 1/10 of a second and then starts over again. The essential code is:

```
i = 0
while True:
    clock.tick(10)                    # Make sure 1/30 second has passed
    display.fill((100, 100, 100))     # Clear the screen
    display.blit(images[i], (0, 0))   # Write current frame
(image) to screen
    i = (i+1)%11                       # Index for the next frame
    pygame.display.update()           # Update the screen
```

If that was all there was to it, then this chapter would be done.

In a game, animations serve many purposes, but it is only in *cut scene* that we display the animation as a full screen sequence of frames. In all other cases, animations form a part of the scene: perhaps a character is walking and the gait is a sequence of frames; perhaps a display on a video screen can be seen by the player; sometimes an effect, like an explosion, results from a collision. Games are a special case for an animator.

Animation forces an artist or designer to think in terms of time and motion. Game design makes a designer think in terms of story, image, and—again—time. As has been said in previous chapters, a game need not *be* real, but it has to *look* real, so the animations that are used in a game must contribute to the look and feel of the game, in that they make the game seem more real, but they should not take valuable computing time away from the rendering or AI components. The motion intrinsic to the animations can make the game much more appealing and lifelike.

Very high-quality games spend a huge amount of time, energy, and money on high-quality animations. The characters in games like *Grand Theft Auto* are nearly perfect in their lifelike qualities at times. What will be discussed here will be just the basics, and the references are intended to lead you to more details if animation is a special interest.

CREATING ELEMENTARY ANIMATIONS

It is probably a good idea to do something first and then discuss the theory later. Animations consist of a sequence of drawn frames, so we'll need some drawing software. The most commonly available drawing program on a PC is Paint, and although it offers only elementary drawing functionality, it is perfectly usable, ubiquitous, and free. As a first project it is important to select something simple to do and yet having some complexities and growth potential. One idea is billiards.

The animation should be linear and two dimensional, and billiards fits the bill. The game has two white (cue) balls and a red one. Each of two players uses one of the cue balls and strikes it with the cue stick, hoping to hit both of the other two balls. What will be animated is one stroke. For a first draft we will need:

- a billiard table drawing, which is a pool table with no pockets
- renderings of the three balls

The Paint program can be used to create the images. The balls can be circles; the table is a green rectangle with markings and a wide boundary. An initial scenario needs to be set up: the ball that will be struck and the direction in which it will move. Once that is done the significant events in the animation need to be determined. A significant event occurs whenever something new happens: in this case when a collision occurs. All of these events are a consequence of the initial configuration, which is what makes this a "simple" animation.

Figure 8.1 shows the renderings of the table and the balls and outlines a plan for the action in the animation. The plan is this: ball 1 is truck by the cue stick and moves along the path indicated by the line until it strikes ball 2. It will bounce off of ball 2, again following the line, until it strikes ball 3. It will bounce off of ball 3 into the corner and bounce out again. Ball 2 will start to move when ball 1 strikes it, moving toward the bottom cushion and bouncing off of it. Ball 3 will also move when struck by ball 1, moving toward and bouncing off of the left cushion.

In animation, as in life, the events occur in a particular order, and it is important to get it right. The events are collisions, and in this animation, they are:

1. Ball 1 collides with ball 2. Ball 2 starts moving.
2. Ball 2 collides with the cushion, bounces.
3. Ball 1 collides with ball 3, ball 3 stars moving.
4. Ball 3 collides with the cushion, bounces
5. Ball 1 collides with the cushion, bounces.

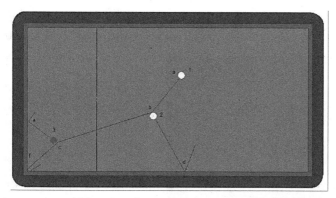

FIGURE 8.1 Initial configuration and plan for the billiards animation. The lines indicating the paths are approximate at this point.

The animation will be constructed based on these events, which are the basis for what we call *key frames*. The key frames will be drawn as the first task in the construction process. Then the animation frames that represent times in between the key frames are drawn—these are called *tweens*.

The first key frame is the initial setup and will be called key frame 0. The second, key frame 1, represents the collision of ball 1 with ball 2, and will show the contact between the two balls. From this frame can be determined the directions the balls will take for the next few frames. As shown in Figure 8.2 the bounces can be determined geometrically from the motion of ball 1 and the precise point of contact. We don't have to do any math; just make the angles look right. The rule is the struck ball will move along a line that joins the centers of the two balls. The striking ball moves away along a line that is 90 degrees to that of the struck ball. This situation is diagrammed in Figure 8.2 also.

The second key frame will show ball 2 striking the cushion. Ball 1 will have moved toward ball 3 during this time too. Ball 2 will rebound with an outgoing angle equal to the incoming angle.

Key frame 3 will show ball 1 striking ball 3. The rules for this impact are the same as for the previous (and all) ball-ball collisions. Ball 2 will have to move farther along its track also. The remaining collisions are ball-cushion collisions and are just like the previous one.

The next step, now that all key frames exist, is to determine the timing. First, let the overall animation take three seconds. We need to determine how much the ball slows down during each time period and how speed is transferred during collisions. If the speed is divided equally for any ball-ball collision and none is lost on a cushion bounce, neither of which is strictly true, then the timings can be approximately determined and all key frames can be put in their places. Time 0 is the beginning of motion for ball 0 and is the time of key frame 0.

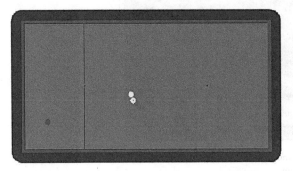

FIGURE 8.2 (Left) Key frame 1, showing the first collision. (Right) The geometry of a ball to ball collision: ball2 moves along a line joining the ball centers and ball 1 moves away at 90 degrees to that line.

Between the points **a** and **b**, ball 1 is moving at full speed (call it speed = 1). At that point ball 1 and ball 2 move at half of that speed. Ball 2 moves at that speed from then on, but ball 1 again shares its speed when it hits ball 3 (point **c**). Now balls 1 and 3 are moving at 0.25 speed, and ball 2 is moving at 0.5 speed.

If we get a ruler and measure the distances of the paths, we'll be able to determine a time frame for the key frames. Figure 8.3a shows the speeds of the ball and the lengths of each path, while Figure 8.3b shows the time needed at the given speeds to travel the path. All distances are relative to the **a-b** distance, which will be treated as 1. It does not matter which portion we choose to be equal to 1; everything works out the same. The longest path in terms of time is **a-b-c-f**, which sums to 9.4 time units. Let's make the total number of time units a nice round 10 and have all of the balls bounce a short distance off of the cushion. This means that 10 time units is three seconds; 3 seconds at 24 frames per second is 68 frames, or 6.8 frames per time unit. Thus, the number of frames between **a** and **b** will be 6.8 (we can round to 7), between **b** and **c** will be very nearly 30, and so on. That is the last critical thing that we need to finish the animation—the number of frames between each key frame.

A table of key frame times and frames between them would look like this:

Key Frame	Time	Frame	Delta
0	0	0	0
1	1	7	7
2	3.8	26	19

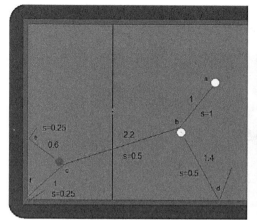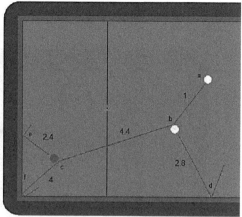

FIGURE 8.3 (Left) Distances between key frame events and the speed along the path segments. (Right) The relative time spent on each path segment.

Key Frame	Time	Frame	Delta
3	5.4	37	30
4	7.8	53	13
5	9.4	64	27

The column labeled *delta* tells us how many frames are between key frames and allows us to do the drawings. So between key frames 0 and 1 there are 7 frames in all.

Now we simply draw the correct number of frames showing balls on the correct background (the table) separated by the correct amount of space; that is, for key frames 0 and 1, the tweens are drawings of the cue ball moved 1/7 of the distance each time. Using Paint, one way to do this is to use a ruler to measure the line on the screen, divide the distance by the number of frames, and mark the positions along the paths with colored dots or lines. Move the ball to the mark, remove the rest of the marks, and save the frame; repeat this.

Numbering the marks is a good idea, because it allows recovery from program crashes, power failures, and other disasters. Figure 8.4 shows the marks used for part of the billiards animation. Note that the rule markers don't have to be precise. The tweens between any pair of key frames can be assigned to teams of artists, and because the action has been carefully scripted, the result should be acceptable. A lot of famous cartoons (Bugs Bunny, for instance) were constructed using key frames drawn by the director, usually the best animator available, and then assigning the tweens to less senior people.

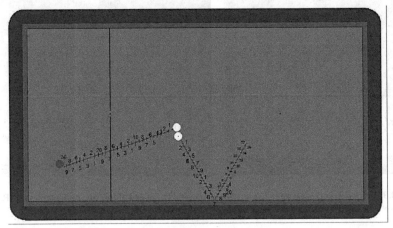

FIGURE 8.4 Marking the points on an image where the balls will be when frames are captured. Move the balls to the locations for each frame (1, 2, 3...) and then erase the markers and save the frame.

Paint has some serious limitations as an animation tool. It has no timing facilities at all, does not handle transparency, and can't even rotate objects except by 90 degrees. *Photoshop* can deal with transparency and rotation and has much more advanced image editing facilities; it can be expensive though. *Flash* is designed to do animations and can do everything you might want, but it is also costly and is disappearing from the Web.

The other way to conduct an animation is called the *straight ahead* method, in which the artist draws the first frame, then the next, and so on in order. Using this method is fine if the entire thing is done by a single artist and if no serious errors are made. It's quite hard to fix a single frame, and it would be likely that the animation would have to be redone from the point of the error. We'll look at this method later in the chapter.

The complete billiards animation can be found on the disk, and it is available as a GIF, MP4, and AVI file. The GIF is the original and is cleanest.

ANIMATION MATH

In order to be good at animation, an artist must have an understanding of how things move. Living things move in a different way from non-living things, and all have a "natural" motion from the perspective of a human viewer. Viewers tend to be uncritical of the math and physics and more critical of the general quality of the perceived motion, but movement that is technically incorrect is less likely to be acceptable. Let's look at simple cases of movement of inanimate objects.

Balls and rocks and feathers move in the environment as described by Newton's Laws of Motion, of which there are three:

1. Inertia. Every object that has weight will remain in its current state of motion until a force is applied to it.

2. Constant acceleration. An object accelerates in the direction of the force applied to it. The greater the force, the greater the acceleration given to the object. For a given force, the greater the mass of the object, the smaller will be the acceleration. The famous equation that describes this is $F = m * a$.

3. *For every action there is an equal and opposite reaction.* If a force is applied to an object, the object reacts with an equal and opposite force on whatever applied the force. For instance, if your kick a ball, it pushes back on your foot.

What do all of these rules mean in the context of animation? They define what is meant by reality and reasonableness in terms of object motion. The first law has been observed by everyone mainly as *friction*. We don't expect that a box that has been pushed will move forever, because that's not what we see. We do expect it to slow and stop because of friction, and that force is present in all motion observed before the twentieth century. If we'd been living in outer space our whole lives, then the first law would appear to us in a more literal fashion—objects that move do tend to continue to move. Friction is not a major issue in space, at least not for basic linear motion.

The second law defines how things move when they are pushed or pulled, and again our interpretation of motion that we see is defined by what we have seen before. This law is most obvious in falling objects. An object thrown into the air slows, stops, and falls back because the force of gravity acts on it. An object thrown up and horizontally moves in a parabola, the vertical motion behaving as previously described and the horizontal motion behaving according to the first law. Of course, there are other equations that relate speed, position, and acceleration, and those are essential to determining object positions, but they are almost always related to forces applied.

The third law is more subtle and is illustrated in day-to-day life as reaction to collisions. Objects that collide don't generally just stop moving, they *bounce*. An obvious example is the game of pool. The cue ball strikes another ball and imparts some of its speed to the other ball, making it move. The other ball kicks back and slows the cue ball and nearly always makes it change direction. Cartoon animations exaggerate this effect and sometimes have the objects distort in shape during a collision and then return to normal form.

Motion Equations

The elementary math that describes motion is known to most people intuitively. Distance, velocity, and time are related in an obvious way. When driving a car at 60 miles per hour (MPH) for one hour, we end up driving for 60 miles. It seems simple enough, and all drivers know this. The equation is:

$$distance = speed * time$$

or

$$d = v * t$$

Physicists use the letter **v** to represent speed very often. It stands for *velocity* and is different from speed technically, but for now it will be treated the same. Objects in an animation must adhere to this relationship, or they will look strange.

Acceleration is less intuitive. It is the change in velocity as a function of time, and we do see it every day: a car starting to move when a light changes from red to green is accelerating. Elevators accelerate when the door closes and start to move up or down. Dropped objects accelerate downward and then again when they strike the ground and stop moving. In general, an object having acceleration **a** for a time period **t** satisfies:

$$speed = acceleration * time \; or \; V = a * t$$

If the object has a speed v_0 before it starts to accelerate, then that has to be considered, and the relationship becomes:

$$v = a * t + v_0$$

Finally, we can find the distance traveled by an accelerating object:

$$d = \frac{1}{2} at^2 + v_0 t$$

This is very important, because it provides the way to compute the position of an accelerating object at any time. Falling and bouncing objects are accelerating and are the most common examples, so let's consider an object, a ball, which is falling; the acceleration due to gravity is a=32 ft/sec^2. Assume that it is dropped, so $v_0 = 0$. At intervals of 1 second we have:

$$d = \frac{1}{2}at^2 + v_0t = 16t^2$$

time	distance (ft)
1	16
2	64
3	144
4	256
5	400
6	576

Clearly the distance between consecutive positions of the ball is not equally spaced. An animation of the falling ball would have to be drawn with this fact in mind. Now consider the situation of a ball being thrown upward. There is now an initial velocity, and the acceleration opposes that velocity; that is, the velocity starts as negative (meaning moving upward), against the force of gravity. A fastball can be thrown with a speed of up to 106 MPH, but let's reasonably assume that the ball is thrown upward at 35 MPH, which is 103 ft/sec. This velocity opposes the acceleration given by gravity and so will be positive while acceleration is negative. Again, at intervals of 1 second we have:

$$d = \frac{1}{2}at^2 + v_0t = 16t^2 - 103t$$

time	$\frac{1}{2}at^2$	v_0t	distance (ft)
1	-16	103	87
2	-64	206	142
3	-144	309	165

time	$\frac{1}{2}at^2$	v_0t	distance (ft)
4	-256	412	156
5	-400	515	115
6	-576	618	42
7	-784	721	-63

According to this table, the ball moves upward for a little over 3 seconds and then falls back. At time t=7 the ball is 63 feet below where it was originally thrown. At what time does the ball stop moving upward? When the velocity becomes zero, and using $v = a*t + v_0$, that time is:

$$0 = 32*t - 103$$
$$103 = 32*t$$
$$t = \frac{103}{32} = 3.21 \, seconds.$$

Figure 8.5 shows this ball-throwing example as points drawn on a grid. A critical thing to notice is that when the ball is moving its fastest, the distance between consecutive drawn points is the greatest. That's because in the fixed

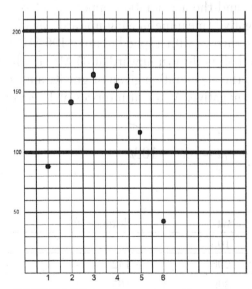

FIGURE 8.5 Ball-throwing experiment. The position of the ball at selected points in time.

interval between calculation times, the ball moves farther when it moves quickly. This is quite a simple idea, but it is critical in an animation, where only fixed interval samples are seen.

One more bit of theory and then we can draw something else. A question of some interest is *where is the ball in the middle of any time interval?* At time t=1.5 the ball will have a height of between 87 and 142 feet, but where exactly is not known from the graph. We can use the equation to figure it out, but as animators we are interested in the position relative to the other two points. Is it in the center? No.

Let's look at the dropping ball again. The equation covering this was $d = \frac{1}{2}at^2$, and we know that at time t=1 it has fallen 16 feet and at t=2 it has fallen 64 feet. At t=1.5, half of the time between those two points, $d=8*1.5)^2 = 36$ feet. This is 20 feet from the first point (t=1) and 28 feet from the second, or 20/48 of the distance between the two points, or almost 0.4 of that distance. So, when drawing the tweens, the tween in the middle in terms of time should be drawn 40% of the distance between the two key frames. This process can be repeated for other tweens; although it is not exact it will be close enough. As a result, the distance between the balls in successive frames will increase, which is correct according to intuition.

In summary, basic physics can be used to calculate the positions of objects in frames. In particular, the tweens can be generated using the fundamental motion equations for objects undergoing simple motion: falling, rolling, and so on.

REACTIVE ANIMATIONS

What will be called *reactive* animation is likely the most common sort to be found in a video game. Simply put, it is an animation that represents a reaction to an event in the game: for example, an explosion or fire after a collision, or the shattering of a brittle object that has fallen. These tend to be quite brief and not necessarily easily modeled by physics. A car crashing and exploding is an example. The animation is short, often has a random component, and can be accompanied by an external sound effect.

Many such animations are built with simple tools using a straight-ahead methodology. That works pretty well because they tend to be very short, running between 1–2 seconds, which is 24–60 frames. Each drawing is a variation, sometimes a slight one, of the previous frame. Using computer tools it is possible to start drawing a particular frame using the previous one by just moving parts of it around.

Consider an animation of a balloon popping. Start with a balloon, as shown in Figure 8.6. In each successive frame parts of the balloon from the previous frame are erased and moved. Because the balloon is exploding, the parts should be moved away from the center. The explosion itself takes frames 15 through 23, which are the ones shown in the figure. It should be clear how successive frames have been built. The Paint tools *erase* and *select* are used to remove parts of the balloon and move other parts away from the center, giving an expanding volume of smaller balloon parts.

The same technique can be used to build short animations of explosions, impacts, rocket exhaust, and other event-based visuals. Each frame is a random variation of the previous one, and this works well so long as the animation is short and not repeated. If played in a loop the animation loses its randomness,

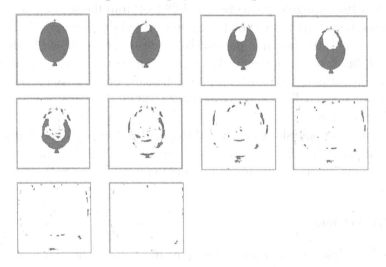

FIGURE 8.6 Drawn frames for the balloon-popping sequence. Each frame is a variation of the one before, created by a random edit with the overall plan in mind.

and the viewer can see details not intended. These are like sound effects; if they are played too often they lose their impact, so multiple short animations could be the solution.

Reactive animations will occupy a small portion of the screen for a very short time. It is important to place the frames in the correct spot in each frame. Consider an animation of a small explosion, perhaps a hand grenade. This must be seen at the location where the grenade was located just before it explodes, meaning that it could be drawn anywhere on the screen depending on the play in the game.

In terms of software, the need for animations in specific locations implies the need for software that will manage the animation, just as we had software to manage the sound clips. An animation not only consists of a set of frames but also a current frame being displayed, a location, a frame rate, and possibly an orientation, in the case of 3D games. We need a way to start and stop animations too, and some might be linked to a sound that is to be played simultaneously; sound can be a part of an animation, but for reactive animations it is never an integral part of it.

Let's design an animation manager for games, starting with what we know right now. It will possess an array of frames (images) and a way to read them in. Included will be a way to normalize the frames; they should clearly all be the same size. We'll need a way to play and stop the display of frames, and they will be displayed at a specified point on the screen. Sound will also be managed. Here is what an outline of this, implemented as a `class`, would look like:

```
class animate:
    def __init__ (self,xx, yy):
        self.xpos = xx          # Position to place the animation
        self.ypos = yy
        self.frames = ()        # Images for this animation
        self.nextFrame = 0      # Next frame to be played
        self.Nframes = 0        # Total number of frames
        self.soundName = ""     # Name of the sound file for this
animation
        self.playing = False

    def play (self):
    def stop (self):
    def pause (self):
    def setPosition (self, x, y):
    def getPosition (self):
    def setSoundName (self, s):
    def addFrame (self, p):
    def draw (self):</CODE>
```

To use an animation in a game, an instance of the animation class would first be declared. The frames would then be read in. It is common to have a pattern in the file names of the frames that can be recognized by a program and read in automatically. We will have a text name ending in digits and then "." and the suffix that defines the image file type ("jpg," "gif," etc.). For the balloon animation the files are "balloon00.png," "balloon01.png," and so on in an obvious sequence. The animation class is given each of the animation frames in proper order, and it saves them in an internal tuple. The animation will be drawn starting at the x and y coordinates provided when the class was instantiated, but this position can be changed using the **getPosition** and **setPosition** methods.

To play an animation, instantiate it and set the initial position, then add the frames. Call the **play** method to start playing it, and ensure that a call to its **draw** method occurs someplace within the main loop. The **draw** method causes the current frame to be rendered into the graphics window. The animation frames will be displayed in order and will loop until either **stop** or **pause** is called.

Example:

```
ac = animate (20, 30)              # Instantiate
        . . .
for i in range(1,N):  # Read the images that represent the
animation
        im = pygame.image.load(" image file name N ")
        ac.addFrame (im)
        . . .

ac.play()

while True:
        . . .
    ac.draw()
```

As a complete example of the use of this class, imagine that we have a game that uses an initial screen with a small animated feature—a jet of gas or steam. The screen will consist of a graphic, and on top of this will be played our animation. Figure 8.6 shows the screen with the animated section outlined. The frames of the animation are played sequentially, in this case as a loop, after being translated to window coordinates (28, 156), the area corresponding to the

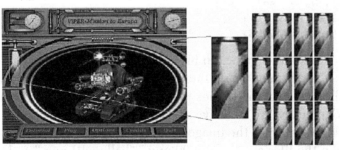

FIGURE 8.7 Animating a portion of a screen. The steam jet is translated to the correct position before display.

box. After initialization, each frame is displayed there in succession using the following code that uses the `animate` class:

```
import pygame
import animateClass

pygame.init()
clock = pygame.time.Clock()
display = pygame.display.set_
mode((800, 512), pygame.SRCALPHA,
32)

ac = animate (28, 156)
background = pygame.image.load("002.
jpg")


for i in range(0, 17):
if i<10:
im = pygame.image.load

("b00"+str(i)+".jpg")
else:
im = pygame.image.load

("b0"+str(i)+".jpg")
ac.addFrame (im)

ac.play()

while True:
clock.tick(10)
display.blit(background, (0, 0))
ac.draw()
pygame.display.update()
```

This animation software object seems reasonable given what we know right now. It may change a little as more requirements are seen to be needed by other types of animations. The frames of the jet animation are built starting with a small image cut from the screen. This image has the steam added to it and is saved, then the steam is varied a bit and it is saved as a successive frame, and so on until enough frames (in this case 17 in all) are created. In that way the background remains constant and compatible with the rest of the existing background. Another way to do a similar thing is to use steam frames having a transparent background color.

The animation is placed into the background where it belongs. There is no reason that there could not be many animations playing at the same time, as will be seen later in this chapter.

Using Real Images

Until now the animations have consisted of drawn images linked together in a sequence. There is no reason why a real image cannot be used at the starting point. There are two main ways to do this: to vary a real image a bit, as we've been doing with drawings, or to use a short video that has been converted into a still-image sequence.

If a single real image is to be used as a starting point, the process is similar to the one we've used before: manipulate the original image to become a second frame, then the third, and so on. It's a bit trickier to edit captured images and keep them looking real. Part of the problem is light and shading, which in real images is continuous, and part is boundaries between objects in the scene, which in captured images are not precise.

Consider the example of a candle. Some images of a burning candle could be taken using a cellphone camera. Taking enough to be used as consecutive frames in an animation is possible in this specific case, because candles don't change much between two images a few seconds apart. The flame may not behave as we wish in these frames, and so editing one or two into a sequence of twenty-four to forty-eight is probably a more practical idea. These images can be used as the basis for a set of animation frames: each one can be edited, shearing the flame, changing its shape and color, and so on.

Using real video data is another viable alternative. The first step is to extract the still frames from a video image, and this requires special software tools. An excellent video creation/extraction tool is VideoMach, which has a free downloadable version and which is very inexpensive in its paid form. A usable copy of this software is included on the accompanying CD.

Extracting frames is exceptionally simple: load the video and **save as** (for instance) *jpg*. The result is a collection of JPEG files in the save directory that are consecutive frames from the video, and these are named "00.jpg," "01.jpg," and so on. These files can be played as if they were an animation, and it will look just like a video so long as the frame rate is the same as in the original video, usually 30 frames per second.

VideoMach can also take a set of frames and create a video in one of a dozen formats, including gif and avi, and this is a valuable facility for previewing the animations before inserting them into the game. Simply create and play an AVI file or use the built-in preview facility to see how smooth the frame transitions are, whether the lighting is good, and if there are artifacts. Figure 8.8 shows *VideoMach* being used to make an *avi* version of the balloon-popping animation.

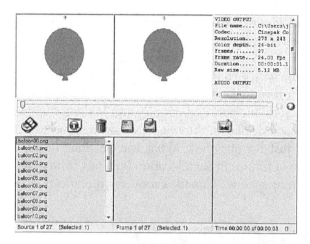

FIGURE 8.8 Using *VideoMach* to create an AVI video file from individual frames.

Microsoft's *MovieMaker* tool can similarly create a video from still frames, but it requires the user to specify the duration of the frames manually, so it is somewhat less convenient, and it can't save in the same variety of formats. Mac's *iMovie* can also export still frames from a video.

AMBIENT ANIMATIONS

Ambient animations are used to provide interesting background activity. An animation of a computer screen or data display that appears on a control panel in the background would be an example. So would smoke or sparks from damaged equipment. These very frequently have to loop, and so they cannot represent an obvious pattern if that can be avoided. They also are required to be playable in many locations simultaneously. A control console can use the same animation in many positions as digital readouts so long as they are not identical simultaneously; they may need to be played out of sync. They also may need to be rescaled, skewed, or rotated too.

Making such animations is similar to making a reactive animation. It's the playback that can be distinctive. The needs of such animations will be important in continuing the design of the `animate` class. Consider, as a practical example, the creation of a control room for a spacecraft launch. In practice there will be scores of active screens visible, but let's limit it to five. The image that will be used for the background is shown in Figure 8.9, and it is in fact a still photo of the Russian control room for the International Space Station. The three large screens at the front and a couple of smaller ones will have animated displays. The screens will be the location of the animated displays, and they are colored green in the original image. The green simply marks the locations and is not needed for the display; this is not *green screen* technology.

The two small screens in the lower part of the image are essentially rectangular and can be overwritten with an animation as we've done before. Since the screens look like computer terminals, we can make a set of frames that show text, images, and windows scrolling past and popping up. Making a large set of such animations, one for each display in the image, would be time consuming and not worth the effort just for an effect. What can be done instead is to display the same sequence of frames in each location but start from a different point and maybe at different speeds. This idea requires modifications to the `animate` class.

FIGURE 8.9 The control room background image showing "green screen" areas where animations will play (background image from NASA).

The ability to play the same animation in more than one place implies the need for an operation that makes a copy of an animation. Each copy could be placed at a distinct location in the scene. The animate class does this through a method called **copy** in a module named **copy** that returns a reference to a new *animate* object having the same properties as the one cloned. So, the assignment:

```
ad = copy.copy (ac)
```

creates a copy of **ac** that can be located elsewhere and displayed separately. The frames are the same. The code simply creates a new *animate* instance and initializes all of its local variables to those of the instance being cloned.

That solves part of the problem. Next, we need the ability to slow down the display of frames for an animation, and to begin playing the sequence of frames anywhere we choose. For sequencing a new procedure named **setNext()** has been created which simply sets the value of the next frame to be played. Play normally starts at frame 0, but a call to **setNext(12)** will begin play at frame 12. Now, two adjacent screens can play the same animation and seem as if they are distinct.

The procedure **setRate** slows down play of the animation; **setRate(1)** is the default, which plays frames at a rate of 1 per call to **display()**. A call to **setRate(2)** means that two calls to **display()** will be needed to change the frame displayed, and **setRate(4)** means that four calls to **display()** will result in a change to the frame. The larger the parameter to **setRate()**, the slower will be the rate at which frames will be displayed.

The three large screens in the scene present a new problem: they are not actually rectangular. They are in real life, naturally, but they are being observed from above and to the side, so perspective has given them irregular shapes. How can we play a rectangular image frame in such a space? By using texture mapping.

In the animation frame in Figure 8.9, the large green screens are not rectangles. Each pixel in each of those screens must be drawn from a pixel in a rectangular image, so we need to define a mapping between the quadrilateral on the screen and the rectangle that is the image, or texture, to be drawn. There are many ways to do that, including perspective transformations, bilinear interpolation, polynomial warping, and so on. Most graphics systems will do this mapping automatically if the coordinates that correspond to the corners of the quad and the image are provided. Pygame does not offer that facility, so in the animation class, a method named **setSize** is provided that gives the corners of the image in screen coordinates. When draw is called a mapping of pixels to the screen takes place so that irregular shapes can be filled with images.

When calling **setSize** a list of x,y coordinates is provided, beginning at the upper left and moving clockwise. It only maps images onto quadrilaterals, so there will be eight parameters. For example, the large green screen in the center of Figure 8.9 has screen coordinates (267, 73) (478, 73) (471, 225) (276, 224). Setting this up as an animate class animation would be:

```
ac = animateClass.animate (0, 0, display)    # Create the instance
for i in range(0,35):  # Read the images
    if i<10:
        im = pygame.image.load("screen1/00"+str(i)+".jpg")
    else:
```

```
    im = pygame.image.load("screen1/0"+str(i)+".jpg")
  ac.addFrame (im)
ac.setSize (267, 73, 478, 73, 471, 225, 276, 224)  # Set the
location
```

In Figure 8.9, there are five green screens that are intended to hold animations. All can be played in their proper places at the same time: simply create the five instances and read the images, call **setSize** for each one specifying their location and shape, play them, and then call **draw()** for each one within the main loop. A program that does this is named **control.py** on the accompanying CD.

CHARACTER ANIMATION

Creating animations of living creatures is among the hardest tasks in video games, and animating humans is the most difficult. It's because living things move in very complex ways, and viewers are very familiar with how that motion should look and are therefore quite critical of flaws. Character animation is a specialized subject, and we will look at the most commonly needed type here: gait.

If your game has a human character, it will need at the very least to walk around the game space. The legs and arms must behave as we human observers expect them to. We will need to build a short animation of the character taking a single complete step, and then this can be played whenever the character moves. Of course, the avatar may need to jump, shoot, reach, crouch, or do many other tasks, but character animation is a complex skill that depends to a great extent on the artist's abilities.

Animating gait is a matter of creating a sequence of drawings that shows the arms and legs of the character walking in a normal way. From the illustration in Figure 8.10, a set of workable steps is shown. First (top) is a set of key frames, in this case showing the right arm and leg of a stick figure during a single full step. Next the left arm and leg are added and tweens are created (middle). Finally, the character can be fleshed out over the skeleton and colors or textures added. The final sequence here has just enough detail to be useful both as an example and as an avatar. This avatar is carrying a pack of some kind on his back.

When the avatar is moved, for example by pressing the right arrow or the "d" key, the frames are played in sequence and the position of the avatar is moved to the left, giving the desired effect. The frames can be redrawn or simply flipped horizontally to allow the avatar to move to the left.

FIGURE 8.10 (top) Key frames for a gait, right side only. (Center) Tweens for the gait. (Bottom) A set of frames for a single stride.

This discussion of character animation is intentionally trivial. Although the actual display of frames is simple and uses methods that have been discussed in detail, the creation of the frames can be profoundly complex. If you have the ability to create realistic motions in a frame sequence, then your games will profit from this skill. If not, it can be learned or (perhaps better) people with that skill can be engaged to work for you. The cost is small, and the improvement in the quality of the result can be priceless.

CUT SCENES

A *cut scene* or *full motion video* (FMV) is an animated narrative that explains a part of the game's story or background. It is played on the full screen like a movie. There is often one at the beginning of the game, and often one that serves as a transition between levels. They are made obvious by a change in aspect ratio to a more cinematic 1.85:1 from the standard computer screen value of 1.6:1. No interaction with the game is possible during a cut scene.

These can be made in any way one chooses, even with live action video. The issue again is how to play it. Cut scenes can have a much higher image quality than the game proper, and to read and display single frames would take far too much time and memory to be practical. What you must do is create an animation, save it as a video file, and play that file at the proper place in the game. This section of the book could be called "How to use Python video classes and functions to display video in a game." To play videos we use a trick.

Pygame used to have a *movie* class but is was removed. It apparently caused more trouble than it was worth. So, how can we play a cut scene? It must again be done frame by frame. However, it is not necessary to read all of the frames into memory first, which could use a great deal of space. Instead we can read the frames just before we display them and reuse the same image for each frame. Playing a video in this way means playing the sound concurrently, so the cut scene video would have to be processed in the following way:

1. Each of the frames would have to be extracted into a distinct file.
2. The audio track needs to be extracted into a .wav or .mp3 file.

Here's some code that will do this:

```
import pygame

pygame.init()
clock = pygame.time.Clock()
display = pygame.display.set_mode((800, 512), pygame.SRCALPHA,
32)

pygame.mixer.music.load("xx.mp3")   # Read the sound track as an
MP3 file

i = 0
pygame.mixer.music.play(0)              # Start playing the sound
while i<=253:
    for event in pygame.event.get():
        if event.type == pygame.QUIT:
            exit()

# Read the next frame

    if i<10:
        im = pygame.image.load("screen1/00"+str(i)+".jpg")
    elif i<100:
        im = pygame.image.load("screen1/0"+str(i)+".jpg")
    else:
        im = pygame.image.load("screen1/" + str(i) + ".jpg")
    i = i + 1

    display.blit(im, (200,140))              # Display the frame

    pygame.display.update()
```

```
        clock.tick(30)

pygame.quit()
```

There are other modules that can accomplish this. They include *moviepy*, *pygame-vlc*, *PyMedia*, and others. Each must be downloaded and installed before use.

ANIMATIONS IN THE BOAT RACE GAME

There are not very many animations in the boat race, and fortunately they are all brief. They include:

1. The wake of a boat under power
2. Birds
3. An explosion
4. Flags

WAKES

This will be a white trail behind a boat when it is moving under power. It should move in somewhat random ways so as to seem like a water wave. There's no need for key frames here; straight ahead animation is fine. Start with one of the boats and a background of blue water from the terrain map. Copy the boat into the image and then draw a set of white and grey extensions from the rear of the boat, saving each one as a separate numbered file. Paint or any drawing program can be used; this is a relatively low-resolution game. Figure 8.11 shows a part of this process.

The final step is to isolate the wake animations. Simply clip them out of the Paint image, making certain that all are the same size and that the entire wake is captured each time. Figure 8.12 shows some of the individual wake frames. When the boats are under power, these will be drawn behind them.

SUMMARY

In *key frame* animation the frames that define the motion are created first, and then the frame in between those (*tweens*) are drawn. This lends

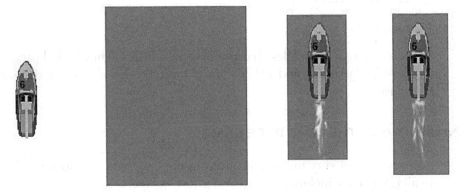

FIGURE 8.11 Creating animation frames for a boat wake using Paint. (a) A boat. (b) Water background. (c) Random white areas drawn to represent the wake.

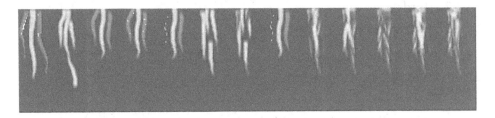

FIGURE 8.12 Sample frames from the wake animation.

itself to a production line system that uses multiple animators. In addition, we can more easily synchronize key moments in the action with specific frames. However, the use of many artists can lead to inconsistent drawings. In *straight-ahead* animation we create the first frame, then the second, then the third. This leads to artistically exciting images and is good when there is a lot of action. On the other hand, there is a lot of pressure on the animator, as this method requires a great deal of concentration. It's also hard to correct, and some kinds of specific timing are hard to do (e.g., lip synch).

Basic physics can be used to calculate the positions of objects in frames. In particular, the tweens can be generated using the fundamental motion equations for objects undergoing simple motion: falling, rolling, and so on.

A *reactive* animation is likely the most common sort to be found in a video game, and it represents a reaction to an event in the game: an explosion after a collision, for example. *Ambient* animations are used to provide interesting background activity. An animation of a computer screen or data display that appears on a control panel in the background would be an example. A *cut scene* is an animated narrative that explains a part of the game's story or background. It is played on the full screen like a movie.

Creating animations of living creatures is among the hardest tasks in video games and should be avoided if possible or hired out to a professional if not. Avatar motions depend on character animation and need to be good.

EXERCISES

1. Make a short (<10 second) animation of a ball bouncing. A basic solution could be a loop, but really it should bounce to a lower height each time and finally end up resting on the ground.

2. Make a short animation of a ball bouncing down some stairs. You may use the animation from exercise 1 as a start.

3. Create a video file from one of the animations in exercises 1 or 2. Use any tool you like, but document the process you used in a brief (< 5-page) document.

4. Take some images of water flowing from a faucet. Create a short animation of this flow and display the frames as an animation. Using any tool you like, create a video file of this animation.

5. Make a video of water flowing from a faucet and extract the frames. Select twenty-four or so and play them in random order in a small window as an animation. How does it look different from a video of the water flowing?

6. Observe the gait of any animal. Try to create an animated gait for this creature. Play it back and try to find flaws—keep a written description of the process and what you found.

7. An entertaining way to make an animation is the *stop motion* or *stop frame* technique, in which actual objects in an actual scene are moved a bit, photographed, and moved again. Miniatures are often used. Make a stop frame animation using any material at your disposal and turn it into a video file. Plan the animation using key frames.

8. A common tool used in the creation of animations and films is the *storyboard*. This is a sequence of drawings, usually including sketches of the key frames, that tells the story of the animation. It helps with the design, and it is used to present the idea to the production group. Make a storyboard for any 30 seconds of animation you choose: a cartoon, perhaps. Part of the value of a

storyboard is in its presentation so, if you can, present your storyboard to a small group.

RESOURCES

Wideo: An online animation creation tool. You must sign up, but it is free. *http://wideo.co/*.

How to animate flames: *http://www.youtube.com/watch?v=f_cNlQocaV8*.

Site for downloading inexpensive images for use as textures: *http://www.dreamstime.com/*.

VideoMach video creation tool: *http://gromada.com/videomach/*.

UnFREEz tool for making animated GIFs: *http://www.whitsoftdev.com/unfreez/*.

Macintosh *iMovie*: *http://www.macworld.com/product/412943/imovie-09.html*.

MovieToImage for getting stills from an iPhone. It's a $1 app. *http://www.macworld.com/product/599549/movietoimage.html*.

GOM Media Player can save stills from a video too: *http://player.gomlab.com/eng/download/*.

Apple's *QuickTime*: *http://support.apple.com/kb/dl837*.

GSvideo: *http://gsvideo.sourceforge.net/*.

Storyboard That, an on-line storyboard creation tool. *http://www.storyboardthat.com/*.

Gaits of a horse for animation:
https://www.youtube.com/watch?v=2f2oSAqvrsg
https://www.youtube.com/watch?v=sF2h5Enyaos

REFERENCES

1. Garry Faigin. (1990). *The Artist's Complete Guide to Facial Expression*. Toronto, Canada: Watson-Guptill Publications.

2. Maureen Furniss. (2008). *The Animation Bible*. New York, NY: Abrams.3. Kit Laybourne. (1998). *The Animation Book*. New York, NY: Three Rivers Press.4. Brian Lemay. (2006). *Layout and Design Made Amazingly Simple*. Oakville, Ontario: Animated Cartoon Factory. *http://www.brianlemay.com/Books/layout.html*.

3. Lynn Pocock and Judson Rosebush. (2002). *The Computer Animator's Technical Handbook*. San Francisco, CA: Morgan Kaufmann.6. Chris Webster. (2005). *Animation: The Mechanics of Motion*. Burlington, MA: Focal Press.

4. Tony White. (2006). *Animation from Pencils to Pixels*. Burlington, MA: Focal Press.

5. Tony White. (1986). *The Animator's Workbook*. New York, NY: Watson-Guptill Publications.

6. Richard Williams. *The Animator's Survival Kit: A Manual of Methods, Principles, and Formulas*. London, UK: Faber and Faber.

## CHAPTER 9

C2H6O – FINAL STEPS

The Jet Boat Race game requires a few more systems and components in order to be complete. First, it is not yet a game! The boats have to follow a specific path in order to successfully pass the finish line and score. The game must track that. It is more fun to track the times of each boat and display them in real time. This has not been done. There is no official start of the game, and no record is kept of passing the finish line, or of the winner.

Most of the sounds are not being played. The animations are not either, so when two boats collide a message is printed; there is supposed to be an explosion.

A mini-map would be fun too, and it is not too difficult to implement. It's common in race games to be able to see where all of the boats are.

Finally the game should be tuned a bit so that it does not give an advantage to any boat, and so that play moves along quickly.

ANIMATIONS

There are two main animations in this game: the explosions and the wake from each boat. These were created in Chapter 8 but have not been used yet.

Wakes

All of the animation frames can be stored in a single image, and the game will extract the needed frame just before it is displayed.

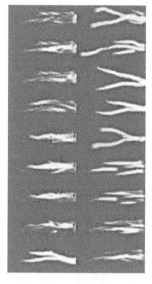

FIGURE 9.1 The animation frame image for boat wakes.

The *wakes.png* image includes eighteen frames where each frame is 83x35 pixels. To draw a frame in position i of row j:

```
display.blit(im, (100, 100), (i*83, j*35, 83, 35))
There are 18 frames, we can generate a random frame number and
then convert it into a pair of (i,j) indices:
k = int(random.random()*18)
i = k//9
j = k%9
```

There is another step needed, because the boats are rarely oriented along a vertical or horizontal axis. The frame, which is a *surface* in pygame, must be rotated so that it aligns with the axis of the boat, and must be translated so that it is positioned at the rear of the boat before it can be blitted to the main surface. In Chapter 2, there, was an explanation of how to orient the boat sprite, which was used in Chapter 7. Now we have to add the animation to the back end of the boat, but when the boat changes direction it should still rotate about the boat's center, not the combined center of the boat and the wake.

Accomplishing this is pretty simple. Use a new *Surface* (named **r** in the code) that is wider than the combined images of the wake and the boat by 1/2 the size of the boat (40 pixels). Copy (blit) the boat image into **r** at location 83, the size of the wake, and copy the wake image at 0. Then rotate and display **r** at the needed location. Code to render at the center of the display *Surface* is:

```
r = pygame.Surface ((251, 35), pygame.SRCALPHA)
          . . .
k = int(random.random() * 18)    # Which wake image?
i = k // 9
j = k % 9

r.blit (boat, (83,6)     # Copy boat to r
  r.blit (wakes, (0,6), (i*83, j*35, 83, 35))  # Copy wake
  boatr = pygame.transform.rotate(r, angle)    # Rotate
  sx = boatr.get_width()
  sy = boatr.get_height()
  display.blit(boatr, (250-sx/2, 200-sy/2))    # Display
```

This code draws the wake using random frames.

Explosions

When a boat collides with the shore, it tries to find a way off of the beach using a method discussed in Chapter 7. When two boats collide with each other, they destroy each other. They are carrying a lot of fuel and their engines are hot. There will be an explosion and the boats will disappear. They will reappear at the starting position, where their chance of winning is small.

A small collection of explosion animations was generated using a program, and this provides a selection that can be used for collisions. Players can tell if the same one is used over and over. When a collision happens the first step is to select an explosion animation at random. There are five animations.

Next the animation should start to play along with the sound of the explosion. Each animation has sixteen frames, and these should be displayed in sequence in place of the boats that collided. A new state called EXPLODING will be added to the NPC class that will result in the next frame in the animation being displayed instead of the boat sprites. The display method must be modified to test whether the state is EXPLODING and, if so, display the animation instead of the sprite.

After the final frame is displayed, the two boats involved must be placed at their original starting positions. This is a simple matter of setting their position and orientation to the initial values. If one of the boats is the player's boat then, of course, the screen view will change and remain centered on that boat.

Playing the explosion animation is the same as playing the wake animation. The frame of the explosion is extracted from a larger image that contains all of the frames; in this case the explosion frames are 64 x 64 pixels and there are sixteen frames in each sequence. In addition, when the animation starts a corresponding sound is played.

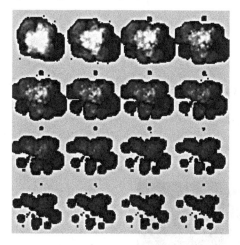

FIGURE 9.2 The animation frame image for an explosion sequence, explode3.gif. These are in GIF format because they have a transparent background.

There are five different animation sequences for the explosion, named **explode1.gif** to **explode4.gif**, and **explode5.png** (Figure 9.2). The sound files are **exp01.wav** and **exp02.wav**. When an explosion occurs one of the five sequences is selected for use so that all explosions don't look the same. There is a test program named explode.py that tests the animation and sound code outside of the game. This is a common practice. The program sets off an explosion at a point where the user clicks the mouse. This works fine, so it can be added to the game.

In the game itself the explosion will take the place of the two colliding boats. The boats will not be drawn, and the frames of the explosion will replace them. When the collision is detected, the boats enter the EXPLODING state and the sound begins to play. In the EXPLODING state the boats are not drawn, and instead the current explosion frame is displayed. When all frames have been drawn, the two boats are placed at the starting line again and the game resumes.

Inside of the **draw** method for a boat we see:

```
if self.state == self.EXPLODING:
    self.showNextExFrame(ccx, ccy)
else:
    display.blit(pygame.transform.rotate
(self.r,self.angle),(ccx,ccy))
```

so that if the boat is exploding, the boats are not drawn. **ShowNextExFrame** displays the explosion:

```
def showNextExFrame (self, x, y):
      global im, s1, kimage


    i = self.frame/4
    j = self.frame%4
    display.blit(im[kimage], (x-32, y-32),
                  (i*64, j*64,64,64))
    self.frame = self.frame + 1
    if self.frame >= 16:
        self.state = self.NORMAL
        self.reset()
```

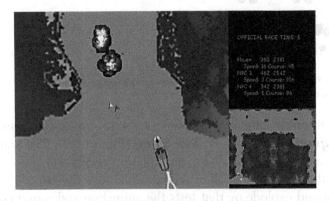

FIGURE 9.3 An explosion happens when two boats collide.

The class variable **self.frame** represents the number of the current frame to display, and **kimage** is the index of the explosion. Finally, when the last frame is displayed, the boat is reset by putting it back in the state it was in at the start of the game. The method that does this is **reset**.

Determining a Boat Collision

The boat class (**npc**) has a method that determines whether a collision is pending (**boatCollision**), and this has been discussed in depth. What it lacks is a method that determines if a collision has actually occurred, which is a precondition for an explosion.

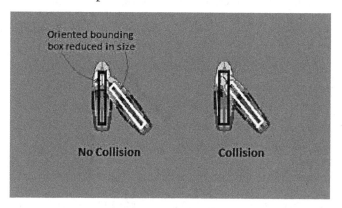

Oriented bounding box reduced in size

No Collision　　**Collision**

FIGURE 9.4 Determining when two boats collide.

Each boat has a bounding box computed and saved for each iteration. A simple collision detection method would be to determine if the boxes of any two boats overlap—these are *object-oriented* boxes, so it will work okay. The game should allow for some degree of "bumping," so this may be too severe a condition. The box can be made smaller to permit some overlap.

The object-oriented bounding box for each boat is stored as four points: ul, ur, lr, and ll (upper left, etc). These points are determined for each iteration using a call to the method **update_box** in the **npc** class. A global function **box_intersect** does the math to determine whether the boxes intersect each other, and if so then the explosion, sound, and state change are done. In the main game, loop we check all boats against each other:

```
if screenState == PLAYSTATE:
    move()
    for i in range (0,3):        # Check boat collisions
        for j in range (i+1,3):
            if boatCollided (i,j):            # Boom
                boats[i].savedx = boats[i].x
                boats[i].savedy = boats[i].y
                boats[j].savedx = boats[j].x
                boats[j].savedy = boats[j].y
                boats[i].state = boats[i].EXPLODING # Change boat
states
                boats[j].state = boats[j].EXPLODING
                boats[i].frame = 0
                boats[j].frame = 0
```

```
snd[int(random.random()*2)].play()   # Play   sound
```

If the boats are already in the COLLIDING state, then no more has to be done, or should be. Collision is done like this:

```
def boatCollided (a, b):
    if boats[a].done or boats[b].done:
        return False
    boat1 = boats[a]
    if boat1.state == boat1.EXPLODING:
        return False
    boat2 = boats[b]
    if boat2.state == boat2.EXPLODING:
        return False
    return box_intersect (
        (boat1.ul, boat1.ur, boat1.lr, boat1.ll),
        (boat2.ul, boat2.ur, boat2.lr, boat2.ll)    )
```

While in the EXPLODING state, the **npc** class draw method will replace the rendering of the boat with the next animation frame:

```
if self.state == self.EXPLODING:
    if self.frame == 0:
        self.savedx = ccx
        self.savedy = ccy
    self.showNextExFrame(self.savedx, self.savedy)
else:
    display.blit(pygame.transform.rotate
                (self.r, self.angle), (ccx, ccy))
```

SOUNDS

After building more of the gameplay aspects, the need for more sounds is apparent. Right now, the player's boat has an engine sound and an explosion. However:

-   We still need sound effects of bounces against the shore.
-   We still need explosions when boats are destroyed.
-   We need a starting sequence.
-   We need a finish sequence.

Engine Sounds

Some time was spent in Chapter 6 showing how engine sounds could be created using Audacity. The sounds created in this way have been saved as mp3 files named *engineBoat1.mp3* through *engineBoat5.mp3*. Each engine sound is distinct, and each should be assigned to a different boat in the game. The sound should play as long as the associated boat is under power. For example, the player's engine should play as long as the "w" key is pressed.

A simple modification to the previous control code will do this. Add a global variable **engine_on** that has the obvious meaning. Now if there are any of the "a," "s," "d," or "w" keys pressed, a local variable **eon** will be set to **True**, indicating that the player wants to move the boat (turn the engine on). If it is already on, no problem. Otherwise turn it on (start the sound):

```
if eon and not engine_on:
   start_engine()
elif not eon and engine_on:
   stop_engine()
```

Each check of the keys that are depressed now looks like this:

```
if k[pygame.K_s]:
        speeds[0] = speeds[0] - .1
        eon = True
```

Each time through the event loop, the variable **eon** is first set to **False** so that if the player releases the keys, the engine will shut off. The functions that do the work are:

def start_engine(): **global** engine_on,sound_on,engine1 engine1.play(1000) engine_on = **True**	**def** stop_engine (): **global** engine_on,sound_on,engine1 engine1.stop() engine_on = **False**

There are other sounds, and those will be implemented in more detail after we know more about animation and when more of the game rules have been implemented.

Starting Gun

This is only used at the beginning of the game, and so there is only one file: *start.wav*. This is played when the starting countdown is completed: *gun.wav.*

Finish

There is a sound that plays when the winning boat passes the finish line. This sound is *cheer.wav*, and is an audience cheering.

Bing

When the player reaches a checkpoint, this sound plays to indicate this fact: *bing.wav*.

Audience

There is a background audience sound playing while the race is running: *audience.wav*.

GAME PLAY

The idea of a timer is to determine a time duration between events. In this game it could be used to show the players the elapsed time from the start of the game until someone passes the finish line.

Completing the Race

When the game begins, as specified by the user pressing the *start* button on the initial page, a timer can count down to the actual start. Let that happen 10 seconds after the game begins. After 10 seconds the gameplay timer will begin, but the same timer can be used to count down the 10 seconds at the beginning. The game can be in one of three states: Initial (countdown), playing, and end.

In the initial state the countdown timer is displayed on the play screen, going from 10 to 0. At zero the starting gun is fired, and the game begins. The play screen must now be divided into three states. The countdown state is:

Start

When the *Play* button is pressed on the opening screen, the game enters the play state and the game can begin. The start of the race should not be immediate; the player should have a few seconds to adapt. A second mouse press could be used to start the game, but another option is to do a countdown to the start, perhaps five seconds. After that time has passed, the player's controls will operate and the NPC boats will start moving.

The countdown should appear on the screen after the play button is pressed. The numbers "10," "9," "8," and so on will appear, followed by the traditional gunshot to start the game.

The countdown can be implemented as a new state that is entered at the beginning of the game, after the *Play* button is selected. In this **starting** state none of the controls will operate. Five seconds after the state is entered the countdown will begin, and at the "0" count the race begins.

Timer

There are two ways to keep track of time using Python. Likely the best one would be to use the **time** function, located in the **time** module. It returns the execution time for your program in seconds. So, to time any differential one could do the following:

```
import time
start = time.time()
... code
end = time.time()
time_difference = end - start
```

When the play button on the start screen is selected the code

```
initialTime = time.time()
```

is executed and the variable **starting** is set to true. Now a function named **countdown** is called each iteration, and it returns the current number of seconds since the play button was pressed, but backward from 10. When 0 is reached this function sets starting to **False** and plays the starting sound effect.

```
# Code in move function

if starting:
    k = countdown()
    player.display()
    boat3.display()
    boat4.display()
    pygame.draw.rect(display,

    (0, 0, 0), (500, 0, 200, 400), 0)
    text("Start in    " + str(k) + " sec-
onds", 520, 100)
    return
```

```
def countdown ():
    global initialTime, starting,

    global start
    diff = time.time()-initialTime
    if 10-diff <= 1:
        starting = False
        initialTime = time.time()
        gun.play()
        ambiance.play(loops = -1)
        ambiance.set_volume (0.1)
        return 0
    else:
        return int(10-diff)
```

Notice that when the countdown reaches 0, the **initialTime** is set to the current time again, meaning that now the difference between this and the **time()** value will be the number of seconds the game has been running. This is the game timer.

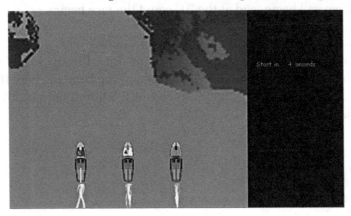

FIGURE 9.5 The starting timer.

The countdown is shown in Figure 9.5.

Intermediate Goals

In order to ensure a fair game, all boats must pass certain checkpoints during the race. The route moves up the initial fjord, moves right to the final island, around that island and left to the first island, and around that and back to the fjord at the far right. The finish line is at the end of that fjord. How can it be ensured that all of the checkpoints have been reached?

There are a couple of possibilities. A boat could reach a checkpoint if it comes within a specified distance of a specific location on the map. There is only one such checkpoint at a time, like waypoints, and when one is reached the next one is selected. Another idea would be to place invisible objects along the path that the boat must collide with. A collision simply marks the relevant portion of the track as having been completed and begins a new section.

The checkpoints are to be marked on the screen with little flags or buoys, and the boats must pass between these flags. They must also pass through them in the correct order. The function **drawWaypoints** draws the flags on the screen, and it is called for each iteration.

One of the NPC boats uses the blue flags, and the other uses the red ones. The player uses the blue flags also.

Finish

The winner of the race is the first boat to cross the finish line, located in the lower right of the terrain map. It corresponds to waypoints 29 and 30, the final NPC waypoints, and when it is reached their position in the race (first, second, or third) and the time needed to complete the race should be displayed. There is a cheer from the crowd after a finish.

FIGURE 9.6 The marker flags, which happen to be at the same position as the waypoints.

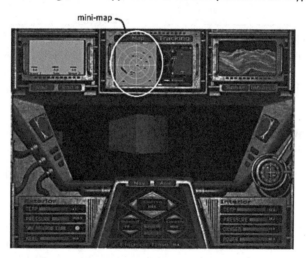

FIGURE 9.7 The play area of the game SMV Rainbow showing a mini-map.

MINI-MAP

A mini-map is a much smaller version of the playing area arranged so that it can all be seen in its entirety, or at least so that most of the play area can be seen. This means that the locations of your opponents can be seen even when they are far ahead or behind you. Other game objects can also be seen with respect to your current position. It's a very common game feature. An example is shown in Figure 9.7 from a game named *SMV Rainbow*, but many driving and combat games have this feature.

To create a mini-map we start with the original terrain image and reduce it in size. In this game the size reduction is 16x, meaning that the mini-map is 200 pixels across. A problem is that there's no place to put it in the drawing area. Anywhere this map goes it will possibly block some valuable game real estate. The answer is to make the drawing area 200 pixels wider, and to draw the mini-map in the lower part of that area. Now the creation of the display is:

```
display = pygame.display.set_mode((700,400),pygame.SRCALPHA,32)
```

The map itself is a copy if the **background** (terrain) map reduced in size:

```
bk2 = pygame.transform.scale(background, (200,169))
```

This image is drawn at location (500, 220) during each iteration. The boats must be drawn on this map too, for the map to be useful. Take the position of each boat on the big map and simply divide by 16, the map scale. Then draw it relative to the upper left of the mini-map (500,220). The player, for example, would be:

```
pygame.draw.circle (display, (255, 0, 0),
    (int(500+player.x/16), int(220+player.y/16)), 2, 0)
```

The player is drawn as a red circle and the NPC boats are blue.

Game Data

The mini-map only uses the lower portion of the expanded area. This leaves some empty space that can be used for other things. Why not display some of the game data here, such as the boat positions, speeds, and courses? It adds more interest to the game. A game timer would be good too. This is a clock showing how far into the race we are at the moment. All of those things will be drawn into the region to the right of x=500 and above the mini-map. Sample code is:

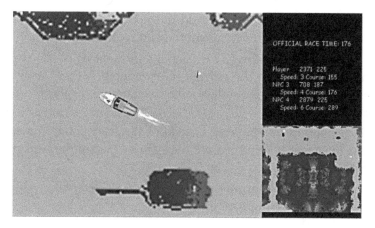

FIGURE 9.8 The new play screen showing the mini-map and playing data.

```
text ("Player     "+str(int(player.x))+"  "+str(int(player.y)),
          520,100)
text ("    Speed: "+ str(int(player.speed*10))+ " Course: "+
             str(int(player.angle)), 520,115)</CODE>
```

TUNING

The concept of tuning a game involves adjusting the parameters of all of the objects so as to make the game more fun. Fun is impossible to define, but we know when we're *having* fun, so this should be possible. What are the tuning parameters of this game? Each waypoint has a speed parameter. These can be varied to make the game more or less competitive. In fact, there could be a different set of waypoints for easy, medium, and difficult versions of the game. The *location* of the waypoints can be changed also. All of the waypoint data resides on a file, so these are easy to modify.

The acceleration and turning speed can change too. These values are constants in the code, but they are easy to change if you have the source. The locations of the checkpoints can be modified, and the required path can be made more or less constrained.

EXERCISES

1. The play testers noted that the passages from the start to the lake and at the end of the game were too narrow. Describe how this could be improved.

2. The wake animations will play over top of other boats and the shore if the situation is right. How could this be changed?

3. The end of the game is unfinished. Add the necessary code to name the finishers and their times and make use of the end screen.

4. There is a file named **flags.png** that contains the images of the two sets of waypoint marker flags. In the current implementation these images are drawn onto the terrain background. Modify the game to display these flags as animations.

5. What would happen to the game if, instead of the flags being drawn onto the terrain as the game is being played, they were a part of the background image? Is that a better way to do this?

6. Use a Python profiler to determine which of the code sections is using the most time. Is it possible to improve that?

RESOURCES

Steering: *https://gamedevelopment.tutsplus.com/tutorials/understanding-steering-behaviors-collision-avoidance--gamedev-7777.*
Pygame animation: *http://usingpython.com/animation/.*
Pygame animation using Spritesheets: *https://codehackersblog.blogspot.com/2015/06/explosion-animation-using-spritesheets-in-pygame.html.*

REFERENCES

1. alter spielend-programmieren. (2011). *The Python Game Book: Scrolling and Minimap. https://www.youtube.com/watch?v=DusPphBj98A.*

2. Bryce Boe. (2006). Line Segment Intersection Algorithm. *http://bryceboe.com/2006/10/23/line-segment-intersection-algorithm/.*

3. Tracy Fullerton, Chris Swain, and Steven Hoffman. (2004). Game Design Workshop: Designing, Prototyping, & Playtesting Games CMP Books, San Francisco.

4. Zack Hiwiller. (2015). Players Making Decisions: Game Design Essentials and the Art of Understanding Your Players. New Riders.

5. Shawn Patton. (2017). The Definitive Guide to Playtest Questions. *https://www.schellgames.com/blog/insights/the-definitive-guide-to-playtest-questions.*

6. Eric Meythaler. (2009). "2D Rotated Rectangle Collision." Gamedev.net. *https://www.gamedev.net/articles/programming/general-and-gameplay-programming/2d-rotated-rectangle-collision-r2604.*

7. Charles P. Schultz. (2016). Game Testing All in One, 3rd edition. Mercury Learning & Information. Dulles, Virginia

10

NETWORKING

A networked game allows many players to participate at one time, and these players need not be in the same room. Multiplayer games are distinct from networked games in that a basic multiplayer game permits multiple people (up to N players, usually no more than four) to use the same computer on which the game software is executing. A networked game allows many more players, as a general rule, and they can be in quite diverse locations. Communications takes place using the Internet.

The usual situation has a special computer somewhere, the game server, which takes logins and moves from players using Internet protocols. A program on each player's computer, called the client, sends the user's actions to the server and displays the actions on the player's computer. It also receives information from the server about the actions of the other players and their locations.

This means that each player can "see" the other players, at least in the sense that all of the avatars are visible on each player's screen. Reality dictates that there must be a small time difference between what a player sees and what the actual situation is as defined by the server, but in an ideal situation this would be small. The time difference is often referred to as *latency*. If this grows too large, then the game becomes unplayable, since each client has a very different idea of where the other players are.

Consider a game where two players were involved, and one was in New York and the other in Chicago. Imagine that the server is in Seattle. The game is a first-person shooter, and both players are in the same region of the game. The server mediates all interactions by the players, but the client on each computer can see what the local player is doing and will update the view very quickly, faster than the server can. Why? The local client can do graphics in microseconds, but the server is limited by the transmission speed between the client and the server.

So, the client-side program of a network game renders the scene, plays sounds, and handles the input from one player. It also receives updates from a server on where all of the objects are in the game and what their state is. In fact, it usually only does so for a small region of the game. It gets updated positions and orientations of objects from the Internet so they can be rendered, and it is informed of new creations and deletions of objects. Finally, it sends player position and orientation data, new creations, and new deletions from the local computer to the server so they can be shared with all of the other players.

In this chapter we'll look at the networking facilities that are easily accessible from Python and use them to build a simple game, a computer version of tennis that resembles the arcade game *Pong*, released by Atari in 1972.

THE GAME: PYTHON PONG

For the few people who are not familiar with the original *Pong*, the game consists of a rectangular play area, a moving ball, and two "paddles." The ball can bounce off of the top and bottom of the play area and also off of the paddles. The paddles are moved up and down by the players so as to prevent the ball from moving past them and exiting the play area from either end. If the ball moves past the left edge of the screen, the right player scores a point, and if the ball exits the right side then the left player gets a point. Balls restart from the middle of the screen someplace.

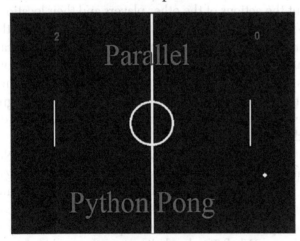

FIGURE 10.1 Background for the parallel pong game.

The basic game can be played by two players, each using a different pair of keys: the left player uses "w" and "s" to move their paddle up and down respectively, and the right player uses the up and down arrows. This game will be implemented first, and then it can be converted into one where each player has their own computer.

This is a very simple game, indeed, although it has all of the ingredients of a computer game. There are three objects: two paddles and a ball. The player uses only two keys and controls one object in only one dimension. The play area is 640 by 480 pixels. It can be coded in about 225 lines of Python using a *ball* class and a *paddle* class.

The Paddle Class

A paddle is a simulation of a ping-pong paddle. In the game it is represented by a simple vertical line. It has the following properties:

xpos - The horizontal position. The left paddle has xpos = 100, and the right paddle has xpos = 540.

ypos - The vertical position. Can be anywhere in the vertical span of the play area. The ypos value specifies the position of the center of the paddle.

color - The color with which the paddle is drawn. In the default game it is white (255,255,255).

size - 1/2 the length of the line the represents the paddle, in other words the length of the line from the center to either end.

disp - The display on which the paddle will be drawn. A Pygame *Surface*.

sx - The width of the display surface (640).

sy - The height of the display surface (480).

score - The score for the player of this paddle.

The class can tell if it is a left or right paddle by the value of **posx**.

The left player uses the "w" key to cause the paddle to move upward, and the "s" key to make it move down. The paddle continues to move while the key is held down. So, as a code example consider the left paddle: the main loop determines whether the "w" or "s" key is depressed and sets a flag **lup** or **ldown**, depending on whether the paddle should be moving up or down:

```
while True:
    for event in pygame.event.get():
        if event.type == pygame.QUIT:
            exit()
        if event.type == pygame.KEYDOWN:          # Right paddle
            if event.key == pygame.K_UP:
                rup = True
            if event.key == pygame.K_DOWN:
```

```
            rdown = True
    if event.type == pygame.KEYUP:          # Left paddle
        if event.key == pygame.K_w:
            lup = False
        if event.key == pygame.K_s:
            ldown = False
```

Then, if the paddle is to be moved, it is done by a method named **changey()** in the *paddle* class:

```
if lup:                                      # Move left if needed
    pleft.changey(-1)
if ldown:
    pleft.changey(1)
```

The parameter indices the direction of motion (-ve is up, +ve is down) and the degree of motion (number of pixels). The **changey** method does not draw the paddle. This is done in the main game loop by calling the **draw** method of each paddle. A somewhat simplified version of **draw** is:

```
def draw (self):
    pygame.draw.line (self.disp, self.color, (self.posx, self.
posy),
                      (self.posx, self.posy-self.size),3)
    pygame.draw.line (self.disp, self.color, (self.posx, self.
posy),
                      (self.posx, self.posy+self.size),3)
    font = pygame.font.Font(None, 36)
    text = font.render(str(self.score), 1, (100, 100, 100))
    if self.posx<320:
        self.disp.blit (text, (100, 40))
    else:
        self.disp.blit(text, (550, 40))
```

This version draws the score as well.

The Ball Class

The ball is a more complicated object than the paddle. It moves continuously, bounces off of other objects, and is responsible for the score in the game. It is represented as a small circle. When it moves off the end of the playing area there is a small pause, and then the ball is drawn somewhere in the middle of the play area and starts moving again.

The ball object has the following properties:

xpos   - The horizontal position.
ypos   - The vertical position.

color - The color with which the ball is drawn. In the default game it is white (255,255,255).

size - Size of the bounding box of the ball (5).

disp - The display on which the paddle will be drawn. A Pygame *Surface*.

sx - The width of the display surface (640).

sy - The height of the display surface (480).

speed - Speed with which the ball moves (pixels per frame).

dx - Change in x position each frame (initially 1).

dy - Change in y position each frame (initially 1).

countdown - The number of frames remaining before a new ball is drawn.

resetDelay - Number of frames of pause after a score is made.

left- The left paddle (an object reference).

right - The right paddle (an object reference).

The ball is drawn using a call to the draw method:

```
def draw (self):              # Draw the ball at the current position
    pygame.draw.circle (self.disp, self.color, (int(self.posx),
                        int(self.posy)), self.size, 0)
```

It is just a filled circle. Ball movement is more complicated. It changes position by **(dx, dy)** each iteration. If it bounces off of the upper or lower edge of the display area, the value of **dy** changes sign. If the ball moves past the left (x=0) or right (x=640) ends of the play area, a point is scored and a countdown is started until the ball starts moving again from the center of the play area. Finally, if the ball hits a paddle, the value of **dx** changes sign.

This code also changes the score for the relevant paddle, and it introduces a small variation in movement after a paddle collision so that movement is somewhat less predictable. Collision with a paddle is tested by the method collision, which checks to see where the ball is relative to each paddle. For example, for the left paddle:

```
if self.posx <= self.left.posx and \
    self.posy<self.left.posy+self.left.size \
        and self.posy>self.left.posy-self.left.size:
    if self.posx < self.left.posx-2:
     return False
    self.dx = -self.dx
     return True
```

```
def move (self):

# Move the ball one step. Check
collisions

    if self.countdown > 0:
#delay post goal
        self.countdown -= 1
        return
    if self.countdown == 0:
        self.posx = 240
        self.posy = random.ran-
dom()*100+200
        self.countdown = -1


    self.posx = self.posx + self.dx
    self.posy = self.posy + self.dy



    #A goal
    if self.posx > self.sx:

        self.left.score += 1
        self.countdown = self.
resetDelay
        if self.posx < 0:
            self.right.score += 1
            self.countdown = self.
resetDelay
```

```
# bounce off of the wall
    if self.posy > self.sy:
        self.posy = self.sy
        self.dy = -self.dy
    if self.posy < 0:
        self.posy = 0
        self.dy = -self.dy

    if self.collision():          #
Paddle collision?
        self.dx = self.dx + \

        (random.random
()-0.5)*0.2



# A slight change after bouncing

        self.dy = self.dy+(random.
random()\

        -0.5)*0.2
        d = math.sqrt (self.dx*self.
dx + \

        self.dy*self.dy)
        self.dx = (self.dx/d)*self.
speed
        self.dy = (self.dy/d)*self.
speed
```

Without the inner **if** statement, the ball could "bounce" if it moved behind the paddle without colliding with it. This has unfortunate consequences as can be seen if this statement is removed.

These two classes implement the game. When one paddle or the other reaches a certain score value, the game is over.

Now let's see how communication is done in Python between computers on a network.

Communication Between Processes

Communication between programs on a network is conducted very much like a conversation. One person (program), the *client*, initiates the conversation ("Hi there!"). The other (the *server*) responds ("Hello. Nice to see you."). Now it is the client's turn again. They take turns *sending* and *accepting* messages until one says "goodbye." These messages might contain email, or FTP data, or TV programs. The communications system does not care what the data is; none of its business, really. Its job is to deliver it.

Data are delivered in *packets*, with each containing a certain amount. In order for the client to deliver the data, there must be a server willing to connect to it. The client needs to know the address of a server, just as an FTP address or email destination was required before, but now all that is needed is the host name and a *port number*. A port is really a logical construction, something akin to an element of a list. If two programs agree to share data by having one of them place it in location 50001 of a list and the other one read it from there, it gives an approximate idea of what a port is. Some port numbers are assigned and should not be used for anything else; FTP and email have assigned ports. Others are available for use, and any two processes can agree to use one.

A module named *socket*, based on the interprocess communication scheme on UNIX of the same name, is used with Python to send messages back and forth. To create an example, two computers should be used, one being the client and one the server. The IP address of the server is required.

Example: Moving a Ball on the Screen

The client will open a communications link (socket) to the server, which has a known IP address. The server will engage in a short handshake (exchange of strings) and then expect to receive a number for the client. The client will send an integer, the server will receive it, square it, and send back the answer. This simple exchange is really the basis for all communications between computers: one machine sends information, the other receives it, processes it, and returns a reply based on the data it received.

The client: will begin the conversation. It creates a connection, called a *socket*, to the server using the **socket**() function of the *socket* module. Protocols must be specified, and the most common ones will be used:

```
import socket

HOST = '19*.***.*.***'     # The remote host
PORT = 50007               # The same port as used by the server
```

```
s = socket.socket(socket.AF_INET, socket.SOCK_STREAM)
s.connect((HOST, PORT))
```

The client must identify the host computer that is the machine running the *server*. Anyone who plays an online game has downloaded the client software that makes that possible, and this software has the server IP address built into it. To test this program we need two computers and we need to know the IP address of the server. This can be found, for the test, by executing the ***ipconfig*** program on your PC. Figure 10.2 shows a possible result.

Port 50007 is used because nothing else is using it. Now the client starts the conversation, just as it appears at the beginning of this section, by sending a message. In this case the message is a string:

```
s.send(b'Hi there!')
```

The **send()** function sends the message passed as a parameter. The string (as *bytes*) is transmitted to the server through the variable **s**, which represents the server. The client now waits for the confirmation string from the server, which should be "Hello. Nice to see you." To receive the message, the client calls another socket function:

```
data = s.recv(1024)
```

which waits for a response from the server. This response will be 1024 bytes long at most, and it will wait only for a short time, at which point it will give up and an error will be reported. If this client gets the response, it proceeds to the next step in the communication process. In this case it should be to receive the (x, y) position of an object on the screen.

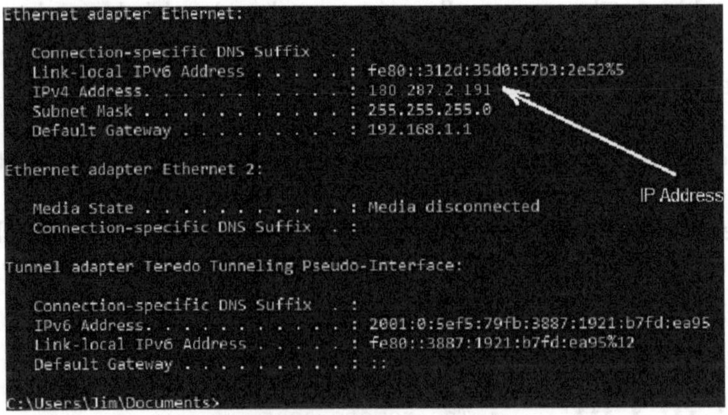

FIGURE 10.2 Output from ipconfig showing your IP address.

Now let's say that we have agreed that the received data will be a pair of integers. The client could read the string, convert it into integers, and use them as screen (window) coordinates at which to draw a ball. Then the client will draw the ball, read another pair, draw again, and so on. The nature of the communication is agreed on in advance and must be followed exactly.

When the exchange of data is complete, the client closes the connection:

```
s.close()
```

The Server: is always listening. It creates a socket on a particular port so that the operating system knows something is possible there, but because the server cannot predict when a client will connect or what client it will be, it simply listens for a connection, by calling a function named **listen()**:

```
import socket
from random import *

HOST = ''    # A null string is correct here.
PORT = 50007
s = socket.socket(socket.AF_INET, socket.SOCK_STREAM)
s.bind ((HOST, PORT))
s.listen()
```

AF_INET and SOCK_STREAM are constants that tell the system which protocols are being used. These are the most common, but see the documentation for others. The **bind()** and the **listen()** functions are new to this discussion. Associating this connection with a specific port is done using **bind().** The tuple (HOST, PORT) says to connect this host to this port. The empty string for HOST implies *this* computer. The **listen()** call starts the server process, *this* program, accepting connections when asked. A process connecting on the port that was specified in *bind()* will now result in this process, the server, being notified. When a connection request occurs, the server must accept it before doing any input or output:

```
conn, addr = s.accept()
```

In the tuple **(conn, addr)** that is returned, **conn** represents the connection, like a file descriptor returned from **open()**, and is used to send and receive data; **addr** is the address of the sender, the client, and is a string. If the **addr** were printed:

```
print ("Connected to ", addr)
```
It would look like an IP address:

Connected to 423.141.12.911

Now the server can receive data across the connection, and does so by calling **recv()**:

```
data = conn.recv(1024)
print ("Server heard '", data, "'")
```

The parameter 1024 specifies the size of the buffer, or the maximum number of bytes that can be received in one call. The variable **data** is of type *bytes*, just as the parameter to **send()** was in the client. The client was the first to send, and it sent the message "Hi there!" That should be the value of the data now, if it has been received properly. The response from the server should be "Hello, nice to see you.":

```
conn.send (b'Hello. Nice to see you.')
```

The same connection is used for sending and receiving. Now the real data gets exchanged. The server will accept integers, sent as *bytes*. It can draw the ball at the specified position:

```
while True:
    data = conn.recv(1024)              # Read the incoming data
    if data:
        xpos,ypos = convertData(data)   # Convert it to integers
        print ("Received ", i)
        drawBall (xpos,ypos)            # Draw the ball
```

The server can tell when the connection is closed by the client, but it is also polite to say "Goodbye" somehow, perhaps by sending a particular code. If the loop ever terminates, the server should close the connection:

```
conn.close()
```

This is a pretty good example of a data exchange and a contract, because there are specified requirements for each side of this conversation which will result in success if done correctly and failure if messed up. Failure is sometimes indicated by an error message, often a *timeout* where the client or server was expecting something that never arrived. In other cases, failure is not formally indicated at all; the program simply "hangs" there and does nothing. For example, if at any time both processes are trying to receive data, then the program will fail. This is a failure in the implementation of the protocol.

Figure 10.3 shows the communication between the client and the server as a diagram. If the client and the server are at any time both trying to accept data from the connection, then the program will fail. In the diagram all data transfers can be seen as transmit-accept pairs between the two processes, and as read-write pairs within the server and write-read pairs within the client.

```
# The client                              # The server
import socket                             import socket

# The remote host                        HOST = '' # A null string is ok here.
HOST = '19*.***.*.***'                    PORT = 50007
# The same port used by the server        s = socket.socket(socket.AF_INET, \
PORT = 50007                                  socket.SOCK_STREAM)
                                          s.bind ((HOST, PORT))
s = socket.socket(socket.AF_INET,\        s.listen()
    socket.SOCK_STREAM)                   conn, addr = s.accept()
s.connect((HOST, PORT))                   data = conn.recv(1024)
s.send(b'Hi there!')                      print ("Server heard", data, "")
data = s.recv(1024)                       conn.send (b'Hello. Nice to see you.')
for i in range (0, 100):                  while True:
    data = str(i).encode()                # Read the incoming data
    s.send (data)                             data = conn.recv(1024)
    data = s.recv(1024)                       if data:
s.close()                                 # Convert it to integer
                                              i = int(data)
                                              print ("Received ", i)
                                          # Square it and convert to bytes
                                              data = str(i*i).encode()
                                          # Send to the client
                                              conn.send (data)
                                          conn.close()
```

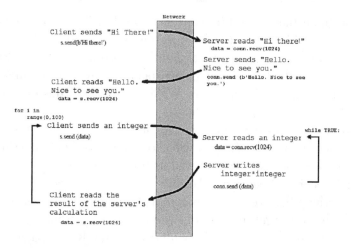

FIGURE 10.2 Typical *communication between the client and the server processes.*

NETWORK PONG

The networked client-server version of this game is played on two computers by two players, with a third computer as the intermediary for communication. Each client program gathers user interface information and sends it to the server. The server shares the result of this information with the clients, in that a keystroke in one client results in a move of the paddle which is sent to the other client as a change in the paddle position. The client has no user interface, and simply acts as an intermediate.

The Client

The game client has a few major tasks:

1. Establish a connection to the server.
2. Determine which paddle it controls using communication to the server.
3. Wait to be told the game has started.
4. Play the game as follows:
   Identify movement of the paddle by the player and transmit this to the server.
   Determine where the ball is and display it at the correct place.
   Tell the server when a point is scored.
   Get from the server the points for each side and display them.
   Get from the server a notice when the game is over.

There is a problem that should be kept in mind, but it can be neglected in implementation until later. That is the question of where the ball really is. Each of the three processes may have a slightly different view of that fact. What this means is that the ball's bounces may occur at different moments in real time on each of the three computers. We'll wait to see if this becomes a serious issue.

We've seen how to establish a connection to the server. The client may have to wait, because the server in this chapter will allow only two clients at a time. A third client trying to connect will have to wait its turn to play.

The client will receive a message indicating which player it is, left or right. That is again something that we've seen before. It waits until the client sends it a message. When the server gets two players who wish to play, as indicated by its receiving messages from two different computers, then it sends a message to both clients saying that the game has begun. It sends the clients the position of the ball.

The client accepts information from the player about paddle motion of the paddle it controls, which it translates into positions and sends to the server. It asks the server for the position of the opponent's paddle and the ball, and then renders the new scene. The paddles need not move, but the ball does, and it is updated each frame. Thus, the ball position updates can be used as a means to time the screen updates: each time a ball update is received amounts to one "clock tick," which triggers a new frame to be rendered by the client.

This is the core of the client code, and a sketch of an implementation would consist of a loop:

```
initialize()
while True:                             void keyReleased ()
    get a message m                         if move paddle up key
    if m is a paddle position                   send server a new
paddle position
        move the paddle                     if move paddle down key
    if m is a ball position                     send server a new
paddle position
        move the ball
        render the frame
```

From this sketch it can be seen that the client does not update its own paddle directly, but waits to hear from the server. The delay on the network could be such that the local paddle position was far ahead of where the server and other client had most recently recorded. This means that a player could see their paddle in one place while the server saw it in another, resulting in points or bounces being recorded that the player could not see. It would be frustrating. Anyone who has played an online game understands the problems that *lag* can bring.

We can also see that a message has a specific meaning or type, and each type has parameters. According to the sketch there are at least two types: paddle position and ball position. There are more, of course. The format of each message can be specific to the content. So:

Message	ID Code	Param 1	Param 2
Paddle position (PPOS)	01	Position y x position is fixed	Which paddle(0 or 1)
Ball position (BPOS)	02	Position x	Position y

In the *initialize* section of code, there is a message sent that identifies the client's designation, left or right:

```
Designation  00               0=left, 1=right
  (DESI)
```

This will be the first message received. The messages consist of four integers (128 bits), the ID code that identifies the kind of message, and three parameters. Each code will have only one bit sent at most. Parameters are 32-bit integers. A message can be sent by calling a function named **sendMessage(a, b, c, d)**.

The Server

The server has the bulk of the communication responsibility. It must wait for a connection to two clients to be established. It tells each client what paddle they control and then sits in the middle of the game, collecting data from each and sending it to both. When the server receives a paddle position from one client, it must send the resulting position to both clients. That is because the server is the ultimate arbiter of paddle position. It determines what the ball position is at each iteration and transmits that position to each client. That is because the server is the ultimate arbiter of the ball position. Because of this, the server determines when a goal is scored and when the game is over. It is responsible for sending these data to the clients.

The server waits for two clients to connect and then assigns each of them a paddle, sending them a *DESI* message. It then delays for a few seconds to give the players time to get ready and then sends a *BPOS* message, placing the ball at a random starting position. It then moves the ball as is done in the standalone game, sending a *BPOS* message after each movement. After each ball movement the server looks for *PPOS* messages from the clients and updates the paddle positions if any are encountered, passing paddle positions to both of the clients as well. When a *PPOS* is received from the left client, the server sends it to both clients—they do not update their paddles until they hear from the server.

When a score occurs, a message is sent to both clients to that effect so that the correct score can be displayed on their respective screens. The server then waits for a few seconds and starts the game again with the ball in a random start position. When one client has scored 21 points, it has won the game, and the server sends a message to that effect to both clients.

We have two new messages:

Message	ID Code	Param 1	Param 2
Goal (GOAL)	04	Left score	Right score
Game over (OVER)	08		

After the game is over, the communication channels are closed. The server can start over, getting two new clients and beginning a new game.

Blocking and Non-Blocking

There are a great many options, protocols, and possibilities when building a communication system using sockets. One important option is whether to use *blocking* or *non-blocking* send and receive operations.

When reading from a socket using **recv**, the default is a *blocking* read, meaning that the function **recv** does not return until it has obtained some data. The program can do nothing else until the data has been received. If the return value is 0, it means that the process at the other end has closed and will never again send any data. A send operation will not return until the data has been sent; sending data means writing it into a buffer in the receiver, and if space is not available, then the sender waits until it is. Blocking can be a problem if it is not known which of multiple processes will send a message. In the current example that's true of paddle positions. Either client can send a paddle position update at any time. These updates must be dealt with as soon as possible, and using a blocking read on the left paddle will delay until a message is set by the left client; meanwhile, the right client could have sent many *PPOS* messages.

A solution would be to ensure that each client sends one PPOS message each iteration, and then awaits a BPOS message from the server. This constrains the reaction of the paddle movement and sends many more messages than needed. Another would be to collect paddle movements so that they could all be sent in a single message after each ball movement was received. Both solutions mean that the sequence of send-receive is predictable, and so the blocking would not cause too much trouble.

A *non-blocking* receive always returns right away, whether or not any data was sent. If data exists the call works as it has before. If there is no data, then the call will throw a **socket.error** exception with the error number (**errno**) of either **EAGAIN** or **EWOULDBLOCK**. Reading from a socket is now a little more complex:

```
def readf (s):
    msg = "error "
    try:
        msg = s.recv(8)
    except socket.error as err:
        if err == socket.errno.EAGAIN or err == socket.errno.
EWOULDBLOCK:   # No data
```

```
            return ""
      else:
           print (err)
           return msg          # an error occurred
      else:
           return msg                # Data was received
```

In the previous code, if no data is received then the program could wait for some time and try again.

Causing the socket to be non-blocking is accomplished by a call:

```
mysocket.setblocking (0)
```

Dealing with non-blocking channels can be a problem, because many conditions have to be tested for any attempted communication. All **recv** calls need to be embedded within tests for errors and content, as previously. There may also be many clients that are in communication at the same time as well. A module named **select** has been constructed which enables non-blocking communication to be dealt with very effectively.

The method **select** take three lists as arguments and returns a subset of each of those three lists as a value. In the call:

```
select (a, b, c)
```

a is a list of objects to be checked for incoming data, **b** is a list of objects to which data will be sent, and for which buffer space will be needed, and **c** is a list of objects that may have resulted in an error. Most often, **c** consists of all of the objects in **a** and **b**. The call returns three lists, so:

```
x, y, z = select (a, b, c)
```

returns **x** as a list of objects that are readable, in that they have incoming data that can be accessed using a **recv** call; **y** is a list of objects that have space in their buffer and can be written to; and **z** is a list of objects that have indicated an error. The game server would have within it, using this scheme, the following code:

```
inputs = [ls, rs]
outputs = [ls, rs]
queues = {}
while True:
     readable, writable, exceptional = select.select(inputs,
```

```
outputs, inputs)
    for s in readable:
        print ("Reading")
        m1 = readf (s)
        if m1 != "":
            print ("[............ ", m1)
    # now update and send ball position
    . . .
```

The game can't do very much except wait for a response from a client if one is not immediately available, so there is no real penalty for using the blocking send and receive. At this point we have a strategy for organizing the communication portion of the network game. We are almost ready to code the game.

Messages

We have defined five distinct messages that the game requires: PPOS, BPOS, DESI, GOAL, and OVER. The connections transmit characters over the sockets, so each message will be a character string. There will be at most two parameters, and each of these will be at most three digits, because they are usually screen coordinates. Thus, eight characters is enough for a message.

Sending a message means taking the message type code and two parameters and converting that into a string that can be sent. The easiest message to format is game over, which has no parameters. It will always be "08000000."

DESI has only one parameter, and that's either 0 or 1. A left DESI is "00000000" and a right DESI is "01000000."

PPOS has only one parameter as well, but there are two paddles. It is sensible to send both the left and right paddle positions in a single message. The implementation of PPOS will have the first parameter represent the left paddle position and the second parameter be the right.

Let's assume that if a parameter is not needed, it will be set to 0. Then any 8-byte message can be formatted using:

```
'{:02d}{:03d}{:03d}'.format(code, p1, p2)
```

So, for some examples:

```
DESI left is 00 000 000
DESI right is 01 000 000
OVER is 08 000 000
PPOS 121,255 is  01 121 255          Left paddle=121, right
=255
BPOS 671,330 is 02 671 330
```

Decoding the messages is pretty simple too. Any string has a 2-character code and two 3-character integers. So, a string **s** can be decoded as:

```
code = int(s[0:2])
p1 = int(s[2:5])
p2 = int(s[5:8])
```

Now we can begin to separate the client and server parts of the game code.

The Pong Client

The client code is most similar to the standalone game code in that it accepts commands from the keyboard and displays the playing area on the screen. The client begins by establishing a connection with the server.

The implementation of the client uses a **communications** class to do a lot of the data transmission to and from the server. It holds the message codes, the server address, and importantly has a method called **initClient** that establishes the link to the server. The first thing the client does is create an instance of the **communications** class that tries to connect. This class also contains the following:

```
def readf(self):            Read a message from the
server
def makeMessage(code, p1, p2):    Construct a message string
def getMessage(s):          Decode a message
def readMessage(self):      Read and decode a message
def sendPPos(self, yl, yr):  Send paddle positions
```

After the connection is made, the client receives a DESI message from the server telling it which side (left or right) the client is playing. Only the key presses appropriate to the client will be processed. If the client is the left side, then the arrow keys will have no effect. The functions **IAMLEFT()** and **IAMRIGHT()** can be used by the client to determine what side it is playing. The two sides also differ in the following ways:

- The paddle being played by each client will be drawn in green.
- The paddle position for the paddle being played is sent to the server.

The game loop for the client is the same up to the point where the paddle motion has to be implemented. Then we have the following code:

First, send the current paddle position to the server.

```
if IAMLEFT():
```

```
    coms.sendPPos (pleft.posy, 0)
else:
    coms.sendPPos (pright.posy, 1)
```

Now get the position of the ball from the server and place the ball in that position.

```
# -------------- Get ball position ------------------
  m1 = coms.readMessage ()    # m1 is a string
  xlst = coms.getMessage (m1)  # xlst is a tuple
  ball.move(xlst[1], xlst[2])
```

Read the paddle positions that the server has. These are really the current positions, because the server determines collisions.

```
# ------------ Get other paddle position --------------
  m1 = coms.readMessage ()      # m1 is a string
  xlst = coms.getMessage (m1)   # xlst is a tuple
  pright.posy = xlst[2]
  pleft.posy = xlst[1]
```

Now read the score from the server. This is used to display on the screen, and to determine when the game is over.

```
# ------------ Get the score --------------------------
  m1 = coms.readMessage ()      # m1 is a string
  xlst = coms.getMessage (m1)   # xlst is a tuple
  pright.score = xlst[2]
  pleft.score = xlst[1]
```

The rest is nearly as before. Draw the background, the ball, and the paddles. In this version the maximum score is 3, which makes debugging easier.

```
display.blit (background, (0,0)) # Display the background
if pright.score > 3:
    gameover = True
if pleft.score > 3:
    gameover = True


  pleft.draw()                 # Draw the left paddle
  pright.draw()                # Draw the right paddle
  ball.draw()                  # Draw the ball
  pygame.display.update()      # Refresh the screen
```

And that's the game. The client does not determine paddle collisions, wall bounces, or scores. The server does this because it is always the owner of all current positions. This means that the server may be a key press or so behind a client due to latency, but it still is the authority concerning the game state.

The code for the client is on the book's disc.

The Pong Server

The server does not display the game. It runs on a computer, perhaps in the background with other processes, and simply arbitrates the two clients. It has the actual **ball** class and **paddle** class, determines bounces and scores, and sends messages back and forth. It has no user interface. Paddle positions are sent from each client and are sent back to the clients after the server processes them.

This means that the entire section of the game loop that handles the user interaction is not needed. The game loop is, in fact, very brief:

```
while True:
    clock.tick(50)
    for event in pygame.event.get():    # Only event should be
QUIT.
        if event.type == pygame.QUIT:
            exit()

# ---------------- Get Paddle positions ----------------------
--------------
    m1 = readMessage(rs)        # Read  paddle message sent by
RIGHT client.
    pright.changey(m1[1])       # Also change the position of the
paddle
    m1 = readMessage(ls)        # Read  paddle message sent by
Left client.
    pleft.changey(m1[1])        # Also change the position of the
paddle

# ------------------------- Move ball, send position ----------
----------------------
    ball.move()   # Move the ball
    sendBPos(ls, int(ball.posx), int(ball.posy))
    sendBPos(rs, int(ball.posx), int(ball.posy))

# ------------------------------ Send paddle pos to clients ------
----------------------
    ls.send(bytes(makeMessage(PPOS, pleft.posy, pright.posy),
'utf-8'))
    rs.send(bytes(makeMessage(PPOS, pleft.posy, pright.posy),
'utf-8'))

# ------------------------------ Send score to both clients ------
----------------------
```

```
sendScore(ls, pleft.score, pright.score)
sendScore (rs, pleft.score, pright.score)
```

The messages passed between the server and the client have be synchronized or one of the blocking reads will simply hang, waiting for data. The game loop for the server must have a send whenever the game loop for the client has a receive, and vice versa. In this case the protocol is:

```
Server                                          Client
Get the paddle positions              Send paddle position
ml = readMessage(rs)                  coms.sendPPos (pleft.
posy, 0)
ml = readMessage(ls)

Send the ball position          Get ball position
sendBPos(ls, int(ball.posx), int(ball.posy))    ml = coms.
readMessage()
sendBPos(rs, int(ball.posx), int(ball.posy))

Send the paddle positions              Get paddle positions
                                  ml = coms.readMessage()
ls.send(bytes(makeMessage(PPOS, pleft.posy, pright.posy), 'utf-
8'))
rs.send(bytes(makeMessage(PPOS, pleft.posy, pright.posy), 'utf-
8'))


Send the score                  Get the score
sendScore(ls, pleft.score, pright.score)   ml = coms.
readMessage()
sendScore (rs, pleft.score, pright.score)
```

Playing the Game

Three computers are used to play this game. First run the server program on the computer having the server's IP address, as used by the clients. Then run a client on each of the other two computers. One will be assigned the left paddle, the other the right. Note that the ball has the same position on each game screen, and when the left player moves their paddle, the movement shows up on the right player's screen.

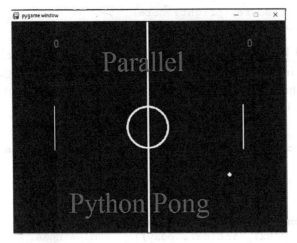

FIGURE 10.4 **Live screen from the pong game.**

RESOURCES

Python Socket – Network Programming Tutorial
https://www.binarytides.com/python-socket-programming-tutorial/
Getting Started with Processing for Android *http://createdigitalmotion.com/2010/09/
getting-started-with-processing-for-android/*
Socket - Low-Level Networking Interface
https://docs.python.org/3.6/library/socket.html
Python - Network Programming
https://www.tutorialspoint.com/python/python_networking.htm
http://realmike.org/blog/2010/12/11/sound-playback-in-processing-for-android/

REFERENCES

1. Todd Barron and LostLogic. (2002). *Multiplayer Game Programming*, 1st edition. Course Technology PTR.

2. A. Freier, P. Karlton, and P. Kocher. (2011). *The Secure Sockets Layer (SSL) Protocol Version 3.0.* Internet Engineering Task Force (IETF). *https://tools. ietf.org/html/rfc6101?ref=driverlayer.com.*

3. Warren Gay. (2000). *Linux Socket Programming by Example*, 1st edition. Que Publishing.

4. Josh Glazer and Sanjay Madhav. (2015). *Multiplayer Game Programming: Architecting Networked Games*, 1st edition. Addison-Wesley Professional.

5. John Goerzen and Tim Bower. (2010). *Foundations of Python Network Programming: The Comprehensive Guide to Building Network Applications with Python*, 2nd edition. Apress.

6. Alberto Leon-Garcia and Indra Widjaja. (2003). *Communication Networks*, 2nd edition. McGraw-Hill Education. Boston.

7. Andrew S. Tanenbaum and David J. Wetherall. (2010). *Computer Networks*, 5th edition [Indian International edition]. Prentice Hall.

A* IN PYTHON

```python
class node:
    def __init__ (self, a, b):
        self.i = a
        self.j = b
        self.parent = None
        self.bestf = 100000
        self.unusable = False
        self.g = 100000
        self.seen = False
        self.mark = False;

    def Mark (self):
        self.mark = True
    def unMark(self):
        self.mark = False

    def updateF (self, f, p):
        if f < self.bestf:
            self.bestf = f
            self.parent = p

    def setUnusable (self):
        self.unusable = True

def initialize ():
    global z

    for i in range (0,10):
        for j in range (0,10):
            z[i][j] = node(i,j);
    """ First maze
    z[2][1].setUnusable()   # Set up the grid
    z[3][1].setUnusable()
    z[4][1].setUnusable()
```

```
    z[5][1].setUnusable()
    z[5][2].setUnusable()
    z[6][2].setUnusable()
    z[6][3].setUnusable()
    z[7][3].setUnusable()
    z[7][4].setUnusable()
    z[8][4].setUnusable()
    z[8][5].setUnusable()
    z[8][6].setUnusable()

    z[1][6].setUnusable()
    z[2][6].setUnusable()
    z[3][6].setUnusable()
    z[3][7].setUnusable()
    z[3][8].setUnusable()
    """
    for i in range (0,9):
        z[2][i].setUnusable()
    for i in range (1,10):
        z[5][i].setUnusable();
    printGrid()

def printGrid():                      # Print the scene
    for i in range(10):
        for j in range(10):
            if i==1 and j==5:
                print("S", end="")
            elif i==7 and j==5:
                print ("E", end="")
            elif z[i][j].mark:
              print ("^", end="")
            elif z[i][j].parent != None:
              print (".", end="")
            elif z[i][j].unusable:
              print ("#", end="")
            else:
              print (".", end="")
        print ()

def h (p):
    return (abs(p.i-goalx) + abs(p.j-goaly)) * 10

def g(p):
    return p.g

def f (p):
    return h(p) + g(p)
```

```python
def inList(p, l):
    for ll in l:
        if ll.i==p.i and ll.j==p.j:
            return ll
    return None

def smallestOpenList ():
    q = openList[0]
    for p in openList:
        if p.bestf < q.bestf:
            q = p
    return q

def neighbors (p):
    nlist = []    # Create a list of neighbors of p
    for i in range(-1, 2):
        for j in range(-1, 2):
            if i == 0 and j == 0:
                continue
            ii = p.i + i
            if (ii < 0 or ii >= 10):    # Range check
                continue
            jj = p.j + j
            if (jj < 0 or jj >= 10):
                continue
            nlist = nlist + [z[ii][jj]]
    return nlist

def unMarkAll ():
    for i in range(0,10):
        for j in range(0,10):
            z[i][j].unMark()

def printCost ():
    for i in range(0,10):
        for j in range(0,10):
            if z[i][j].g>300:
                print ("xxx ", end="")
            else:
                print (z[i][j].g," ", end="")
        print()

z = [[None for j in range(10)] for i in range(10)]
initialize()
startNode = z[1][5]    # Where to begin the path
goalNode = z[7][5]     # The place we are trying to reach
```

```
openList = []          # Open list; a list of points
closedList = []        # Closed list; a list of points
goalx = 7
goaly = 5

startNode.g = 0
print ("Starting f is ", startNode.bestf)
openList.append(startNode)
print (openList[0].bestf)

while (len(openList) > 0):       # While open list not empty
  p = smallestOpenList()        # Select a node from the open list
  if (p == goalNode):           # We have reached the goal.
    print ("Done.")
    printGrid()
    break

  closedList.append(p)          # Add to closed list
  openList.remove(p)            # remove from open
  nlist = neighbors(p)          # Find all neighbors

  for c in nlist:               # Examine each neighbor, named 'c'
    if c.unusable:              # If unusable or
        continue
    if inList(c,closedList) != None: # if it is in the closed
list,
        continue                        # ignore it

    if p.i == c.i or p.j == c.j:  # Distance c to p
       d = 10
    else:
       d = 14
    cost = p.g + d                # New cost of c is old cost + d

    if inList (c,openList) == None:          # c not in the open
list
        openList.append(c)
        if cost >= f(c):
            continue
        c.g = cost
        c.parent = p # Set the parent
        c.bestf = f(c)


  printCost()
  print ("-------------------------------------------------------
----")
```

```
unMarkAll()

p = z[goalx][goaly]
while (p != startNode):
    print ("<        ", p.i,",",p.j)
    p.Mark()
    p = p.parent


printGrid()
printCost()
```

APPENDIX B

C2H6O Jet Boat Race Game Design Document

1.   Game Overview

1.1. Concept – This game will involve the player guiding a jet boat through a course down a river and around a lake and over a finish line, while escaping traps, avoiding obstacles.

1.2. Genre – This is a basic race style game, 2D with overhead view.

1.3. Audience – Any age, but with a younger demographic.

1.4. Game Flow – After moving through the initial screens, the player is signaled to begin the race. The game begins at a small dock with three boats, and initially all move down the river and jockey for position. A lake is entered that has floating pylons to guide the player, each having a number and a color. The number indicates the next pylon to pass in sequence, and the color indicates which boat must pass near to the pylon. The first boat to pass the final pylon wins the race.

1.5. Visual Style – The view of the playing area is from above, and it scrolls to follow the player. It is a typical 2D race game in that aspect. Boats are 21st century jet boats.

2.   Gameplay and Mechanics

2.1. Gameplay

2.1.1. Game Progression – There is one level, and one goal.

2.1.2. Mission/challenge Structure – no specific missions.

2.1.3. Objectives – The overall objective is to cross the finish line before any of the other (NPC) boats. Other goals include:

-   To pass near flags along the route
-   To fuel up to avoid running out of fuel (canceled)
-   To interfere, if possible, with the other boats

2.1.4. Play Flow – The game is focused on the human player. Other boats will attempt to avoid the player. The player must move through the obstacles, pass the markers correctly, and pass over the finish line.

2.2. Mechanics –

The player can control their boat, making it accelerate or turn left or right.

Hitting land slows the boat, which the player must guide back into the water.

The race begins on a river, enters a lake where one lap of a circuit must be made, and ends on another river where the finish line is.

Small flags are floating near the boat's path, and these must be encountered in the correct order so that the player may win. Missing a flag means having to go back.

A clock keeps track of the time that the boat has spent on the race so far. The boat with the smallest time at the finish wins, irrespective of their physical place in the race.

2.2.1. Physics – The game takes place on the surface of the water, which is a high friction surface. Acceleration can be quick, but slacking off on the accelerator will slow the boat quickly. The boat cannot turn too quickly, so moving too fast when a turn is needed slows the player's progress.

2.2.2. Movement in the game – The "q" key accelerates the boat forward, and releasing it will slow the boat. Turns are performed using the "a" key (left) and the "d" key (right).

2.2.3. Economy – There is no in-game economy.

2.2.4. Screen Flow – A graphical description of how each screen is related to every other and a description of the purpose of each screen.

There will be an opening screen (load game assets)

Start screen (play, exit, options, sound)

Options screen – select boats, sound on/off

Play screen

End – win/lose, save score, replay/exit

2.3. Game Options – The player can select a boat that has specific properties of top speed, acceleration, and maneuverability from a small list.

2.4. Replaying and Saving – Game can't be saved but can be replayed and a list of players and scores can be maintained.

3.   Story, Setting, and Character

3.1. Story and Narrative – There is no narrative here, just a race. *Cut scenes before and after the race are real boat racing scenes from actual jet boat races.*

3.2. Game World

3.2.1. General look and feel of world – A 2D plane showing water and land areas, flags, boats, refueling area, and obstacles. The terrain background image is xx.png.

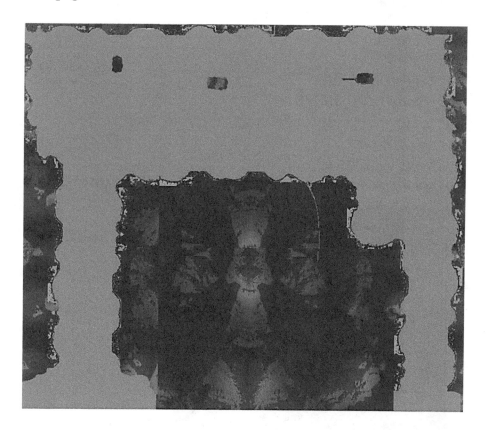

3.2.2. The start area is a dock along a river. When the game begins, the player and NPCs accelerate to the left along the river.

3.2.3. The river opens into a lake that has colored flags and islands to avoid. Blue pylons are needed by the player and one of the NPC boats, the red ones by the other NPC.

3.2.4. There is another river entering the lake which contains the finish line, and it is to be used after circuits of the lake have been performed.

3.3. Characters. NPC boats have various colors and shapes. Boat3 (NPC3) is boat2a.gif as a file.

Boat4 (NPC4) is boat5a.gif.

Each is 88x27 pixels with a transparent background.

4. Levels –

4.1. Levels. Only the one.

4.2. Tutorial Level – Later

5. Interface

5.1. Windows and Transitions

When the game begins the START screen is displayed. (startScreen.jpg)

There are three buttons on this screen: Play, Quit, and Options.

When the Options button is pressed, the Options screen is displayed (optionsScreen.jpg):

The Options screen has a button that turns the sound on or off, and a back button that returns the player to the Start screen.

When the Quit button is pressed the quit screen is displayed, which shows the credits. Any mouse click will terminate the game program.

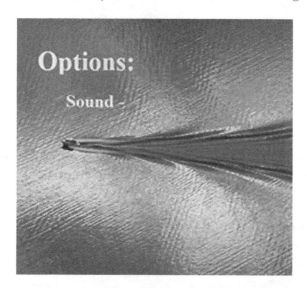

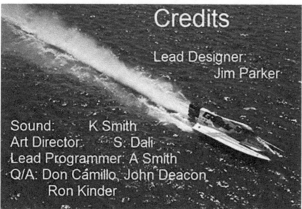

When the Play button is pressed the Play screen is displayed. This is the main play area and is where all of the remaining game aspects occur. The game screen is 700 by 400 pixels. 500 x 400 show the game play, and 200 x 400 show a mini-map and other game data on the right side of the screen.

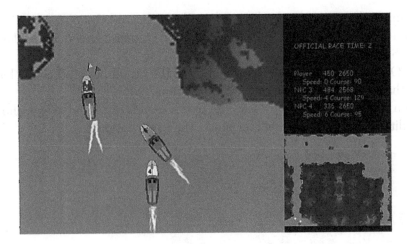

5.2. Visual Assist. HUD.

Camera is above the player's boat.

HUD (mini-map) is in the lower right corner and shows a wider area with other boats and scene features. Above that is a text area showing the current position, speed, and course of each boat.

5.3. Control System – Keyboard

The "q" key moves the player's boat forward. The "a" key turns it left, and the "d" key turns it right. The described actions continue as long as the key is depressed.

5.4. Audio

Music

No music

Starting gun – gun.wav

End indicator – People cheering. finish.wav

Flag indicator – a "bing" noise sounds when the player reaches a new flag. (bing.wav)

Engine noise – Plays while the player has depressed a motion key (engine1. wav)

Ambiance – crowd noise plays once the game starts (audience.wav)

5.5.   Help System – a single help screen can be opened at any time by typing the "h" key. *Contents later.*

6. Artificial Intelligence

6.1. Player and Collision Detection

A boat can collide with another boat or with the shore.

BOAT-BOAT COLLISION

When two boats collide they explode and start over from the beginning. An explosion animation plays and an explosion sound is started.

Collisions are based on object-oriented box intersections. These boxes are somewhat smaller than the bounding box (size to be determined by play test).

There are five different explosion animations, selected as a sequence during play. They are represented as sprite sheets (explode1.gif, explode4.gif, explode5.png).

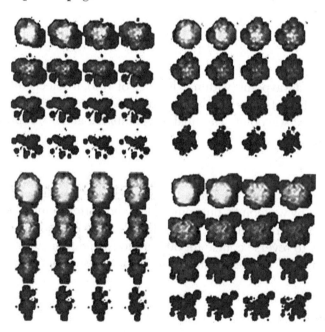

These have 16 individual frames that are 32 x 32 pixels. The sound of the explosion is exp1.wav or exp2.wav, and is selected at random.

BOAT-SHORE COLLISION

A collision with the shore is detected by using the corner points of a boat's bounding box. If any of these fall on a terrain pixel that is not the same color as water (33,174,173), then a collision is indicated.

6.2. Pathfinding

The NPC boats each have a set of waypoints to follow. NPC3 (boat3) follows the odd waypoints, and NPC4 follows the even-numbered ones. These are found on the file paramets.txt, where each line of text contains:

1. The waypoint number
2. Waypoint X coordinate
3. Waypoint Y coordinate
4. Target speed of the boat at that waypoint

Example:

```
1   340 2391 .4
2   325 2385 .6
3   369 1849 .6
4   377 1713 .7
        . . .
```

When the boat reaches a waypoint (within a distance of 100), it selects the next waypoint and slowly adjusts its speed to the next suggested speed and the course to intersect with the next waypoint. The final waypoints (29 and 30) represent the finish of the game.

6.3. Opponent AI

NPC boats will attempt to avoid the other boats, especially the player's boat. NPC boats are guided by waypoints, but sometimes when attempting to evade the player's boat they will run aground. When the shore is intersected by an NPC boat, it attempts to reverse course for 30 iterations, and then attempts to rotate counterclockwise for another 40 iterations. It then resumes its course to the next waypoint.

AVOIDING THE PLAYER

The NPC boats project a ray in front of them for 200 pixels. If that ray intersects with another boat (using the bounding box), then a collision is imminent. The boat enters the AVOID state and turns away from the collision. This is done in a set of 100 steps. It then leaves the AVOID state and resumes a course to its waypoint.

6.4.   Friendly AI None

7. Technical

7.1. Target Hardware – Any desktop

7.2. Development hardware and software, including Game Engine – Python and Pygame

7.3. Network requirements – Later

8. Game Art – Key assets, how they are being developed. Intended style. Game has been seen except for:

Pylons (flags)

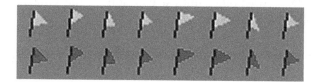

Animations

1. Boat wake. To be drawn behind any boat that is under power (engine on and boat is moving). Can be drawn in a random order. Images are 34 x 83 pixels and include a water background. wakes.gif

All wake frames.

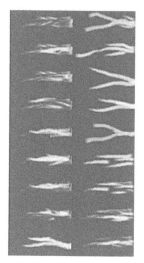

2. Explosion. When boats collide. *http://www.positech.co.uk/content/ explosion/explosiongenerator.html* to create the frames.

See 6.1 for sprite sheets.

9. Game progression

Start – When the player presses the START button on the start screen, the play screen is displayed with no mini-map. Text will count down from 10 to 1 to allow the player to prepare for the start. At the end of the countdown sequence (1 second per step), the full game screen is displayed and the boats can now move.

The NPC boats follow their waypoints until a collision or the end. After a collision they resume following waypoints.

The player may navigate as they choose, but collisions will be detected and dealt with.

- Colliding with another boat results in an explosion and a restart.
- Colliding with the shore stops the boat. The player can turn until the boat is free.

Whenever the player reaches a waypoint, a "bing" sound is played.
Whenever the player holds down the "q" key, the engine sound plays and the boat accelerates to its maximum speed.
Whenever the "a" or "d" key is depressed, the engine sound plays and the boat turns.

THE NPC (BOAT) CLASS FOR THE EXAMPLE GAME

```
# A boat .............................................
class npc : # All class ,local variables
    def __init__(self, x, y, sprite, speed, angle, index):
        self.x = x                  # Current X position
        self.y = y                    # Current Y position
        self.speed = speed            # Current speed
        self.angle = angle            # Current course
        self.index = index            # Index in boats tuple
        self.sound = False            # Engine sound playing?
        self.volume = 0               # Sound volume
        self.targetSpeed = 0          # How fast does the boat want
to go?
        self.targetAngle = 90         # What is the course setting?
        self.sprite = sprite          # The image of the boat
        self.wpt = None               # Next waypoint
        self.name = "NPC 1"           # Name of this boat
        self.NORMAL = 0               #  NORMAL state.
        self.AVOID = 1                #  State where the boat is
avoiding another
        self.COLLIDED = 2             #  State where boat has
collided with the shore
        self.EXPLODING = 4            #  State where the boat is
exploding
        self.state = self.NORMAL      # Current state
        self.ccount = 0               # Current step in AVOID (0 ..
100)
        self.estate = 0               # Current step in COLLIDED
        self.delta = 0                # Angle step in the AVOID
process
        self.frame = 0                # Current explosion frame
        self.r = None                 # Temp surface for rotating
the boat image
        self.player = False           # Is THIS boat the player's?
        self.ul = [1,1]               # Upper left corner of bounding
```

```
box
        self.ur = [1,1]              # Upper right corner of
bounding box
        self.lr = [1,1]              # Lower right corner of
bounding box
        self.ll = [1,1]              # Lower left corner of bounding
box
        self.sternx = 0             # X coordinate of the stern
        self.sterny = 0             # Y coordinate of the stern
        self.prowx = 0              # X coordinate of the prow
        self.prowy = 0              # Y coordinate of the prow
        self.centrex = 0            # X coordinate of the boat
center
        self.centery = 0            # Y coordinate of the boat
center
        self.done = False           # Has this boat finished the
race?
        self.kimage = int(random.random ()*5)  # Which explosion
image to use
        self.savedx = x             # Last x location of the boat
(for explosion)
        self.savedy = y             # Last x location of the boat
(for explosion)
# All methods
    def display(self):              # Display this boat or
its explosion animation
    def showNextExFrame (self, x, y):  # Display the next
explosion animation frame
    def reset (self):               # Restart this boat at
its original position

    #                        Course and speed will change
gradually to the target
    def setSpeed (self, s):             # Set the target speed
    def setCourse (self, a):         # Set the target course

    def setWaypoint (self, w):          # Set the current target
waypoint
    def setName (self, s):              # Set the text5 name of
this boat
    def adjustAngle (self):             # Adjust the boat course
a step to target
    def adjustSpeed (self):             # Adjust speed a step to
target
    def escape (self):                  # Do one step to escape
from a shore collision
```

```
    def normalize (self, vec):          # Normalize a vector
(make is length 1)

    #                              Could a boat collision
between I and j occur?
    def boatCollision(self, i, ddx, ddy):

    def avoid(self, i, ddx, ddy):       # Perform a step in
avoiding another boat
    def update_box(self):               # Update the bounding box
for this boat, step
    def playerStep(self):               # Move the player's boat
one step, all tests
    def nextStep (self):                # Move an NPC boat a
step, all tests
```

INDEX

A

AABB. *See* Axis Aligned Bounding Box
Accuracy, 18–19
Action games, 8
ADC. *See* Analog to digital converter
Advent, 8
Adventure games, 8
Age of Empires, 6
AI. *See* Artificial intelligence
Ambient animations, 225–228
Analog to digital converter (ADC), 160
Angry Birds, 13, 28
Animation01.py, 208–209
Animations, 208–233
   ambient, 225–228
   in boat race game, 231
   character, 228–229
   C2H6O Jet Boat Race, 237–242
   cut scenes, 229–231
   elementary, creation of, 209–214
   math, 214–219
   reactive, 219–225
   wakes, 231
Arc, 53–54, 55
Architecture, 10

Area test, 123
Artificial intelligence (AI), 31, 104–127, 136–137,
   143–146
   C2H6O Jet Boat Race, 193–201
Aspect ratio, 64–65
A*search, 146–150
Audacity, 168–170
Audio concepts, 157–161
Audio software, 168–170
Audio system, 27–28
Autonomous control, 130–136
Avoidance behavior, 133–135
Axis Aligned Bounding Box (AABB)
   collision detection using, 116–117, 118

B

Back-face culling, 121
Backgammon, 1
Ball clause, 254–256
Beta testing, 204
Bind, 259
Blitting, 57–58
Block map method, 119
Board games, 3
Boat race game

animations in, 231
collision detection in, 123–127
C2H6O Jet Boat Race, 40–45, 70–72, 179–206, 236–250
Bots, 104
Bouncing a simulated ball, 78–79
Bounding boxes, collision detection using, 114, 116–118
Broadbase collision detection, 108, 109–120
   geometric tests, 110–112
   operational methods, 109–110
   space subdivision, 118–120
   using bounding boxes, 116–118
   using enclosing circles, 112–116
Broadcast-listener, 33–34
Buttons
   C2H6O Jet Boat Race, 182–184

C

Capita vel Navia, 91
Car, controlling, 131–136
   avoidance behavior, 133–135
   cruising behavior, 132–133
   waypoint Representation and Implementation, 135–136
Card games, 3–4
   randomness in, 90–96
Casual games, 8
Cellular phones, 13
Channels, 161, 162, 164–165
Character animation, 228–229
A Christmas Carol, 4
Circle, 56
Circle-circle collisions, 114–116
   closest point on a line to a specified point, finding, 115–116
Civilization, 13
clock.tick, 77–78
Cognitive simulation, 104
Collision detection, 104–127
   in boat race, 123–127, 240–242
   broadbase collision detection, 108, 109–120
   C2H6O Jet Boat Race, 193–196
   narrowbase collision detection, 120–122
Color(s)
   class, 55
   gradient creation, 51–52
   pixels and, 67–70

transparent, 59–61
Computer games, common aspects of, 9–10
Conflict, 4–15
Copy, 226
Core Techniques and Algorithms in Game Programming, 27
Crazy Taxi, 14
Cross product, 111
Cruising behavior, 132–133
C2H6O Jet Boat Race, 40–45, 70–72, 179–206, 236–250
   animations
      explosions, 238–242
      wakes, 237–238
   artificial intelligence
      boat, avoiding, 199–200
      colliding with the shore, 200–201
      collisions, 193–196
      navigation, 196–197
      waypoints, 197–199
   boat class, 192–193
   design document, 41–45
   game play, 244–247
      completing the race, 244
      finish, 247
      intermediate play, 246
      start, 244–246
      timer, 245–246
   mini-map, 247–249
      game data, 248–249
   play screen, 187–190
   prototype 0, 180–181
   prototype 1, 181–187
      buttons, 182–184
      end screen, 186
      options screen, 185–186
      play screen, 186
      screens, 181–182
      start screen, 184–185
   prototype 2, 186–187
   sound, 201–203, 242–244
      audience, 244
      bing, 244
      collisions and explosions, 203
      engine sounds, 202–203, 242–243
      finish, 203, 244
      starting gun, 203, 243
   testing, 203–206

tuning, 249
user control, 190–192
Cut scenes, 229–231

D

Dance Dance Revolution, 8
Desktop computers, 10–11
Dice, randomness in, 90–96
Display, 55, 227
display.blit, 69
Distance attenuation, 171–172
Donkey Kong, 8
Doom, 8, 18
Dot product, 111
Double Dash, 15
Dragon Slayer, 8
Draw, 55, 222, 228, 240
Drawing text, 58–59

E

Elder Scrolls Online, 8
Enclosing circles, broadbase collision detection
using, 112–116
Entertaining, 2
Events of game loop, 79–87
better game, 86–87
keyboard, 82–83
mouse, 81–82
on-screen button, 84–85
simple game, 85–86
Explosions
boat collisions, determination of, 240–242
C2H6O Jet Boat Race, 237–242

F

Fermi, Enrico, 96
Fidelity, 18–19
Fighting games, 8
Fill, 55
Final Fantasy XI, 8
Finite state machines, 136–144
air state, 141–142
attacking state, 142
damaged state, 142
defending state, 142–143
patrolling state, 143
in practice, 137–140
searching state, 143

skidding state, 143
start state, 141
state and "what do we do now" problem, 140–141
stopping state, 144
Flash, 214
Flight simulator, 7
FMV. *See* Full motion video
font.render, 59
For loop, 64
Frequency, 158
Friction, 215
FSAs. *See* Finite state machines
Full motion video (FMV). *See* Cut scenes

G

Gambling, 90–92
Game, definition of, 1–2
Game Boy, 12
Game Coding Complete, 27
Game consoles, 11–12
Game design, 28–30
mechanics, 29–30
Game design document (GDD), 39, 40, 179
C2H6O Jet Boat Race, 41–45
Game Developer's Conference, 17
Game genres, 6–9
action, 8, 9
role playing, 7–8
simulation, 7
sports, 6–7
strategy, 6
Game loop, 74–100
events, 79–87
randomness, 87–96
random value generation, 96–98
reality and intelligence, simulation of, 98–100
time and intervals, 74–79
Game state, 32
Game testing, 203, 204
GDD. *See* Game design document
Gebert, Nigel, 175
Geometric level of graphics system, 26–27
Geometric tests, for collision detection, 110–112
getPosition, 33, 222
get_pressed, 83, 191
GHz. *See* Gigahertz
Gigahertz (GHz), 158
Global entities, 34–35

Global state of the game, 32
Golfing games, 6–7
Google Docs, 40
Graphics, 15, 47–72
    pipeline, 25
    system. *See* Graphics system
Graphics system, 24–27
    geometric level, 26–27
    object level, 25–26
    optimization, 27
    rasterization level, 27

H
Half Life, 15, 156
Halo, 15, 156
Hertz (Hz), 158
Hidden computer games, 30
Hitchcock, Alfred, 156
Hockey Pong, 136
Horror games, 8
Hz. *See* Hertz

I
Image transformations, 64–67
    rotation, 65–67
Images
    negative image, 63–64
    pixels, 62–63
    Pygame, 61–64
im.get_at, 62
im.get_height, 61
im.get_width, 61
iMovie, 225
im.set_at, 63
Intelligence and reality, simulation of, 98–100
Interaction, 9
Interesting games, aspects of, 13–19
    conflict, 14–15
    fidelity/accuracy, 18–19
    graphics and sound, 15
    interface, 16–17
    pace/scale, 17–18
    props, 15–16
    venue, 13–14
Interface, 16–17, 33
Interior angle test, 123
Intervals of game loop, 74–79
isArmed, 184

K
Key frames, 211
Keyboard events, 82–83
Key_pressed method, 83
KHz. *See* KiloHertz
KiloHertz (KHz), 158
Kinetic games, 3, 8

L
Latency, 251
The Lawnmower Man (film), 4
Line, 52–53, 55
Listen, 259
Little Big Planet, 15
    conflict, 15
Logitech Wingman, 17
Loudness, 158
Lua, 35

M
Mac
    iMovie, 225
Macs, 10
Managers, 33
Mario Kart, 134
Mathematical games, 3, 4
Mechanics, 9, 29–30
Megahertz (MHz), 158
MHz. *See* Megahertz
Microsoft
    MovieMaker, 225
A Million Random Digits (book), 96
Mini-map, 247–249
Mixer, 161, 162
Monopoly, 13
Motion equations, 216–219
Mouse button events, 81–82
mousePressed, 182
mouseReleased, 182
MovieMaker, 225
Moviepy, 231
Multiple inheritance, 35
Myst, 8

N
Narrowbase collision detection, 120–122
    ray/triangle intersection, 121–123
Navigation and control, 129–152

A*search, 146–150
  basic autonomous control, 130–136
  C2H6O Jet Boat Race, 196–197
  finite state machines, 136–144
  pathfinding, 144–146
  stochastic navigation, 151–152
Negative image, 63–64
Networking, 251–272
  See also Pong
Newton's Laws of Motion, 215–216
nextStep, 198
Nim, 4
Nintendo, 12
Nintendo Switch, 12
Non-player characters (NPCs), 129, 131, 144, 192,
    196, 198, 200, 206, 245, 248
Note paper page creation
  lines and curves, 53–55
  pixel level graphics, 50–51
NPCs. *See* Non-player characters

O
Object level of graphics system, 25–26
Object oriented bounding box (OOBB)
  collision detection using, 117–118
Objects, 9, 10
Odd intersections test, 123
On-screen button, 84–85
OOBB. *See* Object oriented bounding box
Open, 259
Opponents, 104, 105
Options button, 183–184
optionScreen, 182

P
Paddle class, 253–254
Paint, 210, 214, 220
Parcheesi, 1
Pathfinding, 144–146
Pause, 222
Photoshop, 214
Pitch, 157, 158
Pixel level graphics, 49–52
  color gradient creation, 51–52
  note paper page creation, 50–51
Pixels, 62–63
  and color, 67–70
  See also Pixel level graphics

Planetside, 9
Platforms, 10–13
  cellular phones, 13
  desktop computers, 10–11
  game consoles, 11–12
  portable consoles, 12
  tablets, 11
Play, 2, 9, 222
Playing the game, by rules
  artificial intelligence, 31
  broadcast-listener, 33–34
  game state, 32
  global state, 32
  hidden computer games, 30
  managers, 33
  push/pull (client server), 32–33
  shared and global entities, 34–35
PlayStation, 12
Playtesting, 203, 204
Polygonal objects, collisions in, 107–109
Polygons, 56–57
Pong, 35–39, 252–271
  ball clause, 254–256
  communication between processes
    moving a ball on the screen, 257–261
  network, 262–272
    blocking and non-blocking, 265–267
    client, 262–264, 268–269
    messages, 267–268
    playing the game, 271
    server, 264–265, 270–271
  paddle class, 253–254
Portable consoles, 12
Portal, 9, 28, 30
Positional audio, 170–176
  2D positional sound, 172–176
  distance attenuation, 171–172
Probability, 92–93
  calculations, 93–96
Props, 15–16
Pseudorandom numbers, 88, 97–98
Push/pull (client server), 32–33
Puzzle games, 8
Pygame, 47
  blitting, 57–58
  drawing text, 58–59
  essentials, 48–49
  game loop, 74–100

image transformations, 64–67
images, 61–64
lines and curves, 52–55
pixel level graphics, 49–52
pixels and color, 67–70
polygons, 56–57
sound in, 161–176
transparent colors, 59–61
pygame-vlc, 231
pygame.draw.circle, 69–70
pygame.event, 79–87
pygame.event.get, 82
pygame.font.Font, 59
pygame.image, 62
pygame.image.load, 61
pygame.init, 54, 55, 76
pygame.KEYDOWN, 82, 83, 191
pygame.key.get_pressed, 83
pygame.KEYUP, 82, 83
pygame.QUIT, 81, 82
pygame.Surface, 68
pygame.time, 76–78
pygame.time.delay, 76, 77
pygame.time.wait, 77
pygame.transform.rotate, 65, 66
PyMedia, 231

Q
Quantization, 24

R
Racing games, 6–7
Rag doll physics, 7
Rand Corporation, 96
Random value generation, 96–98
    pseudorandom numbers, 97–98
Randomness, 87–96
    dice and cards, 90–96
Rasterization level of graphics system, 27
Ray casting, 126–127
Ray/triangle intersection, 121–123
Reactive animations, 219–225
    using real images, 224–225
Reactive Grip controller, 17
Real-time strategy games, 6
Reality and intelligence, simulation of, 98–100
Rect, 56
Rhythm games, 8

Role playing games (RPG), 7–8
Roller Coaster Tycoon, 7
Rotate, 199
Rotation of images, 65–67
Royal Game of Ur, 1
RPG. *See* Role playing games

S
Sandbox, 9, 15
Scale, 17–18
Schell Games, 205
SCRALPHA, 60
screenState, 182, 184
screen_to_terrain, 194
Send, 258, 260
set_at, 55
setExist, 33
set_mode, 48, 55
setNext, 227
setPosition, 222
setRate, 227
Shared entities, 34–35
Shooters, 8
shoreCollide, 194
showNextExFrame, 240
Sign, 86
Silent Hill, 8, 9
SimCity, 7
The Simpsons Hit & Run, 15
The Sims, 9, 14
Simulation
    cognitive, 104
    of reality and intelligence, 98–100
Simulation games, 5, 7
Small studio, 167–168
SMV Rainbow, 247, 248
Socket, 257–258
Software testing, 203–204
Sony PSP Slim, 12
Sound, 15, 156–176
    C2H6O Jet Boat Race, 201–203
    options, 162–165
    own sounds, creation of, 165–170
    positional audio, 170–176
    in Pygame, 161–176
    recording, using cell phones and MP3 devices,
        166–167
    volume, 163–164

Space Invaders, 29, 75
Space subdivision, collision detection using, 118–120
Sphere *vs.* plane collision, 113–114
Sports games, 6–7
Sprouts, 4
SRCALPHA, 60
Star Trek (film), 4, 18
startScreen, 182, 184
Stochastic navigation, 151–152
Stop, 222
Straight ahead method, 214, 219
Strategy games, 6
Super Mario Bros, 12
surface, 55
surf.fill, 61, 68
Survival horror games, 8

T
Tablets, 11
Terrain texture generation tool, 71
terrain_to_screen, 125, 199
Testing, 203–206
3D games, 18, 23–25
    animations, 221
Timing of game loop, 74–79
tkinter, 47
Tower defense games, 6
transform, 64–67
Transparent colors, 59–61
Trivia games, 8
Tuning, 249
Tweens, 211
Twitch games. *See* Action games
Two-player chase game, 1
2D game, 23–25

2D positional sound, 172–176
Tycoon games, 7
    conflict, 14

U
Update, 55
USB interface, 16

V
Venue, 13–14
Video game architecture, 21–28
    audio system, 27–28
    graphics system, 24–27
Video Lottery Terminals, 88
VideoMach, 224–225
Virtual reality, 4–6
Vita, 12
Volume, 158

W
Wakes, 231, 237–238
Warcraft, 6
Waypoint
    C2H6O Jet Boat Race, 197–199
    implementation, 135–136
    pathfinding, 134–135
    representation, 135–136
Word games, 4
World of Warcraft, 13

X
Xbox, 12

Z
Zoo Tycoon, 7, 14
Zork, 8